Keys to Success

Keys to Success
How to Achieve Your Goals

Carol Carter
and
Sarah Lyman Kravits

Prentice Hall
Upper Saddle River, New Jersey, 07458

Library of Congress Cataloging-in-Publication Data

Carter, Carol.
    Keys to success : how to achieve your goals / by Carol Carter and Sarah Lyman Kravits.
        p.   cm.
    Includes bibliographical references and index.
    ISBN 0-13-231135-6
    1. College student orientation—United States—Handbooks, manuals, etc. 2. Study skills—Handbooks, manuals, etc. 3. College students—United States—Life skills guides. I. Kravits, Sarah Lyman. II. Title.
LB2343.32.C37   1996
378.1'98—dc20   95-39333
                                                                                                                                        CIP

Acquisitions Editor: Elizabeth Sugg
Production Editor: Eileen O'Sullivan
Director of Manufacturing & Production: Bruce Johnson
Managing Editor: Mary Carnis
Graphs: HRS
Designer: HRS
Marketing Manager: Frank Mortimer, Jr.
Cover Design: Wendy Helft
Copyeditor: Patty Boyd
Art Director: Marianne Frasco
Illustrator: Rob Peters
Editorial Assistant: Kahdijah Bell
Formatting/Page Make-up: Stephen Hartner
Printer/Binder: Banta, Harrisonburg
Video Production: Steven Feldman

© 1996 by Prentice-Hall, Inc.
A Simon & Schuster Company
Upper Saddle River, NJ 07458

All rights reserved. No part of this book may be reproduced, in any form or by any means, without permission in writing from the publisher.

Printed in the United States of America

10 9 8 7 6 5 4 3 2 1

ISBN 0-13-231135-6

Prentice-Hall International (UK) Limited, *London*
Prentice-Hall of Australia Pty. Limited, *Sydney*
Prentice-Hall Canada Inc., *Toronto*
Prentice-Hall Hispanoamericana, S.A., *Mexico*
Prentice-Hall of India Private Limited, *New Delhi*
Prentice-Hall of Japan, Inc., *Tokyo*
Simon & Schuster Asia Pte. Ltd., *Singapore*
Editoria Prentice-Hall do Brasil, Ltda., *Rio de Janeiro*

DEDICATION

We would like to dedicate this book to two very understanding and supportive men, Rubén Iñiguez and Garth Kravits; to our wonderful families, the Carters, the Lymans, and the Kravitses; and to all of our helpful and patient friends. We couldn't have done it without you.

Contents

CHAPTER 1 YOU ARE "HERE": AIMING FOR "THERE" 3

The 1990's Student 4
Education and Success 7
Strategies to Start You on Your Way 10
  Becoming a Better Learner 10
  Concentrating on the Present 10
  Tapping into Your Resources 11
  Facing Your Fears 16
Summing Up 18
Applications 19
Key to Your Personal Portfolio 25

CHAPTER 2 SELF-AWARENESS: KNOWING HOW YOU LEARN 27

Self-Image 28
Attitude 29
Habits 31
Learning Styles 32
  Are You Active or Reflective? 33
  Are You a Sensor or an Intuitor? 34
  Are You Visual or Verbal? 34
  Are You Sequential or Global? 35
Likes and Dislikes 36
Abilities 38
Summing Up 40
Applications 41
Key to Your Personal Portfolio 52

CHAPTER 3 MAPPING YOUR COURSE: GOALS, PRIORITIES, AND TIME MANAGEMENT 55

Goals 56
  Identifying your Purpose 56
  Placing Goals in Time 57
  Types of Goals 59
Priorities 60
Time Management 61

Daily and Weekly Goal-Setting   61
Your Schedule   62
To-Do Lists   64
Procrastination and other Time Traps   65
Handling Change   67
Reevaluating and Modifying Your Goals   67
Shifting Your Priorities   69
Adjusting Your Schedule   70
Summing Up   70
Applications   71
Key to Your Personal Portfolio   79

Chapter 4   Opening Doors: Thinking Critically and Creatively   81

Critical Thinking   82
How You Think   82
The Value of Critical Thinking   84
Your Mind's Four Major Processes   84
Creating and Innovating   84
Inquiring   87
Problem Solving   88
Decision Making   88
Two Important Door Keys   91
Intuition   91
Perspective   91
Summing Up   93
Applications   94
Key to Your Personal Portfolio   99

Chapter 5   Word Keys: Communicating Through Writing   101

Reading   102
Make Reading a Part of Your Life   102
Follow Specific Reading Techniques   104
Note Taking   106
Writing   111
Essays and Papers   115
Establish the Subject   116
Specify the Topic   116
Gather Information   116
Plan the Construction   116

      Write the First Draft   117
      Revise and Revise Again   117
      Finalize   118
Summing Up   118
Applications   118
Key to Your Personal Portfolio   125

CHAPTER 6   MIND KEYS: RETAINING WHAT YOU LEARN   127

Listening   128
Concentration   129
Memory   131
Test Taking   134
      Preparing for Tests   134
      Taking Tests   136
      Types of Tests   137
Working With Numbers   139
Summing Up   141
Applications   141
Key to Your Personal Portfolio   147

CHAPTER 7   MAINTAINING THE ESSENTIALS: TAKING CARE OF YOURSELF   151

Maintaining a Healthy Body   152
      Eating Right   152
      Exercise   154
      Sleep   155
Maintaining a Healthy Mind   156
      Dealing with Stress   156
      Depression   158
Health Traps   159
      Alcohol   160
      Tobacco   160
      Drugs   160
      Eating Disorders   162
Managing Addiction   163
      Facing Addiction   163
      Substance Abuse Affects Others   165
Sexual Issues   166
      Birth Control   166
      Sexually Transmitted Diseases   167

Sexual Harassment   168
Summing Up   169
Applications   170
Key to Your Personal Portfolio   175

CHAPTER 8 PERSONAL POWER: ASSURING PROGRESS   177

Integrity   178
   Values   179
   Ethics   179
The Four Power Boosters   182
   Motivation   182
   Commitment   182
   Responsibility   184
   Initiative   185
Handling Success and Failure   186
   Dealing with Failure   187
   Dealing with Success   188
Summing Up   188
Applications   189
Key to Your Personal Portfolio   194

CHAPTER 9 THE PEOPLE CONNECTION: RELATING TO OTHERS   197

Human Resources   198
   In-school Resources   198
   Out-of-school Resources   199
Mentors   201
Communication   201
   The Communication Cycle   202
   Ways You Communicate   203
   Strategies for Better Communication   205
Personal Relationships   207
Group Relationships   208
Your Diverse World   209
   Racism and Discrimination   210
   Be Part of the Solution   212
Summing Up   212
Applications   213
Key to Your Personal Portfolio   218

CHAPTER 10   REALITY RESOURCES: MANAGING FINANCES AND WORK   221

Budgeting   222
Working Now   225
     Positive and Negative Effects   226
     Job Listings and Networking   228
     Career Investigation   230
Financial Aid   230
     Loans   231
     Grants and Scholarships   232
Banking Services   233
Smart Spending and Saving   234
Savings Strategies   234
Credit   235
Summing Up   238
Applications   239
Key to Your Personal Portfolio   244

CHAPTER 11   YOUR LIFE: MOVING AHEAD   247

The Master Key: Lifelong Learning   248
When You Fall Short of Your Goals   249
Handling Conflict and Criticism   251
     Conflict   251
     Criticism   252
Making a Difference   254
     Your Imprint on the World   254
     Valuing Your Environment   255
Living Your Mission   255
Applications   257
Key to Your Personal Portfolio   263

REFERENCES   265

INDEX   269

Foreword

I could tell you that *Keys to Success* will make you into a straight-A student with little effort. I could also tell you that this book holds a recipe for increasing your brain power by 75%. I could tell you these things but they would not be true. What I will tell you is that *Keys to Success* provides you with valuable information that you must put to use in order for it to make a difference in your education. The act of reading this book will not make you a better student, but utilizing the skills, hints, and information you receive by reading it can lead to your success.

Getting your education is a difficult and complex process. The goal of *Keys to Success* is to make it easier for you, the student, to get a grip on your education by exposing you to ideas and strategies that many students don't begin to think about until it is almost too late. If someone reads *Keys to Success* and then puts it down, not applying anything they read to their education, the book won't do any good. If, however, someone reads this book and endeavors to incorporate what they read into their education, the book then is priceless.

One of the most important things I have learned while attending college is that active participation is vital. If you involve yourself in everything you do, you glean from it all that is possible. Passivity will hinder your education. The person who raises their hand in class to offer an opinion or ask a question will gain an infinite amount more out of that class than will the person who just sits and watches. Your participation in *Keys to Success* will work the same way.

Keys to Success contains exactly what its title suggests. The "keys" are present here in this text. However, they are only implements provided to help you unlock and discover your education. You might think of it in this way: A key lying in your drawer is just a piece of metal. Looking at this key does not change that fact. It is only when you lift the key, insert it into the lock, and turn it that it becomes valuable. The keys are being given to you here. All you have to do is use them.

—**Aziza Davis, student editor** for *Keys to Success*
at Rutgers University

Key Advice

BALANCING WORK AND SCHOOL

Carla Kay Berg, Capital University. "Finding time for school and work and everything else in college can be difficult. As long as you schedule everything, making sure that there are no conflicts, everything will work out. I try to know ahead of time what I have to do and where I have to go for the day. My first priority is always school, and if I need to spend more time studying, something else from my schedule will get cut."

Amy Katherine Reid, University of North Carolina at Greensboro. "It's hard to keep track of both school and work activities. I had a job where I worked 15 hours a week. Sometimes I even tried doing homework at my job, which was impossible. Eventually, I had trouble with one class because I was working so much. My parents then made me drop some work hours. I was lucky to have a flexible employer, because he understood my situation. Although I didn't want to lose any work hours, I started working a little less, and I worked more on the weekends. Even those few hours made a big difference, and I started doing better in the course."

Aida Ramos, St. Mary's University. "I have a work-study job, which is in the afternoons. I have to work until 5:00 p.m., and at that point I start my school work. Sometimes I have meetings for clubs or other activities in the afternoon, and I have to take time off from work and make up the hours later. Finding time for both school and work can be very difficult. But I never let work become more important than school."

HANDLING ISSUES WITH PROFESSORS AND TEACHING ASSISTANTS

William Cooper, Mesa State College. "It is very important to get to know your instructor personally, so they can attach a name to a face, and know who you are. Often the easiest way to solve a problem is to go to the instructor's office. If you continue to meet regularly, and the instructor gets to know you, he or she can see your strengths and weaknesses, and help you as professional educators."

Vanessa Vergara, Hamline University. "I had an English professor who seemed very distanced from the students. When I had trouble getting feedback from her on a paper, I just saw it as a challenge for myself. If students are having trouble with a professor or class, they should talk to other students who have taken that class before, or talk to other professors who may feel more free to talk with you because they're not the ones giving you a grade. One of the biggest problems students make is not getting to know their professors or not approaching them for help."

Merlene Converse, Biola University. "If you have a problem with a professor, there are a lot of options you have before considering dropping the class. Students can talk to a professor, but if that doesn't work, they can always approach student assistants, look for tutoring, or discuss it with other students. Chances are, you're not alone, and other students in that class are probably having the same problem. If so, you can approach the professor as a group."

Study tips

William Cooper, Mesa State College. "I'm a logical, visual learner. I had a Chemistry professor who always put an outline of his lecture on the overhead, which was very helpful for me. I had another Biology professor who wrote notes out all over the board in a very jumbled fashion, which was much more difficult for me to follow. I used to rewrite my notes for that class, and put them in outline form or reorganize them after class."

Raymond Monhart, Ashland University. "If I have trouble writing a paper, I always pay attention to the comments the professor writes on the paper, and re-do it. I usually re-write papers more than once, often two or three times, but they really improve."

Susan Elizabeth Wood, Purdue University. "I think schools were more quiet when I went, so now I need a quiet place to study. Some people need music or background noise, but I have to go somewhere quiet and be by myself. Sometimes I read aloud and talk things out, even changing the inflection in my voice to keep it interesting. Hearing as you read really helps. Making the information personal by writing about it or reflecting about it helps more. Using more of your senses when you study helps the information stay with you longer."

Matt Caflisch, University of Minnesota. "Even when I don't like the subject matter of classes that I'm required to take, I can always get through the course because I make sure to attend every session and try my hardest to take notes in class."

William Cooper, Mesa State College. "I typically don't study for tests except for a quick review, because I study regularly all along. I don't cram or spend hours trying to memorize. I go to every class, take notes, and clear up any misunderstandings right away. I want to be tested on what I really know, not my ability to memorize. This helps me with test anxiety because first of all, I'm not tired from studying all night; secondly, I have everything organized in my head, which makes me more comfortable about the test. If it's an essay test, I make a mental outline before I start writing, so all of the information is organized."

Returning or non-traditional students

Lois Humphrey, Brescia College. "As a non-traditional student, I really need to keep sight of my goals. I've spoken to friends who are also thinking about returning to school. I tell them that time will pass regardless of what they do. Twenty years will go by, and they might as well have a college degree to show for the passing of time—even if they have to take one class at a time."

Susan Elizabeth Wood, Purdue University. "In one course I took, my professor told me to cancel all my plans for the weekend. He was right! I spend every waking moment of my weekends on homework. I was also involved in other church and community activities. Doing well in school was a priority for me, but people had to learn to forgive me for not being in two places at the same time. People who are struggling with this really need to talk to someone. A lot of us think we're the only ones who have these problems, but many people have a hard time with returning to school. If it means dropping courses and picking them up another time, then do it. You have to realize you can't get everything right all the time. Don't be too hard on yourself."

Christine Carol Richardson, Southeastern Oklahoma State. "It's never too late to go back to school. But don't keep waiting — don't wait to figure out what you want to study or what classes you want to take. College helps you figure out what you want to do. You won't regret going back."

Key Advice

SEEKING HELP FROM COUNSELORS AND ADVISORS

Amy Katherine Reid, University of North Carolina at Greensboro. "I would encourage all students to talk with a counselor or advisor, but don't expect them to know exactly what your situation is. Treat them the way you want to be treated. When I went to see my advisor, she told me to take some courses that I wasn't real enthusiastic to take. But in the long run, it turned out better than I expected, and I ended up learning a lot."

Vanessa Miller, Biola University. "I had a counselor who was a nice person, but didn't know enough about my major or goals to give me the best advice. Now, if I feel like I'm in the wrong class or have another problem, I go straight to my advisor in my major, who knows more about what I need. But just to be sure, I always try to be aware of what I need to do myself."

Nancy Replogle, Lake Erie College. "I'm acquainted with a young woman who was having a lot of problems with her family and with school, and she was suffering from depression. I don't think she knew who to turn to. She was very frustrated with school, and her family didn't seem to want to listen to her or have time for her. A lot of students don't know who to talk to about their problems, and they distrust that whoever they tell will go to a dean or a coach. They are very careful about discussing their problems, but they don't realize that talking it out is exactly what they need to do."

MONEY MATTERS

Joshua Durkin, Oral Roberts University. "If students start early in planning for funding their college education, they can get lots of help. I evaluated my status in my junior year of high school. Scholarships can be offered through work, activities, church, and other affiliations which are willing to provide a lot of help for college students. It's essential to attend any financial aid meetings to get as much information as you can. Also, don't be afraid of student loans. Finally, if you are awarded a financial aid plan, get a work-study job. Remember that there is often more funding available once you are in school. I got involved wherever I could in student leadership positions and activities, because that's what organizations look for in awarding scholarships."

Vanessa Miller, Biola University. "Students planning to go to college, especially high school students, need to plan ahead for financial aid. Students need to do the best they can in their grades, in activities, or in sports, and then look for scholarships in those areas. There is a lot of money out there available to students, and there are so many opportunities that everyone can find some help."

Carla Kay Berg, Capital University. "It is important to be as active as you can in college, both inside and outside of the classroom. You should get everything you can get out of college, especially since it has so much to offer. You're paying a lot of money for your education, so you should take every opportunity to play an active role in it."

Preface

You're taking the time, the effort, and in most cases a decent amount of money to provide an education for yourself. It's a big deal. Being a smart consumer means making sure you're receiving something of value for everything you're giving—and that includes getting something out of this book you've bought. We've spent a great deal of time talking to and surveying students across the country; what we've learned is that you are concerned about your future, you care about the value of an education, and you want honest and direct guidance on how to achieve your goals. Imagine us, the authors, sitting across from you at a table. Get to the point—ask us why it's worth your time and energy to read *Keys to Success*, and ask us to be straight with you. We'll do our best.

How will these skills help me in school?

Every skill described in this book helps you to build your ability to make the most of what your courses offer. You need to believe that you are worth educating. You need a strong sense of who you are and what you want to begin to discover the right course of study. You need to have good study skills to retain what your instructors give you to learn in and out of class. You need to know how to stay healthy so that you are in class and awake every time you need to be. *Keys to Success* can guide you to build skills in all of these areas and more. All kinds of educational opportunities lie right in front of you.

The exercises at the end of the chapters have four important features: critical thinking skills that you develop by applying what you learn in the chapter to your own life and experiences; cooperative learning which gives you a chance to learn from each other and build your teamwork and leadership skills; journal writing which provides an opportunity for you to express your thoughts and improve your writing ability; and a personal portfolio that helps you to build a paper trail of important work and useful information.

We also talk about the resources that may be available to you at your school, helping to guide you through an exploration of what you can find and how it can help you. They're there for you—it's up to you to use them.

Does this book do me any good after I'm done with school?

You will want to keep *Keys to Success* around for a long time to come—because everything that helps you make the most of your education can also help you make the most of your working life. We know that you are concerned about the competitiveness of the job market, your career, and your quality of life, and we have made a point to relate the strategies you will read about to both school and workplace success. For example, you need to know how to communicate with your instructors and fellow students just as much as with co-workers and supervisors. **Learning is a lifelong process** that, if you keep it up, will build your knowledge and enrich your experiences. More about that in later pages.

You don't know me—how can you give me what I need?

One thing we recognized right off the bat is that every person, every instructor, and even every education is incredibly unique. We knew one point of view wouldn't apply to everyone. Therefore, we have included a variety of perspectives. You will see quotes from students and professionals of many different ethnic, cultural, and educational backgrounds. You will find examples that deal with all different situations—students with or without families, different financial needs, different lifestyles, schedules that include classes at different times, different interests, etc. We've done our best to find a niche for everyone—and if you think we haven't found yours, we encourage you to let us know.

We also focus on your uniqueness early in the book when you will be able to identify your individual learning style, based on the pattern of your answers in a questionnaire that shows how you prefer to learn. Based on your profile, you will be able to relate information throughout the book to your particular style.

I want to know what else I'm getting out of this. How can one book help me find success in my life—what can it do for me?

Some of the material deals specifically with issues that can come up in your life, such as personal health, dealing with your relationships, working through addictions, and values. However, your best tool is a belief in your ability to know who you are, follow your chosen path with determination, and earn the success that you want. As you focus on topics like self-esteem and thinking skills, you will learn how to boost your personal power. Whether you strive for a job offer, a successful relationship, a level of financial comfort, or anything else, knowing how to tap into your own power will pull you through.

You are responsible for your education, your growth, your knowledge, and your future. The best we can do is give you some great suggestions and strategies and ideas and structures that you can use as you go—then, it's up to you to use them. *So dive in—read on*—use whatever fits your particular situation, needs, and wants. You've made a terrific start by choosing to continue your education—now make it work for you by taking advantage of all it has to give you.

Acknowledgments

We owe a debt of gratitude to the following professionals for their technical expertise, advice, and excellent guidance:

Patty Boyd, returning student
Susan Chin, DeVry Institute of Technology, Georgia
Barbara Cox, Cox Consultants, California
Robin Diamond, Livingston College, Rutgers University, New Jersey
Eloise Doxie Dixon, Xavier University, Louisiana
Kevin Dohrenwend, Middlesex County College, New Jersey
Scott Drakalich, Essex County College, New Jersey
Alyce L. Eason, Austin Peay State University, Tennessee
Pat Taylor Ellison, Minnesota School of Business, Minnesota
Richard Glazer, Westchester Community College, New York
Dawn L. Leonard, Charleston Southern University, South Carolina
Carol Lindquist, Manhattan Community College, New York
Frank Lyman, Ph.D., University of Maryland/Howard County Schools, Maryland
Randall Price, University of Rio Grande, Ohio
Theresa B. Robinson, Middle Tennessee State University, Tennessee
Jon A. Schlenker, University of Maine at Augusta, Maine
Gwen Spencer, Seattle Pacific University, Seattle, Washington
Earle Wilke, Pennsylvania Institute of Technology, Pennsylvania

In addition, we are grateful for the hard work and input of many individuals affiliated with Prentice Hall: Elizabeth Sugg, our editor; Eileen O'Sullivan, our Production editor; Stephen Hartner, for Formatting and Page Make-up; the design group at HRS; Illustrator Rob Peters; Marketing Director Frank Mortimer, Jr.; National Accounts Manager Jackie Fitzgerald; Sales Director Todd Rossell; intern Christine Mueller; the people involved with the Keys to Success Seminar campaign; and the Prentice Hall sales force.

A final word of thanks goes to everyone else who made this project possible. Your contributions have been most appreciated.

Supplements

Instructor's Resource Kit. Complete package of course information including: course outlines and syllabi; exercises to encourage interaction; articles; lecture anecdotes and hints; evaluation techniques; tests; transparency masters; and more.

Overhead Transparencies. Related course lecture material on acetates.

Job-Search Folder. A workbook that prepares students for career changes and advancements, or beginning new careers. This brief guide either supplements the textbook or is sold separately. It covers résumé preparation, company research, and networking along with many other topics.

Student Key Advice Video. A selection of motivational clips from students, learners, and professionals coordinated with the text material. This professional quality video was prepared especially for Prentice Hall.

NCS Testing Program. Career Assessment Inventory that compares occupational interests and personality preferences with individuals in hundreds of careers.

Simon & Schuster College Online. Access through the Prentice Hall Internet Web-site or America-on-Line to chat sessions, Auditorium presentations, and critical issues pertaining to coursework.

Keys to Success Magazine, Webster's New World Compact Dictionary, America-on-Line introduction package, and other materials are available options for student textbook packages.

About the Authors

Carol Carter is Vice President and Director of Student Programs at Prentice Hall. She has written *Majoring In The Rest Of Your Life: Career Secrets for College Students* and *Majoring In High School*. She has also co-authored *Graduating Into The Nineties* and *The Career Tool Kit*, and is publisher of a magazine for students issued each semester by Prentice Hall entitled *Keys To Success*. In 1992 Carol and other business people co-founded a non-profit organization called LifeSkills, Inc., to help high school students explore their goals, their career options, and the real world through part-time employment and internships.

Sarah Lyman Kravits comes from a family of educators and has long cultivated a strong interest in educational development. A writer and actor, she recently co-authored *The Career Tool Kit* with Carol and has served as Program Director for LifeSkills, Inc., a non-profit organization that aims to further the career and personal development of high school students. In that capacity she helped to formulate both curricular and organizational elements of the program, working closely with instructors as well as members of the business community. Sarah holds a B.A. in English and Drama from the University of Virginia, where she was a Jefferson Scholar, and an M.F.A. in Acting from Catholic University.

Photo Credits

Chapter Opening Photos

Chapter 1: Skier in Alaska going over ledge. Credit: Mark Newman, Source: Phototake, NYC. **Chapter 2:** Hikers rest on large rock near the White Rim 4WD Trail–Canyonlands National Park, Utah. Credit: David Hiser, Source: Aspen, Inc. **Chapter 3:** Hot air balloon–Pittsfield, NH. Credit: William Johnson, Source: Stock Boston. **Chapter 4:** Classroom situation at Tufts University in the Chemistry Department. Credit: Seth Resnick, Source: Stock Boston. **Chapter 5:** Man with laptop computer. Source: Comstock. **Chapter 6:** College students studying around table at Boston Institute of Intercultural Communication. Credit: Frank Siteman, Source: Rainbow. **Chapter 7:** People doing step aerobics. Credit: David Young-Wolff, Source: PhotoEdit. **Chapter 8:** Jogger. Credit: Michael Philip Manheim, Source: Photo Network. **Chapter 9:** Kent State University, Ohio—college students walking. Credit: Ron Sherman, Source: Stock Boston. **Chapter 10:** CNN—Cable News Network Media/News Room—Atlanta, Georgia. Credit: Chromosohm/Joe Sohm, Source: Allstock. **Chapter 11:** Red hang glider. Credit: Rod Kaye, Source: Stock South Inc.

Interior Photos

Chapter 1: Student at Clark Library–UCLA, Los Angeles, CA. Credit: Phil Schermeister, Source: Allstock. **Chapter 2:** African-American teenage girl in mirror. Credit: Coco McCoy, Source: Rainbow. **Chapter 3:** African-American college student studying. Credit: Phyllis Picardi, Source: Stock Boston. **Chapter 4:** Detroit immigration—men studying. Credit: Tony O'Brien, Source: Stock Boston. **Chapter 5:** Female college student reading. Credit: Kindra Clineff, Source: Allstock. **Chapter 6:** Students testing in community college class—summertime—Austin, TX. Credit: Daemmrich, Source: Stock Boston. **Chapter 7:** Group therapy session on mental health for teen leaders and community adults. Credit: Daemmrich, Source: Stock Boston. **Chapter 8:** Female Asian student smiling. Credit: Kevin Morris, Source: Allstock. **Chapter 9:** Professor with students at blackboard. Credit: Shopper, Source: Stock Boston. **Chapter 10:** Young Asian couple paying bills. Credit: Frank Siteman, Source: Rainbow. **Chapter 11:** Anheuser Busch Recycling Center. Credit: Wes Bobbitt, Source: Blackstar.

Keys to Success

C H O O S

1

You Are "Here:" Aiming for "There"

Welcome to your education. Even if you've been a student for many years, every new situation brings unfamiliar challenges. You may wonder what you are getting yourself into as you explore the changes that accompany life as a college student. Whatever you feel at this moment—excitement, hesitation, worry, anticipation, or any combination of emotions—know first that you've earned your place here. You have a right to an education, no matter who you are. Given that right, it is your responsibility to use your education and its resources to build your knowledge and personal power. You have already taken the first step just by being here. No matter what uncertainties and insecurities you feel, by choosing to pursue an education you have given yourself a strong vote of confidence.

This book will help you fulfill your potential as a learner by giving you keys—ideas and strategies—that can help you continue to learn throughout your life. When you use these keys to maximize your knowledge and abilities, you can take charge of your choices. In this first chapter, you will learn about the diversity in personal profiles and needs that characterizes the *1990's student*. As you explore the benefits and demands of being in school, you will discover the connection between *education and success*. Finally, you will study *strategies* that will help you move ahead on the road toward your goals—*becoming a better learner, concentrating on the present, tapping into your school resources*, and *facing your fears*.

THE 1990'S STUDENT

As a group, the student body has become increasingly diverse in recent years and will continue to diversify. Although many still enter college directly after high school, the old "standard" of the student finishing a four-year college education at the age of 22 is a standard no longer. Some students take longer than four years to finish. Some students complete part of their education, pursue other paths for a while, and return to finish later in life. Some go right into the workforce after high school and decide to pursue a college degree after many years. The education "game" has new rules.

Who is pursuing an education today? According to the National Center for Education Statistics, these are the facts about you and your fellow students.

- Enrollment from 1982 to 1992 showed the most growth in the female student population (25 percent) and students over the age of 25 (34 percent). NCES projects that the older student population will grow another 14 percent from 1990 to 1998. (Digest of Education Statistics, 1994)

- In 1989-90, 42 percent of all undergraduates were 24 years old or older. The majority of these older students were married and had dependents other than a spouse. One-quarter of all female undergraduates in their 30's were single parents. Most older students attended part-time, approximately 69 percent, and 46 percent worked full time while studying. (NCES Profile of Older Undergraduates Contractor Report, 1989-90)

- Minorities comprise an increasingly larger percentage of the student population. In 1976, 15.7 percent of students were minorities, compared to 22.5 percent in 1992. (Digest of Education Statistics, 1994)

- More minority citizens are in school. From 1982 to 1992, enrollment increased 26.6 percent for African-Americans, 83.9 percent for Hispanics, 98.5 percent for Asians or Pacific Islanders, and 35.1 percent for Native Americans or Alaskan natives. Enrollment for white non-Hispanics increased by only 8.7 percent. (Report, February 1994, on Trends in Enrollment in Higher Education Fall 1982 through Fall 1992, taken from the Integrated Postsecondary Education Data System [IPEDS] "Fall Enrollment" Surveys between 1986 and 1992)

- Only just above half of the students, 52 percent, were enrolled in four-year institutions. The rest attended two-year or less than two-year schools. (1989-90 Integrated Postsecondary Education Data System)

- In the academic year 1989-90, 56 percent of undergraduates were enrolled full-time, while 23 percent were enrolled less than half-time, leaving 21 percent who studied more than half-time but less than full-time. (1989-90 Integrated Postsecondary Education Data System)

- Approximately three-fourths of undergraduates reported working at some time during their enrollment in the academic year 1989-90. About 40 percent reported working full-time. (1989-90 National Postsecondary Student Aid Study)

- Students are taking longer to get the bachelor's degree. The percentage of college graduates who completed the degree within 5 years of graduating from high school was 57 percent in 1991 compared to 67 percent in 1977. (Condition of Education Report, 1993)

Note the trends that surface as you read this data. **The student body is more ethnically and culturally diverse. People are attending schools for different lengths of time and at different points in their lives. More students are working while in school.** Today's students are challenging the educational system to come up with ways to satisfy their diverse, unusual, and ever-changing needs. The more you develop your own study and coping skills, the more you will be able to adapt and survive.

Why are students in school today? There are as many different combinations of reasons as there are students. If you ask yourself why you are here, you might have more than one answer, perhaps something like some of the following:

- Everybody in my family gets an education past high school.
- I can't live how I want to on the money I make from my current job.
- I don't feel ready to jump into the working world yet.
- I don't have any marketable skills.
- I am recently divorced and need a change.
- I got a scholarship.
- I have a family member/friend in this field and they like it.
- My parents pushed me into it.
- I have a baby on the way and need to increase my salary.
- I am studying to pursue a specific career.
- It's what I can afford right now.
- I don't really know.

All of these answers are legitimate, even the last one. Being honest with yourself is crucial if you want to discover who you are and what life paths make sense for you. Whether you pursue an education out of personal interest or necessity, you have an opportunity to learn.

What do students want out of life? Look beyond the present reality of your studies. If you could peer into a crystal ball at your future, what would you like to see? Your response to such a big question will probably be whatever fits at the moment. You might come up with something different in a month or a year when you are in a different state of mind, situation, or environment. As you continue to change and grow throughout your life, your desires change as well. The smaller goals that you define as you move through this course will combine to give you a "big picture" look at your more general, long-term goals.

Dreams are as unique as the dreamers; therefore, there are as many ideal life plans and lifestyles as there are people. As you have seen in the statistical data as well as by looking around you, students enrolled in college are an incredibly diverse group. Parents of young children frequently attend classes with empty nesters. Native-born Americans encounter immigrants and naturalized citizens from all corners of the globe. Those who are just learning English sit alongside those who grew up speaking it. People

Real World Perspective

Q Susan Elizabeth Wood, student at Purdue University in Michigan City, Indiana

I graduated from high school in 1965, and will graduate from college around 30 years later. I went to college right after high school, and I quit after one semester because I hated it. But going back to school is something I always wanted to do. I told myself that the second time I wanted to try harder and prove to myself that I could do it. I had worked lots of jobs, and I felt like I had to make myself more employable and marketable. The way to do that was with a college background. The time seemed convenient, so I thought I'd just try one course. Then I tried three, then four, and even five.

Things have really changed since 1965. I was a good student in high school, but when I came to college I hadn't had classes for a very long time, and what I remembered wasn't enough. Also, when I went to take a Biology course, I found out how much things have changed since I last studied science, and how much has been discovered. How can I make up for lost time? What can I do to catch up with the information that has accumulated over the last thirty years? I'm finally back and pursuing my education and I want to stay on track. I am doing this for myself and I know that returning to school isn't crazy. I want to study what interests me and to accomplish my goal of earning a degree, but I don't want to get bogged down in subjects that give me trouble.

A Earle Wilke, Ph.D. Counselor in Media, Pennsylvania.

Returning to school as an adult student is a gift and a new beginning. It is a second chance at redesigning all or part of your life and your future. Instead of focusing on what you should have done, think about what you need to be doing here and now. Take each day as an opportunity to build your vision of a future—one thought at a time, one class at a time, one test at a time. Staying on track means having a plan and following it, learning how to meet and to master the demands and skills essential to the task. School is a long distance race that will test your commitment. You will have to overcome failure, frustration, confusion and exhaustion, but if you persist you will reach your goal.

Returning adults are the new majority. Returning students have a rich storehouse of life experiences and can see connections between work and school. What will bring you success in the classroom? Walk, don't run. Evaluate how you manage your time prior to going to school, and in school. Learn how to prioritize. Focus on issues like child care and close personal relationships. Set up a study plan from day one and follow it.

My study group students offer these suggestions. First, network with other serious students regardless of age; select these people by answering the question, "Who are the students who mean business?" The easiest way to break down barriers is to walk up and introduce yourself. Share your insights, ask questions, and build a support network right away. Second, study your instructor; he or she is a walking, living textbook. Work at establishing a comfortable relationship. Finally, get in the habit of reviewing your work prior to class. Discipline yourself to complete all assignments. Give yourself the best chance possible to successfully fulfill your educational plan.

learning a specific trade study with people who don't know quite yet what they want to do. Students take classes at all hours of the day and night, for various lengths of time, for a variety of different degrees and certifications. **Your ideal lifestyle is whatever would make you the happiest**, not what fits the norm or what would make other people happy.

Think about what satisfies you, challenges you, and spurs your creativity. Consider your ideals in the following areas of your life: family, friends, living quarters, income, schedule, activities, possessions. What are the special rewards that make life worth living for you? Do you want to live in a city apartment or a suburban single-family home? Do you want to work in a large corporation or own your own small, independent business? Would you prefer to spend your free time going to a hockey game or wandering through an art gallery? Do you want to have children, own a certain kind of car, travel, write a book, or live near your parents? The more you know about yourself, the easier it will be to narrow your focus to subjects and career areas that would satisfy you.

Many of your lifestyle choices will eventually help to point toward a career focus. Choosing a career that fits what you want out of life is crucial because most people spend the majority of their lives working—approximately 40 years or more, five days a week, at least eight hours a day. The only thing you will do more in your life is sleep. When you don't like your work, you might not like your life either. Many people drag through their work week and live for the weekend. You can have a good time more than two days out of seven if you pursue a career that keeps you interested, challenged, and satisfied. Even though you might not spend your life at a job, if you undertake the search with similar attention to what you want, you will succeed.

Besides the job itself, other factors come into play when you consider your working life. What hours do you want to work? Do you want to drive or take public transportation? What kind of *perquisites* or "perks" (health insurance, discounts, parking, vacation time) are important to you? Do you prefer to work full-time, part-time, or flextime? Weekdays, weekends, or nights? With a large or small company? In town or in the suburbs? In a structured and formal organization or a relaxed and social atmosphere? How do you want to move up in the ranks? The "landscape" of a job goes far beyond the job description itself.

You don't have to nail yourself down on any of these decisions yet. Just keep your direction in mind as you explore through your reading and course of study. Staying aware of what you want as you go will help you to chart your career course.

EDUCATION AND SUCCESS

It isn't easy to make a decision to take classes, pay tuition, figure out what you want to study, sign up, gather the necessary materials, and actually get yourself to the school and into a seat in a class you have chosen. Many people stall out at any one of a number of places along the way, but you have made it. This accomplishment is just the first part of a lifelong commitment to learning.

Education—the process of developing and training the mind through formal schooling—should be far more than the accumulation of credit hours. If you take advantage of all it has to offer, it can help you find and develop an incredible array of skills and talents, leading you to success in whatever you choose to pursue.

What defines education?

- ❏ **Education is a choice.** You have chosen to improve your mind and skills through the educational process. You have focused your energies on a program that you think will get you where you want to go. Any program, no matter the length or the focus, is an opportunity to set and strive for goals.

- **Education is working.** As a student, think of yourself as a worker. You may not be making a salary by attending class, but you are doing everything else an employee does: following directions, working alone and with others toward goals, completing projects, and receiving evaluations. If you reverse that idea, you will see that workers are also students. On the job you need to keep learning new ideas and skills in order to complete tasks and projects and earn promotions. Information, processes, materials, equipment, and ideas are constantly changing in the workplace.

- **Education is what you make of it.** An Ivy League student who doesn't work hard won't benefit from school as much as will a dedicated learner at a community college. If you make the most of your mind and your educational opportunities, you will realize your potential.

- **Education is change.** Learning means changing for the better and adding to what you already know. By continuing to learn throughout your life you will experience continual change and continual progress.

How can education help you succeed?

- **Education gives you tools to continue learning.** Not only do you learn information, you improve your *ability* to learn via thinking skills, commitment, attentiveness, study skills, curiosity, and other important qualities. You may use specific information only for specific tasks, but you will use your ability to learn in everything you do.

- **Education changes you as it develops your knowledge.** Change, in the forms of development and improvement, brings growth, which fosters success. Learning, change, and success are all continual processes that occur together—the first two create the third.

- **Education improves your quality of life.** Income and employment get a boost from education. The 1994 Digest of Education Statistics reports that between 1980 and 1990, annual income generally rose more rapidly

How Education Boosts Income

Level of Education	Mean Annual Income
Master's degree	$43,032
Bachelor's degree	$35,900
Some college	$27,705
High school graduate	$23,410
Some high school	$18,012

Source: Adapted from the U.S. Department of Commerce, Bureau of the Census, *Current Population Reports*, Series P-60, *Money Income of Households, Families, and Persons in the United States: 1992*, as reported in the *Digest of Educational Statistics, 1994* (published by the National Center for Education Statistics, U.S. Department of Education Office of Educational Research and Improvement)

FIGURE 1-1

for persons with higher levels of educational attainment than for those with lower levels; for example, income for men who had completed four years of high school rose 37 percent compared to 78 percent for men who had completed five or more years of college. Figure 1-1 shows average income levels for different levels of educational attainment. Also, unemployment rates for those with a bachelors degree were 3.2 percent compared with 6.8 percent for those with four years of high school.

❏ **Education shows you what you are capable of.** You don't even know yet half of what you can do! As you rise to the challenges that your education continually presents to you, you will discover that your capacity for knowledge and your roster of abilities are constantly growing. The cycle of development leads to ever-increasing possibilities. As you make new contributions in class, on the job, and in your community, those contributions may then encourage others to offer you diverse opportunities to develop your abilities and use your intelligence.

❏ **Education gives you more power to make future choices.** As you can see in Figure 1-2, education extends your power in two directions: horizontally (introducing you to more available choices) and vertically (giving you more ability to follow those choices to success). For example, a student might take a class that introduces a new and interesting career field. This experience may lead the student to choose a class in that field that increases spe-

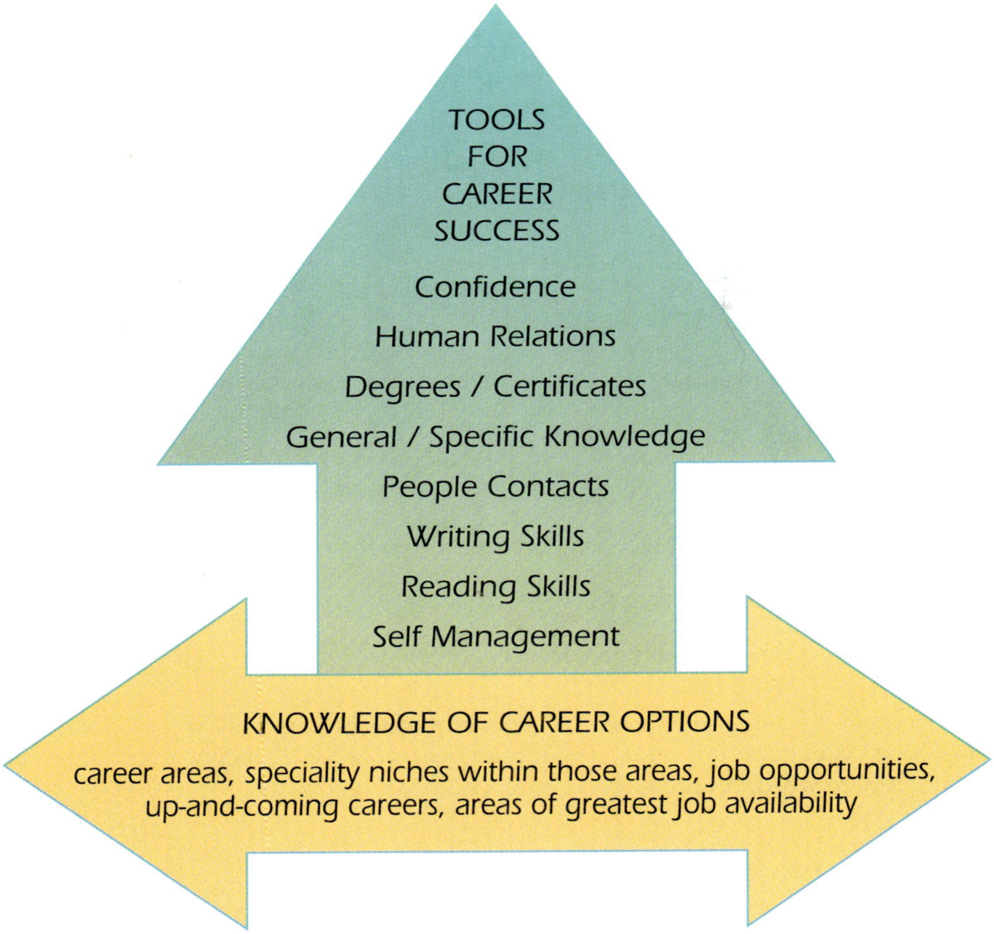

TOOLS
FOR
CAREER
SUCCESS

Confidence

Human Relations

Degrees / Certificates

General / Specific Knowledge

People Contacts

Writing Skills

Reading Skills

Self Management

KNOWLEDGE OF CAREER OPTIONS

career areas, speciality niches within those areas, job opportunities, up-and-coming careers, areas of greatest job availability

FIGURE 1-2

cific knowledge and skill level. If the student went on to major and work in that field, two classes would have changed the course of a life.

Furthermore, the Digest says that education affects both community involvement and personal health. Education helps to prepare individuals for participation in their communities by informing them of political, economic, and social conditions. Education also increases knowledge about health behaviors and preventative care; therefore, educated people may be more likely to see doctors regularly and to practice healthy habits.

Strategies to Start You on Your Way

You have to be ready to learn before the learning can happen. A student who isn't yet open to learning probably won't benefit from even the most innovative teaching techniques. These four strategies—*Becoming a Better Learner*, *Concentrating on the Present*, *Tapping into your School Resources*, and *Facing your Fears*—will help you take in new information more freely and make the most of your natural abilities.

Becoming a Better Learner

Although everyone has a unique learning style, a topic which you will explore in the next chapter, there are some basic rules of learning from which anyone can benefit. As elementary as they seem, they can help students of all ages take responsibility for what they learn.

- Keep an open mind.
- Listen carefully.
- Ask questions.
- Concentrate.
- Attend class regularly, on time, and with necessary supplies.
- Do the work assigned.
- Ask for help when you need it.
- Study at a time and place that lets you work efficiently.
- Prepare adequately for tests.
- Reward yourself when you succeed.

You will expand your knowledge on many of these topics as you read through upcoming chapters of this book. These rules demand a lot of energy, time, and dedication. You're worth the effort.

Concentrating on the Present

Start by considering why *not* to focus on the other two options: the past and the future. The past—well, it's over. Nothing that has already taken place can be changed.

The best that you can do is to learn from experience and use that knowledge to make improvements and better choices in other situations you encounter. On the flip side, the future is a complete unknown. As much as you prepare for what you think might or should happen, you can never really predict the course of events. The unexpected may pop up and leave you breathless.

The present, on the other hand, isn't in yesterday's trash or on a high shelf. It's lying in the palm of your hand ready for action. For example, you have a big mid-semester project due in a week. You want to do well to compensate for a couple of mediocre test grades from earlier in the semester. How do you proceed?

- ❏ You could dream or despair about your future final grade in the class.
- ❏ You could dwell on your past test grades and make yourself miserable.
- ❏ You could focus all of your energy on doing well on the project.

What would the third choice bring you? Investing your energy in your project could have a number of positive results. You would derive personal satisfaction for a job well done. More than likely, your instructor would reward your efforts with a grade which would raise your average. Your success would reinforce your belief in yourself—a quality that can fuel your efforts through the rest of the semester. Past, present, and future are all connected; by doing your best with the present, you can positively influence both the impact of your past and the promise of your future.

Tapping into your Resources

Resources are tools inside and outside of school that help you make the most of your education. As a student, you are making a big investment of your money and your time. Whether you study for six months or six years, you owe it to yourself to find out what benefits are available to you.

Table 1-1 is a summary of the resources you may find, listed along with the areas in which they can serve you. Every school will have some combination of these elements; to explore your school's offerings in detail, find a copy of your Student Handbook (printed by schools yearly to inform students of available resources). Take advantage.

The **library** deserves a special notice here. Your library is probably the most comprehensive resource available to you. Some schools have only one library; others have one or more central libraries in addition to smaller libraries that focus on specific material for an individual department (an arts and architecture library, a math and sciences library). If you take time at the beginning of your academic career to become acquainted with everything the library has to offer, you will save yourself hours of searching and a great deal of stress in the future.

Trying to find specific information in a library can be daunting. It's hard to know where to begin, and you can't benefit from the information available to you unless you can find it. Start by finding out if your library offers tours. A library tour is a terrific introduction to all of the different sections of the library: where they are located, what they offer, and how to use the materials they store. A tour can give you the orientation you need to feel comfortable navigating through the library on your own. If no tour is available, ask a librarian to give you an overview. Your library may have printed information that can help you as well.

When you are confused about where to go, the reference section is your best bet. The reference section is like the brain of the library. Within it are materials that act as a clearinghouse for information, helping you find out exactly where to look for what you need. Here you will find whatever system the library uses to catalogue its own holdings: a card catalogue, microfiche and microfiche viewers, or computer terminals that hook into a com-

You are "Here:" Aiming for "There"

TABLE 1-1

Resource	School	Personal	Job/Career	Financial	Active Involvement
Advisors/counselors	Assistance with balancing studying and work, choosing classes, getting over academic hurdles, selecting a major	Help with working out your personal problems	Advice on knowing yourself well enough to choose a job that fits you		
Library/Media Center	Academic catalogues, books on study skills, reference materials	Self-help books	Publications about general and particular job market info (books, papers, mags)	Brochures/books on financial aid, scholarships and loans, budgeting	
Instructors/Professors	Help with understanding class material, fulfilling requirements, studying	During office hours, are available to talk to you	Can help direct you in their fields, may have personal contacts for you		
Administration	Can help with academic problems, course selection, educational focus	Can help sort through personal issues with members of faculty or other administrators	Can be a source of valuable contacts	Can direct you toward financial aid opportunities	
Clubs—Academic, Arts, Athletic, Women's Issues, Minority Issues, Special Interest	If an academic club, can help broaden your knowledge/experience in a particular area of study; can help you balance school with other enriching activities	Provide opportunities to build strong and supportive friendships and alliances	Can help you develop skills, build knowledge, make new contacts		Depending on club focus, opportunities to serve on committees serve the community, plan functions, create shows or presentations, participate in athletic events, build a support system, exhibit support for others
Bulletin Boards	List academic events, class info, changes and additions, teacher office hours, academic club meetings and activities	List self-help group meetings	List career forums, job sign-ups and employment opportunities, seminars	List financial aid seminars, job opportunities, scholarship opportunities (application and deadline information)	List opportunities to participate in clubs, meetings, sports events, games, parties, seminars, community service events

STRATEGIES TO START
YOU ON YOUR WAY

TABLE 1-1 *continued*

Resource	School	Personal	Job/Career	Financial	Active Involvement
Health Services	If psychological services available, can help relieve school-related stress	Provide wellness care (regular examinations), illness care, and and prescriptions if necessary		Provide opportunities for low-cost and/or free care and prescription medications	
Telephone Hotlines	If school-related, can help you sort through academic issues	Advice and someone to talk to about personal problems—relationships, substance abuse, family issues, physical abuse, etc.			If you volunteer to staff a hotline yourself, an opportunity to help others work out their problems and feel more in control of their lives
Support Groups	If school-related, a chance to benefit from hearing how others have both stumbled and succeeded in school—and a chance to share your own stories	A chance to share stories, listen to ideas about how to make changes, feel like you're not the only one out there with a problem			An active, involved way to address your problems and help others at the same time by talking about your experiences—a chance to learn from one another
Career/Job Placement Office			Job listings, help with résumés and interviews, possible interview appointments, general factual info about the workplace—where the jobs are, salaries, etc.	Can add to your financial aid package through job opportunities	
Publications	Information for when you need to research a subject	Articles about day-to-day issues	Articles about the current job market	Information about financial conditions, jobs and scholarships	If you work on a school or local publication, a chance to be involved in the process of getting information to the public

TABLE 1-1 *continued*

Resource	School	Personal	Job/Career	Financial	Active Involvement
Tutoring	If you seek a tutor, help with any of the academics that confuse or overwhelm you / If you tutor, a chance to solidify what you already know		If you volunteer to tutor, a chance to find out if teaching and working with people is for you		If you tutor, a chance to help other students around you
Financial Aid Office			Job opportunities within your school environment (work/study and others)	Information and counseling on loans, grants, scholarships, financial planning, and balancing a budget	

puterized catalogue such as the OCLC (Online Computer Library Center) Union Catalog. Materials in catalogs are organized in three ways: by author, by title, and by subject.

In addition to standard reference materials, such as encyclopedias, almanacs, thesauruses, atlases, and dictionaries, you will find books that list information sources. For example, the *Business Periodicals Index* and *The Reader's Guide to Periodical Literature* list articles cross-referenced by periodical name or subject. Government publications and books like *Information USA* list government agencies and information sources; many contain statistics and articles developed through federal studies and operations. You can find reference books that help you find information in almost any field, from listings of dentists to U.S. historical documents to electrical code regulations.

Your reference room may provide computerized research tools. Many libraries now use ProQuest, a periodical reference system that enables you to locate articles stored on CD ROM and print them directly from the disk. Other sources that focus on specific subjects, such as the Biography Index or Dissertation Abstracts, have been put onto CD ROM. The *ROM* of CD ROM stands for *read only memory*; therefore, the information on a particular CD ROM cannot be altered or updated. CD ROM services provide libraries with updated disks regularly.

Electronic databases open up a world of knowledge. Online services such as DIALOG (with access to over 300 databases), ORBIT, and BRS help guide you through many different databases in search of specific information. For example, databases such as ERIC (Educational Resources Information Center) and D&B-Dun's Electronic Directory of Education store an extensive array of information, including statistics and fact sheets, library listings, directory listings, and articles written by professionals and scholars. You can locate databases on medical care (Medline, National Institute for Mental Health) job searches (U.S. Employment Opportunities, Career Placement Registry) finances (Consumer Credit Letter, Financial World), and much, much more.

Following are some additional hints for library use.

Don't hesitate to ask questions. The people who work at their library know their way around. A two-minute question may save you a couple of hours of random searching, and less research time means more productive thinking time.

Hunt down resources as soon as you receive an assignment. Chances are, many other classmates are looking for the same information. If you procrastinate, you may find that what you need has been checked out or is in use.

Use interlibrary loan. If you can't find a book you need, you can probably request it through interlibrary loan, a system that gives you access to books from libraries all over. Make book requests through your library. Plan to wait a while; a book from another library can take from a few days to a couple of months to arrive.

Find school-related information. Your library will probably carry course catalogues, student handbooks, and other resources containing information specific to your school.

Plan to spend time. Research is a time-consuming process. If you rush, you may miss out on some valuable information. Allocate enough time to cover all your bases.

You can also create your own small library at home. It won't replace your school or local library, but in collecting reference materials that you know you use often can save you time. "If you find yourself going to the library to look up the same reference book again and again, consider purchasing that book for your personal or office library," advises Sherwood Harris, author of *The New York Public Library Book of How and Where to Look It Up*. "These desktop libraries commonly include a dictionary, a style guide, a small atlas, the *World Almanac*, and, more and more these days, a computer manual or two." Evaluate what you most often need and consider making it your own.

One other relatively new and extensive resource that may be available to you is **the Internet**. The Internet is a collection of information networks connected to each other and to individual computer systems via telephone technology. The Internet can be a powerful research tool, helping you connect with databases, read "home pages" compiled by companies, schools, individuals, and organizations, download documents (transfer them to your own computer terminal's memory), search through catalogues of different libraries, and post messages and inquiries to an extensive array of people in all kinds of specialties.

This book would have to be twice as long in order to discuss everything you can know about the Internet. Your best bet is to focus on the specific services and tools that you need most. "Getting a handle on the Internet is a lot like grabbing a handful of Jello— the more firm you think your grasp is, the more oozes down your arm," says Ed Krol in his book *The Whole Internet User's Guide and Catalog*. "You don't need to deal with Jello in this manner to eat it, you just need the right tool: a spoon. And you need to dig in and start eating. The same is true of the Internet. You don't need to be an expert in telephone lines, data communications, and network protocols for it to be useful—You just need to know how to use some tools and start working on them."

Here are some tools you might want to use, depending on what is available to you.

TELNET allows you to log on to other computers on the Internet and is useful if you want to access databases, library catalogues, and many public services.

Electronic mail (e mail) lets you send typed messages to people at all corners of the Internet.

FTP (File Transfer Protocol) is a tool that allows you to access archives for the purpose of moving files from other computers to yours. If you want to have a copy of a legal document, an article, or some free software, you can download them through FTP.

The **World Wide Web** is a flexible tool for Internet exploration. It allows you to browse through a network of documents or "pages," most of which contain a mix of text and graphics.

Usenet is a network of newsgroups, places where people post their comments about all kinds of topics. Each newsgroup has its own specific topic; they are so numerous that you have a good chance of finding a newsgroup on almost anything that interests you. You can even start a newsgroup if you find that one doesn't exist on your topic of interest.

Gopher is a tool that organizes resources in menu format. Gopher helps you both find and access resources; once you find what you need on a menu, you select it and Gopher hunts it down for you. Because it allows you access to all types of Internet resources and eliminates the need to know exact Internet addresses, it is very user-friendly.

Your level of access to the Internet depends on the sophistication of the computer system you are using. If you have a computer at home, you can acquire a modem (a device that allows your computer to communicate by phone) and sign up for an online service such as America Online or CompuServe that provides Internet access. Your school may have direct Internet access. You may also be able to access the Internet through your work, if your company uses computers and is connected to the Internet.

This is a very brief overview of what you can do on the Internet. Check your library or bookstore for more extensive resources; *The Whole Internet User's Guide and Catalog* is one of the most comprehensive. It is worth your while to get to know how to navigate this vast and rapidly-growing information source. Whether you need to find an article about a new government program, locate a list of substance abuse organizations, talk to librarians about available materials, or find out the latest data on financial aid, the Internet will allow you to do it all from one computer terminal.

Facing your Fears

Everyone experiences fear. As exciting as they might be, new experiences often provoke many fears. Dealing with new people, taking on new responsibilities, wondering whether you can handle the work, figuring out if you have chosen the right school or the right program, worrying about your family and friends expecting too much of you or standing in your way—any and all of this can inspire real fear.

One common fear involves *independence*. The responsibilities of living—making and managing your own money; dealing with shelter, food, bills, and taxes; perhaps taking care of a family or an elderly relative—none of this is easy. Fear of what's involved in living today keeps some people from ever growing up and taking responsibility for anything. You have already faced this fear in one important way by becoming a student. The successful pursuit of an education demands a willingness to explore your limits.

Fear tends to keep people in the starting gate, hesitant to get on with the race. Many people feel safe with the familiar. They have trouble exploring other possibilities because their fears narrow the range of choices. To fight that inertia, address fears as soon as you can; they can take a long time to quiet. Once you name and examine your fears, you can start to work through them. For example, if you dropped out of college years ago and have worked full time ever since, you may fear many different aspects of returning to school, including adjusting your schedule, staying financially sound, meeting new people, having to take tests and fulfill assignments, and being judged by instructors. One way to address your fears gradually is to begin with one course and then gradually, over a year or two, increase your course load while decreasing your work time.

Your mind is powerful. It can convince you that something unknown to you is unreachable; on the other hand, given the chance, it can also propel you ahead into new territory. The old maxim, "You never know until you try," has proven time and time again to be true. Almost every student has had the experience of a dreaded course turning out to be one of the most rewarding in the schedule. In such cases the student conquers fear by putting forth a strong effort no matter how hard the course promises to be.

How do you face your fears? These five steps will help you discover and use your storehouse of courage. Through the course of your reading you will find yourself taking these steps again and again.

1. **Acknowledge your specific fears.** Whether it's self-doubt, the career area you have chosen, your financial status, or a difficult relationship, just the act of naming your fear will take it down a notch.

2. **Decide which fears are real and which conceal something deeper.** If you are scared of your final exam, think it over; do you fear the exam itself or do you fear the fact that if you pass and graduate, you will have to face the real world? If you fear the exam, you can take steps to prepare adequately for it. If you fear the real world, you might make an appointment at the career office to get help with job hunting. Figuring out what you truly fear will help you choose an appropriate strategy.

3. **Decide what plan of attack will help you take control of your fears.** If you feel your skills are inadequate to pursue your chosen career, find

Erase Fear

someone to talk to who is already in the workplace doing what you intend to do. If you are uneasy about your financial situation, develop a realistic picture of your finances by consulting a financial planner or checking related reading material out of your library.

4. **Move ahead with your plans.** This is the easiest step to understand and the hardest to carry out. Here's where having courage is the key to moving ahead. You may find that the drive to overcome fear forces you to work harder, resulting in even greater success than you imagined. You may also discover your fear is so great that you must change your plans, and that information is also valuable.

5. **Talk about your fears with people you trust.** You might be surprised about what fears others have. Often the ideas other people have about gaining control can help you with your own fears. When you share strategies, everybody benefits. You will be happy to know that other people have stumbling blocks just as you do.

Fears are your friends in a strange way. They provide valuable clues to what blocks your success. They tell you where you need a push or extra work, and they also can alert you to when you need to make changes. The more you know about what stalls you out, the more ways you will find to conquer your problems.

> "He has not learned the lesson of life who does not every day surmount a fear."
> Ralph Waldo Emerson, essayist and poet

Summing Up

If you remember nothing else from this book and this class, take the following idea away with you and build your world around it:

In order to be successful, you must take responsibility for your life.

No one book, person, or class can turn everything around and make it happen for you. This book and any other resource your school offers you can only provide ideas, suggestions, and support. You have to live with the paths that you choose. Make choices that make sense for your unique and individual needs.

Responsibility for your life means responsibility for your education. In taking on the responsibility to educate yourself, you aim to learn, get a job, and earn a decent living. Be a smart consumer; squeeze every ounce of opportunity out of your time as a student. Compare it to buying a car. A car buyer takes time to study prices, evaluate options and packages, investigate rebates, and check out repair records of certain makes and models. All of that hard work pays off in a desirable deal.

As a student, try just as hard to get the most for your money by challenging yourself to experience everything your education offers. You are spending a great deal of money, whether it is your own or someone else's. Every time you cut a class you throw money in the trash — anywhere from $35 to $100. Don't let that happen. Demand the most for your money, as well as from yourself, and you will reap the benefits of success.

Chapter 1: Applications

Keys for your Key Chain: Skills Worth Keeping

List here what to you are the five most important keys, or skills, you have learned from reading this chapter.

1. _____
2. _____
3. _____
4. _____
5. _____

Key Into Your Life: Opportunities to Apply What You Learn
Exercise 1 Why Are You Here?

Fact: You are here as a student. What circumstances caused you to enroll? Do any of the answers listed in the chapter fit you? Do you have other reasons all your own? You can have more than one answer; most people do. Write them here.

1._____
2._____
3._____
4._____
5._____

Do you dislike any of these reasons? If so, which ones and why?
_____
_____
_____

Which reasons are most important to you? Why? Rank them in order of importance.
_____
_____
_____

Look again at the reasons most important to you. For each, write here why that reason will help propel you along the path you have set for yourself.

1._____
2._____
3._____
4._____
5._____

Exercise 2 Your Dream

Think about what you want out of life by comparing it to what others want for themselves or for you.

What desires do you share with your family and friends?
_____
_____
_____
_____

What traditional aims that others think you should have don't appeal to you?
_____
_____
_____
_____

What untraditional aims do you have that others around you don't seem to share?
_____
_____
_____
_____

Exercise 3 Brainstorm Your Ideal Life

Take some quiet time to think about your life. Spend a half-hour or so brainstorming about everything that you wish you could be, do, have, or experience. List your wishes on a blank piece of paper.

Areas for you to consider:

❑ Career choices (job, perks, schedule, opportunities)

❑ Lifestyle issues (how you want to live, when you work, when you play)

❑ Finances

❑ Relationships

❑ Serving others

❑ Creativity

❑ Material possessions

❑ Places to work/live/travel

❑ Things to do

❑ Whatever else you think of

Now take a look at your list. You probably have a wide variety of details. To find the big picture, categorize your wishes. You can most clearly see relationships among your wishes by rewriting your list, regrouping wishes by category.

1. *Essential*—to who I am and to my happy life.

2. *Important for Now*—but probably not forever, and could change as my life changes.

3. *Out of Reach*—but something tells me I need to try anyway.

4. *Icing On The Cake*—would be nice, but not essential.

Look at what wishes you have grouped together, especially for category number 1. Ideas or themes may emerge that make sense to you. What themes come up again and again?

Examples of themes include living a city life, helping others, being social, staying close to family, and stability. List your recurring themes. Knowing them will help you to set goals and priorities later on.

_____

_____

_____

Exercise 4 What Obstacles and Fears Hold You Back?

What would get in the way of your achieving your ideal life? What distracts you? What makes you scared enough to turn away? Here are some possibilities:

Other people

Self-doubt; negative self-image

Fear of the expectations of others

Fear of responsibility

Ideas about workplace realities

Procrastination

Fear of failure

Lack of skills

Lack of education

Lack of support from others

Fear of the unfamiliar

Exhaustion and overwork

Comparison of self with others

The first step to overcoming your obstacles and fears is naming them. Thinking about the preceding list and anything else that hinders you, make a list of your five toughest roadblocks. Describe what causes them specifically. The more specific you can be, the more likely you will be able to overcome these roadblocks as you read the other chapters in this book. For example, under the category of "other people," a specific entry might say, "My father has always pressured me too hard and I resist by slacking off." For now, just list your fears and roadblocks; the keys you acquire in upcoming chapters will help you find ways to overcome them.

1. _____
_____
_____

2. _____
_____
_____

3. _____
_____
_____

4. _____
_____
_____

5. _____
_____
_____

Exercise 5 How Well Do You Open Yourself to Learning?

Here again are the rules that help you become a better learner. You may have a different level of success with each one. Rate yourself on a scale of 1 to 5 for each.

1 = Almost without fail

2 = Most of the time

3 = Often

4 = On and off

5 = I could use some real focus on this one

Rules	Rating
Keep an open mind.	
Listen carefully.	
Ask questions.	
Concentrate.	
Attend class regularly, on time, and with necessary supplies.	
Do the work assigned.	
Ask for help when you need it.	
Study at a time and place that lets you work efficiently.	
Prepare adequately for tests.	
Reward yourself when you succeed.	

Write here three rules you want to focus on and improve:

1. _____
2. _____
3. _____

Key to Cooperative Learning: Building Teamwork Skills

Who Can Help You?

Every school is unique and offers its own particular smorgasbord of opportunities. Investigate your school. Consider the list of school resources described in the chapter. Which does your school make available to you? Indicate here by writing *yes* or *no*.

Advisors and Counselors _____

Seminars and Meetings _____

Library/Media Center _____

Instructors _____

Clubs _____

Bulletin Boards _____

Telephone Hotlines _____

Support Groups   _____

Career/Job Placement Office   _____

Publications   _____

Tutoring   _____

Financial Aid Office   _____

Gather in groups of two to four. Each person should select two or three different resources to investigate (make sure no two people explore the same resource). As you do your research, look for specific answers to the following questions (include details that apply to your particular school).

1. Who provides the resource?
2. Where can it be found?
3. When is it available?
4. What can it provide for you?
5. How can you seek it out?

When you have finished, meet once again and share what you have found with each other. Write down the benefits of five of the resources you feel you are most likely to use. Notice how teamwork has given you information about many resources in exchange for working on only a few.

1. _____
_____
_____

2. _____
_____
_____

3. _____
_____
_____

4. _____
_____
_____

5. _____
_____
_____

Key to Self-Expression: Discovery through Journal Writing

School

How do you really feel about your studies right now? Describe the pros and cons of what you are doing, where you think it might take you, your goals, fears, frustrations, and victories—whatever comes into your head.

Key to Your Personal Portfolio: Your Paper Trail to Success

Educational Contract

This is the first item in your personal portfolio. Find a sturdy folder or notebook in which to keep each portfolio item you add as you read through the chapters of this book. By the end of this course, you will have collected concrete evidence of your abilities, education, progress, and qualifications for success in the real world. Your portfolio will come in handy during your tenure as a student as well as in your experiences with the application, interview, and hiring processes of the workplace.

When you accept employment, your employer may draw up a contract that you both read, approve, and sign. That action legally commits you both to fulfilling the responsibilities described in the contract.

In order to get the most out of your education, apply the contract principle to your time as a student. Draw up a "contract" between you and your school. Simply create two lists, one for each of the following subjects:

What you expect your school to provide for you

What you expect yourself to give

Make sure you are specific in your lists. Instead of saying, "I expect a good education," you might say, "I expect instructors who are available to help me" or "I expect classes that challenge me." Your lists can include people, resources, ideas, specific subjects, circumstances and situations, opportunities, anything at all. Don't hold back. Expect the most from yourself and your school, and you will increase your chances of attaining the goals you have set.

When you finish your contract, schedule a meeting with the instructor who is teaching this course. Go over the contract together. Your instructor's insight into what the school can give you will help you decide if your expectations are reasonable. Together you can clarify your contract, making any necessary changes, so that you both have a better idea of what to expect.

E X P L O R

Explore

2

Self-awareness: Knowing How You Learn

When you purchase a new tool or appliance, you want to make sure that you get good use out of it. Generally, you familiarize yourself with your purchase by reading the instruction manual, testing it, and using it safely.

You owe your mind the same care and respect. It is the most powerful tool you will ever possess. If you spend some time getting to know how it operates and what particular conditions and procedures maximize its efficiency, then you will continue to learn and develop throughout your lifetime.

In this chapter you will become aware of yourself and how you learn by defining these different elements of you: your **self-image**, your **attitude**, your **habits**, your **learning style**, your **likes and dislikes**, and your **abilities**. Knowing yourself will allow you to make smart decisions about where to be, what to do, with whom to associate, and how to work. Plus, you cannot believe in yourself until you *know* yourself.

SELF-IMAGE

Take an honest look at yourself. It isn't easy. Most people prefer to imagine what they will be doing in the future rather than look closely at their present situation. Looking ahead plays an important role as you set your goals and work toward them, but you must first make an honest assessment of your starting point. When you try to find an address in an unfamiliar town, you need to get your bearings before you can head in the right direction.

Most people do not perceive themselves accurately. Although a few overestimate themselves, too many people suffer from a poor self-image. If you feel inadequate from time to time, you aren't alone, but that doesn't mean it's a good idea to think poorly of yourself.

What effect can an inaccurate self-image have? Look at people you know who seem to misjudge themselves, thinking that they are less intelligent, capable, or attractive than they really are. Observe how that hinders their ability to make the most of themselves. You do the same to yourself when your self-image doesn't match reality. Your goal is to refine your self-image so that it eventually reflects your true self.

Assessing yourself honestly is crucial because you can create yourself through what you think of yourself. A poor self-image can paralyze you. The less you think you can do, the less you will try to do, and consequently the less you will achieve. In school that may result in poor grades, but in the working world the consequences of poor performance may escalate to job loss, financial woes, and/or depression. Unfortunately,

> **Self-Image,** noun. One's conception or view of one's self (*self* includes one's own identity, abilities, and worth).

Most people don't perceive themselves accurately

most of the messages people send themselves are negative. People can be their own worst critics, often internalizing messages from parents and other authority figures. Realize that such negative "self-talk" is possibly quite far from the truth.

The positive self-image has two components:

1. **Self-esteem** is a perception that you are of value, that who you are and what you can contribute to the world are valuable.

2. **Self-confidence** is a trust in yourself, a belief that you have power to make positive changes in yourself and your surroundings. It puts your self-esteem into action.

You can think your way to success with positive self-talk. Replace negative thoughts (I'm not very smart/I can't do it/I'm not good enough) with positive ones (I have a lot to offer/It won't be easy, but I'm smart enough to figure it out/I am talented). Talk to yourself as if you were talking to another person, someone you care a lot about. You would never talk to a friend as harshly as you talk to yourself at times. People tend to believe what other people say about them, whether negative or positive. Take that to heart and be kind to yourself.

How can you put positive self-talk into action?

Stop negative talk in its tracks and change it to positive talk. If you catch yourself thinking, "I am really stupid," stop and say to yourself, "I can do better than that and next time I will." Negative self-talk is natural but destructive; learning to replace it takes constant work, even when you think you've mastered it.

Take a moment, perhaps every morning in front of the mirror, to pay yourself a general compliment: "I am a terrific, valuable, and powerful person." Or be specific. "I will demonstrate impressive potential at my interview."

Replace *have-to* words, which take power from you, with *want-to* words.

I have to	becomes	*I want to*
I should	becomes	*I choose to*
I'll try	becomes	*I will*
I intend to	becomes	*I promise to*

Want-to words give you power and control because they imply a *personal decision* to act. When you say, "I have to," you're saying that someone else has the power to decide what you do. When you say, "I want to," you're saying that the choice is yours.

Note your successes. Even when you don't think you are at your best, don't let that diminish your victories. As you work for self-improvement, congratulate yourself when you have taken any steps in the right direction, no matter how small. Whether you ace a test, make an important contact, eat more vegetables, win a job, or begin to communicate more honestly, each success helps you believe in yourself. Try keeping a list of your successes in a notebook.

Building a positive self-image is a lifelong challenge. If you work to maintain a bright vision of yourself, it will take you far along the road toward achieving your goals.

ATTITUDE

Attitude,
noun. 1. a state of mind or disposition 2. a manner of acting, thinking, or feeling that shows that state of mind

Your attitude affects everything you do. It can energize you or trip you up because it affects how you see yourself and your world. A positive attitude can open your mind to learning experience, inspire you to take action, and help you contribute to the welfare of others. On the other hand, a negative attitude can hinder learning, stifle initiative, and create stress for others. For example, say you are enrolled in a required course unrelated to your major. If you adapt the attitude that the course is a waste of time, chances are you won't learn much. If, however, you keep an open mind, the course might teach you something valuable or perhaps open a new area of interest for you.

Attitudes come in part from exposure to prevailing views in your family, circle of friends, and local community. Despite those predispositions, you have the power to change your attitudes through your life experiences. People who have grown up in culturally homogenous neighborhoods and then study or work in more integrated environments, for example, may change their attitudes about people of other cultures and races. A student or an employee who can't accept working with different kinds of people will have trouble surviving in an environment that promotes diversity.

Within a general positive attitude you can develop specific attitudes that correspond to the principles by which you live. Treating others as you want to be treated and valuing people of all races, creeds, and colors are two positive attitudes. Many different attitudes are positive. Part of the maturing process involves recognizing that some unfamiliar attitudes have worth and that your own attitudes may change over time. For example, you may have grown up with the attitude that no one can succeed without four-year college education. If later you meet a successful individual who completed a six-month course of study in a proprietary school, you may develop a new positive attitude: Shorter school terms can be practical and just as valuable.

"No one can be positive all the time," says Elwood N. Chapman in his book *Your Attitude Is Showing: A Primer of Human Relations*. "You will naturally have periods of doubt. These temporary periods will not hurt you seriously. But a day-to-day negative attitude that persists over weeks and months will destroy your future." Chapman suggests the following ways to keep your attitude positive.

1. **Let your positive attitude in one area spill over into another.** If you are happy about your progress at school, for example, you may be able to remain more positive about your personal life.

2. **Talk positive to yourself and others.** Find what you can compliment and praise about a situation or person. Avoid constant complaining.

3. **Seek the good in the people around you.** If you make an effort to focus on what is positive about your friends, family members, classmates, and instructors, you are more likely to feel positively about them and to be able to benefit from your associations.

4. **Seek the good in your school or workplace.** Noticing what is negative doesn't usually take a lot of effort, so put some hard work into seeing the positive. What do you like about your environment? What benefits you? What inspires you? The more good you see, the more you can take advantage of it.

5. **Avoid getting dragged down by the negative thinking of others.** The negative opinions that others have don't necessarily apply to you. Stay strong and evaluate situ-

ations for yourself. Protecting your positive attitude will help you make decisions that suit you best rather than ones that please negative peers.

HABITS

Anything that you become accustomed to doing in a certain way, and often on a regular basis or at certain times, constitutes a habit. You might have a habit of showering in the morning, eating raisins for a snack, channel surfing with the TV remote control, leaving your wet towel on the bed, hitting the snooze button on your clock, talking for hours on the phone, or studying late at night. Your habits reveal a lot about you.

So-called bad habits earn that title because they can prevent you from reaching important goals. Some bad habits such as chronic lateness cause obvious problems. Other habits, such as renting movies three times a week, can affect you in more subtle ways. You may learn the hard way that you needed those six hours you spent watching movies for studying or family obligations.

People maintain bad habits because they offer rewards. Many rewards brought on by habits are enjoyable even if later effects aren't so great. Eating pastries every morning might cause you to gain weight, but the reward is that they taste delicious. Going out to eat frequently may take precious dollars out of your budget, but it's so much easier than shopping for food, cooking, and washing dishes. What bad habit of yours has a pleasant effect?

You often have to wait longer and work harder to see a reward for good habits. That makes them harder to maintain. If you were to cut out fattening foods, you wouldn't lose weight in two days. If you were to reduce your nights out to gain more study time, you wouldn't see better grades by the end of the week. When you're striving to maintain good habits, you have to trust that the rewards are somewhere down that road.

Think over your habits. Are there some you would like to break or change? Here is one step-by-step way to do it.

> **Habit,**
> noun. 1. A recurrent, often unconscious pattern of behavior frequently acquired through repetition
> 2. Customary manner or practice

1. **Recognize the habit as troublesome.** This can take serious thought because sometimes the trouble doesn't seem to come directly from the habit. Spending every weekend working around the house may seem like a necessity; however, you may be overdoing it and ignoring friends and family members.

2. **Decide to change.** You might realize what your bad habits are but don't yet care about their effects on your life. Until you are convinced that you will receive something positive and useful from changing, your efforts won't get you far.

3. **Start today.** What's the point of waiting? You could put this off forever—after this week, after the family reunion, after the tax audit, after the semester. Each day lost is a day you haven't had the chance to benefit from a new lifestyle.

4. **Change one habit at a time.** Changing and breaking habits is difficult. Trying to be perfect overnight will only frustrate you. Spending more time with your family, reducing TV time, increasing studying, and saving more money all at the same time can bring on a fit of deprivation, sending you scurrying back to all your old habits. Easy does it.

5. **Reward yourself for positive steps taken.** Use appropriate rewards of course. If you're trying to study more and you earn a good grade, don't reward yourself by slacking off the next week. If you've lost weight, don't celebrate in an ice cream parlor. Choose a reward that won't encourage you to stray from your target.

6. **Don't get discouraged.** Rarely does someone make the decision to change and do so without a setback. Realizing how normal slips are can help you avoid negative self-talk. Being too hard on yourself might build up frustration that tempts you to give up and go back to the habit. Work through the slip by examining (a) why it happened, (b) how to avoid it in the future, and (c) how to try again.

LEARNING STYLES

Your mind has an incredible capacity to take in and process information, even though you might not always give it credit. Unfortunately, the judgments that family members, peers, or instructors make about you can narrow your view of yourself and your abilities. Some people become convinced they are stupid or incapable of learning how to do anything new. Don't believe it. You can continue to learn throughout your life. If you feel you don't fit into the standard educational system, perhaps you learn differently from the way others do.

Think about where you are now and how far you have come. You are fluent in one or more languages. You can read and write at some level. You probably have learned how to operate complicated machinery such as an automobile, computer, VCR, or fax machine. You may take those abilities for granted, but it took time, energy, determination, and a willingness to make mistakes for you to be successful. You have even tackled the difficult task of learning how to get along in the world—how to communicate with others, manage your life, be a member of a family, be a friend, and operate within the community and society.

You possess and can process an enormous amount of information.

Thinking about how much you know will help you understand just what an accomplished learner you are and how you will benefit from staying open to new experiences.

Just as people have different personality traits, they have different styles of learning. What some might interpret as a learning difficulty may be simply a different learning style. You may not have ever thought about how you learn, but you may already know some other of your characteristics such as how you react to different people, events, and situations. For example:

I love to socialize.

I take things personally.

I don't pick up on ideas right away.

I like to be in charge.

I prefer someone to give me direction.

I love getting organized.

I am shy around people.

I enjoy helping others.

There are no right or wrong answers, no good or bad ways to be. The only "right" description is the one that you discover by analyzing yourself accurately and honestly. Then, if there is room for improvement—problem areas you want to target or good areas you want to build upon—you can begin to work on them, step by step.

If you don't give yourself a chance to know what works best for you, you run the risk of forcing yourself into career or personal situations that stifle your creativity, development, and happiness. Have you ever experienced stress and inattentiveness due to a problematic job or a relationship? Did you feel angry, dulled, restricted, lethargic, or agitated? Did the situation change? If so, what happened? Getting out of the situation may have provided you with some relief, although you may or may not have learned why you were unhappy. People often fall into the same troublesome situations time and time again without understanding why. You can break that difficult pattern by learning as much as you can about yourself and about how to maximize your capability for learning.

How do you get from your own randomly built knowledge of yourself to knowing how you learn? Barbara Soloman, the Associate Director of the University Undesignated Program at North Carolina State University, has developed a **Learning Styles Inventory** that can help you. You will have an opportunity to complete a version of her inventory at the end of the chapter, and your answers will help you discover your particular learning style.

"Students learn in many ways," says Professor Soloman. "Mismatches often exist between common learning styles and standard teaching styles. Therefore, students often do poorly and get discouraged. Some students doubt themselves and doubt their ability to succeed in the curriculum of their choice. Some settle for low grades and even leave school. If students understand how they learn most effectively, they can tailor their studying to their own needs. Not only does this help to raise their grades, it also helps to raise their self-esteem as they realize that difficulties they encounter may be due to mismatches between their learning styles and their teachers' teaching styles."

Following are descriptions of the four categories that you will use to map out your learning style; each category has two opposing types. Most people will fit somewhere along the continuum between the two types in each category, although some will be off the map in one direction or the other. As you read, don't think too hard yet about where you fit in; the inventory at the end of the chapter will help you decide more accurately. The suggestions you see for how to work with individual styles have come from Professor Soloman's students, who made recommendations for their own styles from what they learned while exploring how they learn.

Are You Active or Reflective?

Active learners retain and understand information better after they have done something in the external world (outside their brain) with the information. They like to apply the information to the real world, experience it in their own actions, or discuss or explain to others what they have learned.

Student-suggested strategies for the active learner:

❏ Study in a group in which members take turns explaining topics to each other and then discussing them.

❏ Think of practical uses of the course material.

❏ Think of how the material relates to your own experiences, or if you have ever directly experienced something that clarifies how the information works.

Reflective learners retain and understand information better after they have taken time to think about it.

Student-suggested strategies for the reflective learner:

❏ When you are reading, stop periodically to think about what you have read.

- Don't just memorize material; think about why it is important and what it relates to, considering the causes and effects involved.

- Write short summaries of readings or class lectures in your own words. It may take time, but writing can help you to retain the material more effectively.

> "Students still have to work hard to overcome the obstacles that mismatches between learning styles and teaching styles engender, but when they realize it is not because they are just not smart enough, they are encouraged to do the necessary work."
>
> Barbara Soloman, Director of Undesignated Programs at North Carolina State University

Are You a Sensor or an Intuitor?

Sensors prefer concrete and specific facts, data, and detailed experimentation. They like to solve problems with standard methods and are patient with details. They don't respond well to surprises or unique complications that upset normal procedure. They are good at memorizing facts.

Student-suggested strategies for the sensor:

- Ask the instructor how ideas and concepts apply in practice.

- Ask for specific examples of the ideas and concepts.

- Brainstorm specific examples and practices by yourself or with classmates.

- Think about how theories make specific connections with the real world.

Intuitors prefer innovation and theories. They are good at grasping new concepts and big picture ideas. They dislike repetition and fact-based learning. They are comfortable with symbols and abstractions, often connecting them with prior knowledge and experience. Most classes are aimed at intuitors.

Student-suggested strategies for the intuitor:

- If you happen to be in a class that deals primarily with factual information, try to think of concepts, interpretations, or theories that link the facts together.

- Be aware that you are prone to careless mistakes on tests because you become impatient with details. Take time to read directions and entire questions before answering, and be sure to check your work.

- Tell yourself to be more careful and to pay attention to details in school.

Are You Visual or Verbal?

Visual learners remember best what they see: pictures, diagrams, flow charts, time lines, films, and demonstrations. They tend to forget words and ideas that are spoken only. Classes generally don't include that much visual information. Note that although words written on paper or a blackboard are something you see, understanding them easily is part of being a verbal learner. Visual learners learn most easily from visual cues that don't involve words.

Student-suggested strategies for the visual learner:

- Add diagrams to your notes whenever possible. Dates can be drawn on a time line; math functions can be graphed; percentages can be drawn in a pie chart.
- Organize your notes so that you can clearly see main points and supporting facts and how things are connected. You will learn more about different styles of note-taking in Chapter Five.
- Connect related facts in your notes by drawing arrows.
- Color-code your notes with highlighters so that everything that relates to one topic is the same color.

Verbal learners remember much of what they hear and more of what they hear and then say. They benefit from discussion, prefer verbal explanation to visual demonstration, and learn effectively by explaining things to others. Written words are processed as verbal information; therefore, verbal learners learn well through reading. The majority of classes, since they present material through the written word, lecture, or discussion, are geared to verbal learners.

Student-suggested strategies for the verbal learner:

- Get enough sleep and show up on time so that you can take everything in most efficiently.
- Talk about what you learn. Work in study groups so that you have an opportunity to explain and discuss what you are learning.

Are You Sequential or Global?

Sequential learners find it easiest to learn material presented in a logical, ordered progression. They solve problems in a linear, step-by-step manner. They can work with sections of material without yet fully understanding the whole picture. They tend to be stronger when looking at the parts of a whole rather than understanding the whole and then dividing it up into parts. They learn best when taking in material in a progression from easiest to more complex to most difficult. Most courses are taught sequentially.

Student-suggested strategies for the sequential learner:

- If you have a class where an instructor jumps around from topic to topic or skips steps, ask the instructor to fill in the skipped portions or to help you connect topics.
- When you study notes from a class where the instructor presents information at random, don't read your notes as they are. Take time to re-write the material according to whatever logic helps you to understand it best. Even though this takes a while, it will save you study time in the long run.

Global learners learn in fits and starts. They may feel lost for days or weeks, unable to solve even the simplest problems or show the most rudimentary understanding, until they suddenly "get it." They may feel stupid and discouraged when struggling with material which many other students seem to learn easily. Once they understand, though, they tend to see the big picture to an extent that others may not often achieve. They are often highly creative.

- ❏ First of all, just recognizing that you aren't slow or stupid can help.

- ❏ Before you try to study a chapter in a book, read all the subheadings to try to get an overview of where the chapter is going.

- ❏ When you get your first assignment on a new topic, set aside extra time and skim the entire chapter before you begin. That kind of "preview reading," described in more detail in Chapter Five, will save you from going over and over parts that you just can't understand.

- ❏ Instead of spending a short time on every subject every night, try setting aside evenings for specific subjects and immerse yourself in just one subject at a time. Then stay away from that subject for a day or two.

- ❏ Try to relate subjects to other things you already know. Keep asking yourself how you could apply the material and what it has to do with anything else.

- ❏ Don't lose faith in yourself. You will get it, and once you do, you may be able to do more with it than you can imagine.

What's the point? What are the benefits of knowing your learning style? Two stand out.

1. **Success in school.** Since people have different learning styles, they need different strategies in order to efficiently take in class material and make it their own. For example, say you do well in discussion-based classes but not in lecture courses. Knowing your style can help you both understand why that is and apply the appropriate strategies to improve your retention in a lecture situation.

2. **Success on the job.** Any successful worker knows that learning, instead of stopping when you graduate from school, continues throughout your career and can keep you on the path of success. Your learning style is essentially your working style. If you know how you work, you will be able to look for an environment that suits you well. You will also be more able to adjust when you encounter situations that are more difficult for you.

Figure 2-1 gives you an idea of where the majority of students fall within the categories, according to statistics gathered by Professor Soloman.

When you complete the inventory and determine your style, remember that you probably won't fit completely into any one category. Some people even switch back and forth between preferences, depending on what they're doing. The point is to figure out your tendencies and use that information to improve your learning and working, not to box yourself in with a particular label.

LIKES AND DISLIKES

How can you determine what you like? You know many of your general likes and dislikes already. For example, you know

SOURCE: Adapted from 1992 data gathered by Barbara A. Soloman, Associate Director, University Undesignated Program, North Carolina State University, Raleigh, NC.

FIGURE 2-1

- ❏ What qualities you admire in other people.
- ❏ What areas of study you enjoy.
- ❏ What activities make you happy.
- ❏ What kind of daily schedule you like to keep (early riser, night owl).
- ❏ What type of home and work environment you prefer.

Start now to spend some time thinking through your likes and dislikes so that when you begin to make important life decisions, you know what you want.

Does it matter that you study subjects you enjoy and eventually work in a career area that you like? You may know people who work because they have to, at jobs that aren't necessarily their ideals. Some decide to put up with a certain line of work because they need the salary or stability. Some may not have the skills or education to do something they would like better, or perhaps they don't realize they can do better. In addition, the longer people stay in jobs they dislike, the tougher it is to leave. The best bet is to find something you like at the start.

Think about your life. You are asleep approximately 35 percent of the time, and working 40 percent. That leaves 25 percent, much of which goes toward your relationships, home and car maintenance, bill-paying, and fulfilling other obligations. Seeing how little time remains for relaxation and enjoyment will show you how much it makes sense to pursue what interests you. This doesn't mean your studies and your work will always make you deliriously happy. It just means that you can spend your school and work time in a manner that is, in large part, pleasant to you. You will spend eight or more hours a day, five or more days a week, up to 50 or more weeks a year as a working citizen. Choose to make your happiness a factor.

Here are three good reasons to go to the trouble of pursuing subjects and careers that you like.

1. **You will have more energy.** Doing something you like boosts your energy. Think about how you feel when you are looking forward to seeing a special person, participating in a favorite sports activity, or enjoying something entertaining such as a movie or a TV show. When you are doing something you like, time seems to pass very quickly. Contrast this with how you feel about disagreeable activities. The difference in your energy level is immense. You will be able to get much more done in a subject or career area that you enjoy.

2. **You will perform better.** Think back to high school. You probably got your best grades in your favorite classes and excelled in your favorite activities. That doesn't change as you get older. You will always find the most success in work that you like to do, whether in class or on the job. The more you like something, the more you work hard at it—and the harder you work, the more you will improve.

3. **You will have a positive attitude, which contributes to a positive environment.** Even if you perform well, a negative attitude can sour the atmosphere for your co-workers and may ultimately cost you your job. On the other hand, a positive attitude can brighten everyone's day and might even make up for areas in which you lack ability or experience. Think about what it's like to work as a team with others. Just as the moods of your co-workers can energize you or make you miserable, yours may do the same to them. You and your co-workers will both perform better when happy.

Ability,
noun. The power to do something, either physical or mental; skill.

ABILITIES

As you think about what you like, your particular abilities will come to mind, because you often like best the things you can do well.

Some abilities seem to be natural; you learned to do some things without ever having to work too hard. Others you struggled to develop and continue to work hard to maintain your level of expertise. How do you know what your abilities are? Consider

❑ What you have always been able to do well.

❑ What others have always praised about you.

❑ What you have always wanted to do and worked hard to develop.

Here are two more sources of information to consider:

1. **Your learning style.** An active learner might possess good interpersonal skills; a sensing learner might have a talent for details and figures; a sequential learner might excel in organizational and management skills. Your learning style can provide clues to your particular strengths.

Real World Perspective

Q Nicole Kelly, student at Notre Dame College of Ohio in Parma, Ohio

Students don't have a lot of control over how or what a teacher teaches. I didn't realize it right away, but I have been a visual learner my whole life. One day, my communications teacher gave the class some information about the different types of learning styles. The information stuck in my head, and as I thought about what helps me remember class material, I realized that my particular style of learning was probably visual; I feel like I learn a lot better in classes where the teacher uses graphs and overheads in addition to the lecture.

I think my visual learning style has contributed to the problems I have had in classes where the teacher would just talk. I would try to write everything down, but I could not possibly remember everything the teacher said, and my notes were bits and pieces that didn't make any sense. This contributed to my not doing as well as I could have in these types of classes. Not all teachers give information in ways that help me take it in. How do I deal with my own type of learning style so I have more success in the classroom?

A Barbara Soloman, Associate Director of the University Undesignated Program in the Division of Undergraduate Studies at North Carolina State University in Raleigh, North Carolina

You can't change your teachers, but there is a lot you can do to help yourself. One suggestion is to buy yourself a set of colored pens. Decide on one color for main points, one for examples, one for specific facts and others for whatever else is suitable for a particular class. Line your pens up on your desk and as you take notes, use the appropriate color. Not only will this make your notes more "visual," it will also keep you actively involved and thinking as the teacher lectures.

Of course, you cannot remember everything the teacher says. Nobody can; not even a verbal learner. Try this idea: take a ruler and divide your notebook pages in half lengthwise. In class, only take notes on the left half of the page. After class, as soon as possible, review your notes. Perhaps team up with a friend and use both sets of notes. Definitely read your text. On the right side of the page add anything you remember as you review your own notes, your friend's notes, or the text. Use arrows and lines connecting things that go together. Draw your own diagrams whenever you can think of suitable ones.

Reviewing this way on a daily basis takes more time in the short run, but it can save you lots of study time right before the test because you remember lots more.

2. **Your accomplishments.** They don't have to have earned you a trophy. Did you care for a baby nephew? Have you volunteered at a senior citizens' home? Are you handy with house or car repairs? Did you help your family through a financial crisis? Anything achieved that has given you pride in yourself reveals abilities.

As with your likes and dislikes, knowing your abilities will help you find a job that makes the most of them. That kind of job situation has the best chance of making you happy and therefore able to perform to the best of your ability. If you love people and are intimidated by electronics, you wouldn't be wise to aim for a career in computer programming. Once you know yourself, you will be more able to set appropriate goals.

What about your weaknesses?

Your strengths and weak points together define your individuality. Nobody is perfect, and no one is good at everything. You need to keep the whole picture in mind as you search for a place for yourself.

Most people deal with their weak points in one of two ways:

❏ They ignore them.

❏ They dwell on them, causing a poor self-image.

Both are natural, but neither is wise. Ignoring your weaknesses can get you into situations where you won't admit that you can't deliver; focusing on your weaknesses can make you forget you have any strengths at all.

The second tendency is much more common than the first, and usually shows up as negative self-talk. If you have ever been down on yourself, focusing on everything you think is wrong with your life, you know how that dulls your desire to try. Don't be your own worst critic; support yourself with positive self-talk. "I have a ways to go, but I am getting there." "I can learn a lot from this mistake and will improve next time." Talk yourself up—it will allow you to take risks that help you grow. You can even write your positive statements on Post-It notes and put them where you will see them every day.

Rather than focusing on your shortcomings, just acknowledge that they exist and work to improve what you can. A healthy understanding of your weak points can help you avoid situations where they would cause you trouble. If you become shy in large groups, you might seek a small-group environment in school or on the job. If working with words and language has never been your thing, you might want to consider a career in technology. Use your weaknesses to your advantage.

Summing Up

Life is a series of decisions. The more you know about yourself, the more quickly and easily you can choose paths appropriate for you and be on your way. When you are familiar with your learning styles, abilities, shortcomings, and preferences, you will be more likely to make a living in your areas of interest, and the more your studies and your work suit you, the more success you will enjoy.

Chapter 2: Applications

Keys for your Key Chain: Skills Worth Keeping

List here what to you are the five most important keys, or skills, you have learned from reading this chapter.

1. _____
2. _____
3. _____
4. _____
5. _____

Key Into Your Life: Opportunities to Apply What You Learn
Exercise 1 - Your Habits

You have the power to change your habits. List three problematic habits and the effects of each.

Habit	How It Prevents You from Reaching Goals
1.	
2.	
3.	

Out of these three, choose the habit you most want to change. Write it here.

_____
_____
_____

What helpful habit do you want to develop in its place? For example, if your problem habit were a failure to express yourself when you are angry, a replacement habit might be to calmly talk about situations that upset you as soon as they arise. If you have a habit of cramming for tests at the last minute, you could replace it with a regular study schedule that allows you to cover your material bit by bit over a longer period of time.

_____
_____
_____

One way to help yourself abandon your old habit is to think about how your new habit will improve your life. List two benefits of your new habit.

1. _____

2. _____

Set yourself a deadline; give yourself four weeks to complete your habit shift. Keep track of your progress by indicating how well you did on each day. If you avoided the old habit, write an X below the day. If you used the new one, write an N. Therefore, a day where you only avoided the old habit will have an X; a day where you did both will have both letters; a day where you did neither will be left blank.

1 2 3 4 5 6 7 8 9 10 11 12 13 14

15 16 17 18 19 20 21 22 23 24 25 26 27 28

Don't forget to reward yourself for your hard work. Write here what your reward will be when you feel like you are on the road to a new and beneficial habit.

_____

_____

_____

Exercise 2 Your Learning Styles Inventory

This "test" will help you understand your personal learning style. Circle *a* or *b* to indicate your answer to each question. You must answer every question and you must choose *only one* answer for each question. If both answers seem to apply to you, choose the answer that applies more often.

1. I study best
   a. in a study group.
   b. alone or with a partner.

2. I would rather be considered
   a. realistic.
   b. imaginative.

3. When I recall what I did yesterday, I am most likely to think in terms of
   a. pictures/images.
   b. words/verbal descriptions.

4. I usually think new material is
   a. easier at the beginning and then harder as it gets more complicated.
   b. often confusing at the beginning but easier as I start to understand what the whole subject is about.

5. When given a new activity to learn, I would rather first
   a. try it out.
   b. think about how I'm going to do it.

6. If I were an instructor, I would rather teach a course
   a. that deals with real-life situations and what to do about them.
   b. that deals with ideas and encourages students to think about them.

7. I prefer to receive new information in the form of
   a. pictures, diagrams, graphs, or maps.
   b. written directions or verbal information.

8. I learn
   a. at a fairly regular pace. If I study hard I'll "get it" and then move on.
   b. in fits and starts. I might be totally confused and then suddenly it all "clicks."

9. I understand something better after I
   a. attempt to do it myself.
   b. give myself time to think about how it works.

10. I find it easier
    a. to learn facts.
    b. to learn ideas/concepts.

11. In a book with lots of pictures and charts, I am likely to
    a. look over the pictures and charts carefully.
    b. focus on the written text.

12. It's easier for me to memorize facts from
    a. a list.
    b. a whole story/essay with the facts embedded in it.

13. I will more easily remember
    a. something I have done myself.
    b. something I have thought or read about.

14. I am usually
    a. aware of my surroundings. I remember people and places and usually recall where I put things.
    b. unaware of my surroundings. I forget people and places. I frequently misplace things.

15. I like instructors
    a. who put a lot of diagrams on the board.
    b. who spend a lot of time explaining.

16. Once I understand
    a. all the parts, I understand the whole thing.
    b. the whole thing, I see how the parts fit.

17. When I am learning something new, I would rather
    a. talk about it.
    b. think about it.

18. I am good at
    a. being careful about the details of my work.
    b. having creative ideas about how to do my work.

19. I remember best
    a. what I see.
    b. what I hear.

20. When I solve problems that involve some math, I usually
    a. work my way to the solutions one step at a time.
    b. see the solutions but then have to struggle to figure out the steps to get to them.

21. In a lecture class, I would prefer occasional in-class
    a. discussions or group problem-solving sessions.
    b. pauses that give opportunities to think or write about ideas presented in the lecture.

22. On a multiple-choice test, I am more likely to
    a. run out of time.
    b. lose points because of not reading carefully or making careless errors.

23. When I get directions to a new place, I prefer
    a. a map.
    b. written instructions.

24. When I'm thinking about something I've read,
    a. I remember the incidents and try to put them together to figure out the themes.
    b. I just know what the themes are when I finish reading and then I have to back up and find the incidents that demonstrate them.

25. When I get a new computer or VCR, I tend to
    a. plug it in and start punching buttons.
    b. read the manual and follow instructions.

26. In reading for pleasure, I prefer
    a. something that teaches me new facts or tells me how to do something.
    b. something that gives me new ideas to think about.

27. When I see a diagram or sketch in class, I am most likely to remember
    a. the picture.
    b. what the instructor said about it.

28. It is more important to me that an instructor
    a. lay out the material in clear, sequential steps.
    b. give me an overall picture and relate the material to other subjects.

SCORING SHEET

1. Put 1's in the appropriate spaces in the table below (e.g., if you answered *a* to Question 3, put a 1 in Column *a* by Question 3).

2. Total the columns and write the totals in the indicated spaces.

3. For each of the four scales, subtract the smaller total from the larger one. Write the difference (1 to 7) and the letter (*a* or *b*) for which the total was larger on the bottom line. For example, if under "ACTV/REFL" you had 2 *a* and 5 *b* responses, you would write 3*b* on the bottom line under that heading.

4. On the next page, mark X's above your scores on each of the four scales.

CHAPTER 2:
APPLICATIONS

ACTV/REFL Q		SENS/INTU Q		VISL/VRBL Q		SEQN/GLOB Q	
a	b	a	b	a	b	a	b
1 __	__	2 __	__	3 __	__	4 __	__
5 __	__	6 __	__	7 __	__	8 __	__
9 __	__	10 __	__	11 __	__	12 __	__
13 __	__	14 __	__	15 __	__	16 __	__
17 __	__	18 __	__	19 __	__	20 __	__
21 __	__	22 __	__	23 __	__	24 __	__
25 __	__	26 __	__	27 __	__	28 __	__
Totals: __ __		Totals: __ __		Totals: __ __		Totals: __ __	
Difference: ___		Difference: ___		Difference: ___		Difference: ___	

LEARNING STYLE SCALES

ACTV _____ REFL
    7a 6a 5a 4a 3a 2a 1a 0 1b 2b 3b 4b 5b 6b 7b

SENS _____ INTU
    7a 6a 5a 4a 3a 2a 1a 0 1b 2b 3b 4b 5b 6b 7b

VISL _____ VRBL
    7a 6a 5a 4a 3a 2a 1a 0 1b 2b 3b 4b 5b 6b 7b

SEQN _____ GLOB
    7a 6a 5a 4a 3a 2a 1a 0 1b 2b 3b 4b 5b 6b 7b

If your score on a scale is 1 or 2, you are fairly well balanced on the two dimensions of that scale.

If your score on a scale is 3, 4, or 5, you have a moderate preference for one dimension of the scale and will learn more easily in a teaching environment which favors that dimension.

If your score on a scale is 6 or 7, you have a very strong preference for one dimension of that scale. You may have real difficulty learning in an environment that does not support that preference.

SELF-AWARENESS: KNOWING HOW YOU LEARN

Exercise 3 Explore What You Like

This exercise is designed to get you thinking about your personal preferences. For each of the five questions, rate yourself on the scale and then answer the questions that follow.

1. **People** How much do you like to be around people? Circle where you fit in.

   Shy   1   2   3   4   5   6   7   8   9   10   Outgoing

   How much personal interaction would you prefer on the job?

   _____

   How does meeting strangers make you feel?

   _____

   Describe the personality traits of one of your best friends.

   _____

   _____

   Is he/she a good example of the kind of person you most like?

   _____

   Do you prefer the same kind of people for friendships and work relationships? If no, what is the difference between the two types?

   _____

   _____

2. **School** How do you feel about studying and academics?

   Unenthusiastic   1   2   3   4   5   6   7   8   9   10   Enthusiastic

   What are your favorite subjects?

   _____

   Why do these particular subjects interest you?

   _____

   _____

   What have you learned from these subjects that you can apply to your working life?

   _____

   _____

   What do you like about being in school?

   _____

3. **Activities** How much do you participate in activities beyond the must-do's?

   Never   1   2   3   4   5   6   7   8   9   10   Every day

What are your favorite personal activities?
_____
_____

What do you like about these activities?
_____
_____
_____

How does your participation help you develop mentally and/or physically?
_____
_____
_____

Could your participation in these activities help you succeed on the job? How?
_____
_____
_____

4. **Schedule** At what time of day do you function best?

   Night 1 2 3 4 5 6 7 8 9 10 Morning

   When do you attend school and study?
   _____
   _____

   Does your school/study schedule make the most of your best times? If not, describe how you might change it.
   _____
   _____
   _____

   What kind of work schedule do you eventually want to have?
   _____
   _____

5. **Environment** Where are you most comfortable?

   Rural 1 2 3 4 5 6 7 8 9 10 Urban

   What type of environment (busy, quiet) do you prefer for living?
   _____
   _____

   Do you prefer the same type of environment for working? For studying? If not, describe the differences.
   _____
   _____

   Are your present home/school/study environments in line with your needs?
   _____
   _____

   If not, what can you do to change them to your benefit?
   _____
   _____
   _____

SELF-AWARENESS: KNOWING HOW YOU LEARN

Exercise 4 Explore What You Don't Like

It's as important to know what you dislike as much as what you like. Sometimes, you are aware of your dislikes even more than your likes—and they can help you clarify your likes. Describe the situations/qualities in people/things you could do without—whatever comes to mind.

Personal Qualities

1. _____
2. _____
3. _____
4. _____

School

1. _____
2. _____
3. _____
4. _____

Activities

1. _____
2. _____
3. _____
4. _____

Schedule

1. _____
2. _____
3. _____
4. _____

Environment

1. _____
2. _____
3. _____
4. _____

Exercise 5 Determine Your Abilities

Don't say you have no abilities, because you wouldn't be here if you didn't. Take your time and think it through. Talk to people who know you well if you feel that you aren't a good judge of yourself. Abilities can range from writing and computer skills to cooking, keeping organized, getting along with family members, settling arguments, drawing, playing a sport—anything at all. At the end of each of the following questions, condense your answer into one word that characterizes your ability. For example, if you stay on a schedule, you might say you are *prompt*; if you work well with children, you might say you are *caring*.

1. What do you seem to be able to naturally do well?

   _____
   _____
   _____

   A word that describes you: _____

2. What have you worked hard (and continue to work hard) on to be able to do?

   _____
   _____
   _____

   A word that describes you: _____

3. What do other people tell you are your natural abilities?

   _____
   _____
   _____

   A word that describes you: _____

4. What do other people praise you for doing well and working hard at?

   _____
   _____
   _____

   A word that describes you: _____

Exercise 6 Where Do You Need Improvement?

Because people tend to criticize more than they praise (both others and themselves), you might be more aware of your shortcomings than your talents. As you consider these shortcomings, decide which you want to change and which are either too difficult or not important enough to change. Be realistic. You don't want to expend too much energy on areas where you don't need that much improvement, but neither do you want to ignore problem areas.

**SELF-AWARENESS:
KNOWING HOW YOU
LEARN**

1. What activities are difficult for you?

   _____
   _____
   _____
   _____
   _____
   _____
   _____
   _____

2. From this list, what do you want or need to improve?

   _____
   _____
   _____
   _____
   _____
   _____

3. Which of these listed activities are not important to your personal and career goals?

   _____
   _____
   _____
   _____
   _____
   _____

4. Choose one of the areas you want to improve; list the steps you will take.

   _____
   _____
   _____
   _____
   _____
   _____

Key to Cooperative Learning: Building Teamwork Skills

Putting your Abilities into Action

Pair up with a classmate and exchange the four words you used to characterize yourself in exercise 5 for your classmate's. Carefully consider the four words your classmate has given you. Answer the following questions: Which abilities will help your classmate succeed in school? Why? Which abilities might help on the job? Why? When you have come up with answers, share them with your classmate, taking time to explain your answers to each other. Indicate here what you came up with together for *your* personal abilities.

1. Personal Ability _____

    Helps in school because: _____

    Could help on the job because: _____

2. Personal Ability _____

    Helps in school because: _____

    Could help on the job because: _____

3. Personal Ability _____

    Helps in school because: _____

    Could help on the job because: _____

4. Personal Ability _____

    Helps in school because: _____

    Could help on the job because: _____

Key to Self-Expression: Discovery through Journal Writing

The Path of Bad Attitude

Consider a situation about which you had a negative attitude. What was the situation? Was your attitude a reaction to the situation or completely unrelated? What was the impact of your negative attitude? Did it prevent you from enjoying yourself? Did it harm you or anyone else in any way? Did it complicate the situation? If you had that situation to live over again, what would you do differently? How can you apply what you have learned to a situation coming up in the next month?

_____

_____

_____

_____

_____

_____

Self-awareness: Knowing How You Learn

Key to Your Personal Portfolio: Your Paper Trail to Success

Self-Portrait

"Paint" your self-portrait with words, according to what you have explored in this chapter. Discuss your self-image, learning style, attitude, habits, likes and dislikes, and abilities.

You will complete two "portraits." One should be a written portrait of less than one page, single-spaced. The other should be in Think Link style. This will give you one "portrait" of yourself that you relate to easily (the written page for a verbal learner, the Think Link for a visual learner), while the other will help you develop a different style of expression.

You will learn more about Think Links in the note-taking section in Chapter 5, but for your immediate purposes here is a brief overview. A Think Link is a visual construction of related ideas, similar to a map or web. Ideas are written inside geometric shapes, often boxes or circles, and related ideas and facts are attached to those ideas by lines drawn connecting the boxes. The Think Link creates a visual representation of your thought process. For example, in this exercise you may want to create a "wheel" of ideas coming off your central shape entitled "Myself." Then, spreading out from each of those ideas (self-image, learning style, etc.) you would draw lines connecting all of the thoughts that go along with that idea. Connected to "Abilities," for example, might be "singing," "good memory," "get along with people," "math skills." Use the prototype shown here (in Figure 2-2) or create your own.

SAMPLE SELF-PORTRAIT THINK LINK

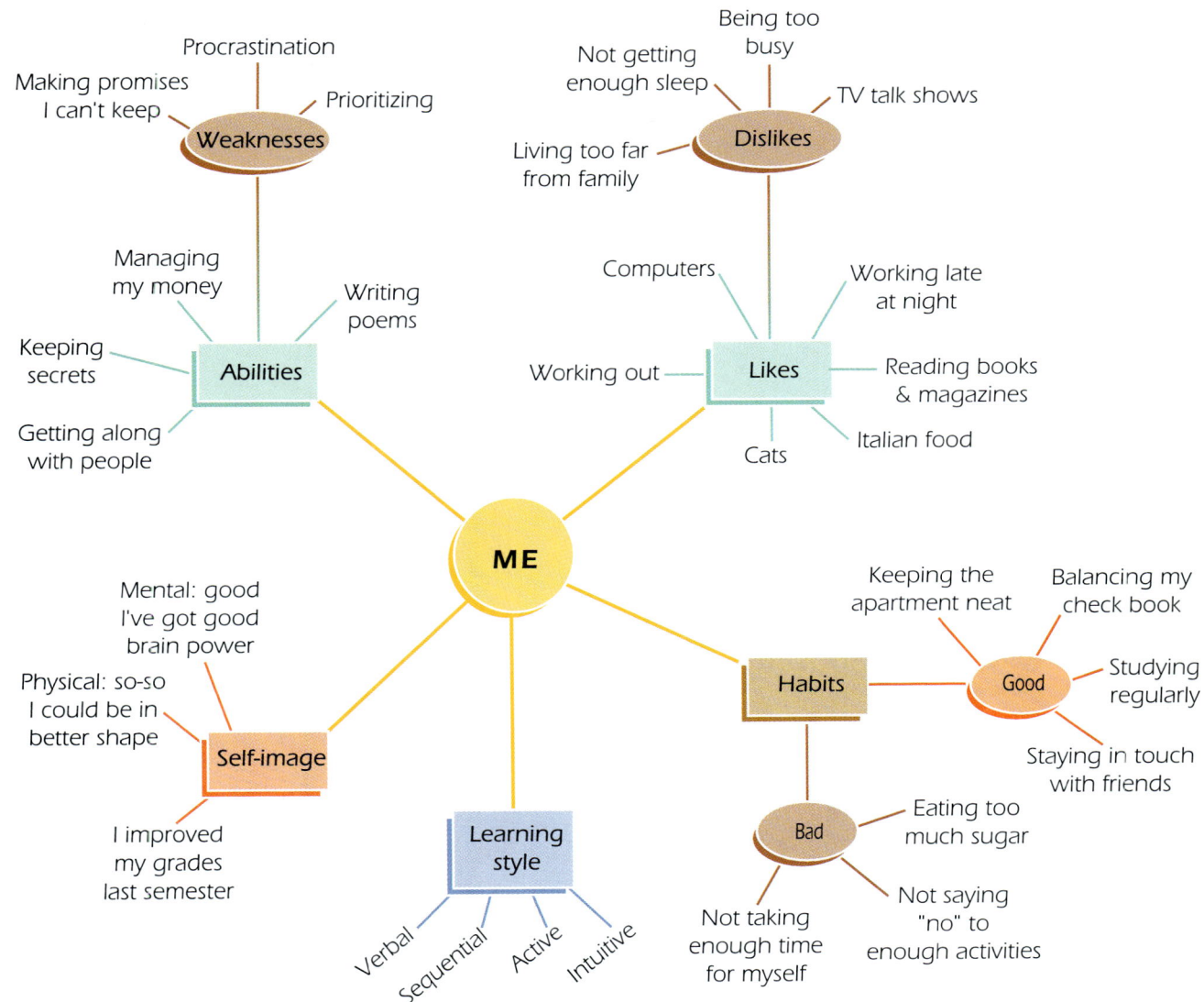

FIGURE 2-2

A S P I R

3

Mapping Your Course: Goals, Priorities, and Time Management

As important as it is to know who you are, self-knowledge is only part of the picture. What makes life truly meaningful is the discovery of what you want to do, to be and the quest to create that life for yourself. Pursuing what you want—out of life, out of college, out of this year, or even out of this week—gives your existence shape and purpose. Through taking responsibility for your life, you claim the power to create that shape yourself. You won't always make the right decisions at the right times, but the more you think through what you want your life to be, the better chance you have of fulfilling your dreams.

In this chapter you will explore *goals* by examining your unique purpose in life, learning how to place your goals within different time frames, and thinking through different types of goals. You will establish your *priorities* through examining the relative importance of your diverse goals. *Managing your time* will give you control over your life as you learn daily goal-setting, how to design and follow a schedule, how to use to-do lists, and how to deal with time traps such as procrastination. Finally, you will learn how to go with the flow of your life's changes in *handling change* as you explore adjustments in goals, priorities, and scheduling.

Goals

> **Goal,** noun. An object, aim, or end that one strives to attain

From the scope of your whole life to the tiniest day-to-day activities, goals will help you see your purpose more clearly.

Identifying Your Purpose

Many people go through their whole lives without ever really thinking about what special gifts they offer to the world or what their purpose is in living. It's easy to lose yourself in the constant barrage of events, duties, and demands that fill your days. If you let the fast lane get the best of you, though, you may look back on your past and realize that you hardly know what you've done or why you did it all. Feeling as though you have no control over the course of your life can leave you empty and unfulfilled. You can avoid that emptiness by periodically taking a few steps back from your life and deciding where you want it to go.

Determining a general purpose is the first step in goal-setting because it gives you a framework within which you can identify your goals. Picking goals at random without a larger framework is like grocery shopping without a list—you can end up with quite a few items you didn't really want while forgetting your true needs. On the other hand, if you remain consistently aware of your purpose, you can make every moment count by taking daily, weekly, monthly, and yearly steps toward your goals under the guidance of that purpose.

One helpful way to determine your purpose is to write a *personal mission statement*. Dr. Stephen Covey, author of the best-seller *The Seven Habits of Highly Effective People*, defines a mission statement as a philosophy that outlines what you want to be (character), what you want to do (contributions and achievements), and the principles by which you live. Dr. Covey compares the personal mission statement to the Constitution of the United States, a statement of principles that gives this country guidance and a strong standard in the face of constant change. "A personal mission statement based on correct principles becomes the same kind of standard for an individual," he says. "It becomes a personal constitution, the basis for making major, life-directing decisions, the basis for making daily decisions in the midst of the circumstances and emotions that affect our lives. It empowers individuals with the same timeless strength in the midst of change."

Here is an example of a personal mission statement.

> **Charles Crawford's mission:** *To use my talents and abilities to help people of all ages, stages, backgrounds and economic levels achieve their human potential through fully developing their minds and their talents. To balance work with people in my life, understanding that my family and friends are a priority above all else.*

Companies often have mission statements so that each member of the organization, from the President to the janitor, clearly understands what to strive for. A company, like a person, needs to establish standards and principles that guide its many activities. If a company fails to identify its mission, a million well-intentioned employees might focus their energies in just as many different directions, creating mayhem and low productivity. For example, here is a mission statement from Northwest Airlines, which they display all around their company building and on the back of each employee's business card. Notice how it reinforces the company's goals of teamwork, leadership, and excellence.

"To build together the world's most preferred airline with the best people; each committed to exceeding our customer's expectations every day."

Another example is from Prentice Hall, the company who publishes this text:

"To provide the most innovative resources—books, technology, programs—to help students of all ages and stages achieve their academic and professional goals inside the classroom and out."

You will have an opportunity to write your own mission statement at the end of this chapter. For now, just consider your purpose. Your efforts to think through your mission can enable you to take charge of your life, putting you in the driver's seat rather than allowing circumstances and events to control you. Much of your success in life will come from determining what you want and taking the initiative to make it happen. If you frame your mission statement carefully, taking your time to determine your true purpose, it can be your guide in everything that you do.

Placing Goals in Time

Why set goals? You are one person with only so much energy. Your commitments can overwhelm you with activity unless you make some conscious decisions. Have you ever had a day flash by so quickly that, although you were constantly busy, it seems like you accomplished nothing? Have you ever felt that way about a longer period of time, like a month or even a year? When you define a goal, large or small, you can focus and direct your energy.

Paul Timm, a best-selling author and teacher who is an expert in self-management, feels that focus is a key ingredient in setting and achieving goals. "People without a sense of purpose lack focus in their lives. They are often guilty of living by wandering around, which may be the single most common cause of poor self-management. Focus adds power to our actions. If somebody threw a bucket of water on you, you'd get wet, and probably get mad. But if water was shot at you through a high-pressure nozzle you might get injured. The only difference is focus." When you focus on what is important to you in life, your goals will become clear to you.

If developing a personal mission statement establishes the big picture, placing your goals within particular time frames allows you to bring individual areas of that picture into sharper focus. Establish first the goals that have the largest scope, the *long-term* goals that you aim to attain over a lengthy period of time, up to a few years or more. You already have experience in setting this type of goal if one of your goals as a student is to receive a solid education. Becoming an educated citizen is an admirable goal that takes a good number of years to reach.

Some long-term goals are lifelong, such as a goal to continually strive to learn new ideas and information. Others have a more definite end, such as a goal to complete a course successfully. When you determine your long-term goals, think in terms of what you want out of life, a career, your educational experience, and your relationships with others. Here Charles has written a long-term goal statement.

Charles' Objective Goals: *To accomplish my mission through writing books, giving seminars, and developing programs to affect opportunities for students to learn and develop. To* *create a personal, professional and family environment which allows me to manifest my abilities and duly tend to each of my responsibilities.*

You may establish long-term goals such as these:

- ❏ I will graduate from school and know that I have learned all that I could no matter what my grade point average may indicate.

- ❏ I will gain real-world experience from a job I now hold or will hold so that I can learn first-hand how to develop practical, effective skills.

- ❏ I will build my leadership and teamwork skills through forming positive, productive relationships with classmates, instructors, and co-workers.

For further focus, to give your long-term goals some detail and to become more immediate in your goal-setting, look at the coming year as a unit of time. What are your objectives for this year? As your long-term goals follow from your personal mission, your *yearlong* goals should follow from both your personal mission and long-term goals. Charles' yearlong goals are as follows:

1. Develop programs to provide internships, scholarships, and other quality initiatives for students.

2. Write a book for students emphasizing an interactive, highly visual approach to learning.

3. Allow time in my personal life to eat well, run five days a week, and spend quality time with family and friends. Allow time daily for quiet reflection and spiritual thanksgiving.

As you can see, Charles' goals are very specific to his personality and interests. Few, if any, other people would have these particular goals. Personal missions and goals can and should be as varied as each individual. That's at the heart of what makes each person unique and special.

Some goals for this year might be:

- ❏ I will earn passing grades in all my classes.

- ❏ I will look for a part-time job with a local newspaper or newsroom.

- ❏ I will join two clubs and make an effort to take leadership roles in each.

Translate your goals into smaller increments of time as well, such as *six months* and *one month*, in order to narrow your focus even further. Within six months' time you can focus on goals such as what you want from your particular classes that semester, what activities you want to emphasize, and how you want your relationships to progress. Within one month you can identify specific tasks that can help you reach those six-month goals. In six months a student might want to accomplish these goals:

- ❏ I will pass Business Writing I so that I can move on to Business Writing II.

- ❏ I will make an effort to meet with some of my co-workers outside of work to ask them their opinions and advice about getting into the news business.

- ❏ I will attend four of the monthly meetings of the Journalism Club.

Finally, the following could be one month goals:

- ❏ I will complete five of the ten essays for Business Writing.
- ❏ I will set my work schedule so that I work three days each week.
- ❏ I will write a piece for the club newsletter, schedule a meeting with my writing instructor, and make a salad for the pot luck barbeque at the end of the month.

As you consider your goals ranging in scope from those you will accomplish over years to those you will take care of in the next month, notice that all of your goal-setting is connected. Look at how each set of the sample goals you have read relates to the others. While your larger goals set the parameters for the smaller goals, your smaller goals clarify and concretize the larger goals. The whole system works together to keep you on track both now and in the future.

Types of Goals

Although your understanding of goals within different time frames will help you understand how to set goals, you also need to consider what types of goals to set. You can draw on the following "databanks" to help you think about what you want out of life.

- ❏ *Likes and abilities*—what you naturally enjoy, do well, and succeed at.
- ❏ *Role models and mentors*—special people whose character and deeds you admire.
- ❏ *Dreams and desires*—what you think about having someday in the future.
- ❏ *Past experience*—what you have seen, heard, and experienced.

> *"Goal setting is a motivational technique that works—it is not a fad. Goals give direction to life. They provide points of reference. But, if a goal isn't written, it isn't a goal—it's a wish. Occasionally wishes come true, but not as often as goals."*
>
> Paul Timm, Ph.D., Chair of the Department of Managerial Communication at Brigham Young University

With those thoughts in mind, you can determine and organize your goals according to five categories: personal, family, school/career, financial, and lifestyle.

1. **Personal.** This category encompasses your character, personality, physical appearance, and conduct. Do you want to be a kind person? Develop a lean, athletic physique? Gain confidence and knowledge? Become less angry? Any missing pieces in your ideal self-portrait can indicate potential personal goal areas for you.

2. **Family.** Goals involving family, actual or projected, belong here. Do you want to stay single? Do you want to marry and have one or more children? If you have already started to build a family, do you want it to grow? Do you want to address problems with parents, improve your relationship with your spouse, or change the way you relate to your family? Do you want to live near relatives or farther away? Set goals that can help you build your ideal family life.

3. **School/Career.** Anything you want to do or be in school or in the workforce belongs to this category. What kind of subjects or career field do you prefer? In school, consider the classes, living environment, instructors, teaching styles, class schedule, and available degrees or certificates. At

work, consider the environment, hours, co-workers, salary, transportation, and company size and style that might be associated with your ideal job. What about moving up? When do you want to graduate, and with what kinds of honors or achievements? Do you want to become a manager, a supervisor, an independent contractor, or a business owner? How much responsibility do you want? Identify goals that can help you earn your ideal education and launch your dream career.

4. **Financial.** How much money do you need to meet your obligations, maintain your chosen lifestyle, and save for the future? Do you need to borrow money for school or a major purchase such as a car? Do you already have heavy monthly bills that you need to reduce? Compare your current financial picture to how comfortable you eventually want to be, and set goals that will help you bridge the gap.

5. **Lifestyle.** Where do you want to live (city, suburbs, country) and in what kind of space (apartment, condominium, townhouse, single- or multi-family house, mobile home)? With whom do you want to live (extended/immediate family, roommates, friends, no one)? Do you want conveniences like off-street parking, laundry, dishwasher, or health club? Do you want cable TV, books, a stereo? How do you like to dress and decorate? What do you like to do in your leisure time? Consider goals that allow you to live the way you want to live.

After all this thought, the most difficult task remains: getting started. Taking action is the toughest step, but as you follow what you have set out to do, you will start to see your hard work pay off.

PRIORITIES

By now you have thought of more than a few goals. If you try to see them through all at once, your energy will give out before you go very far. Working toward goals takes a great deal of time and stamina, so your best bet is to *prioritize* them.

Setting priorities focuses your energy on what's important at any given moment.

If you pursue your goals in no particular order, you might tackle the easy ones first and leave the tough ones for later, regardless of how important some of the harder ones may be. You don't want or need everything to the same degree all of the time.

To explore your priorities, look at the categories that helped you consider your goals—personal, family, school/career, finances, and lifestyle—and think about your personal mission and long-term goals. Right now, what is most important to you to achieve? Does one particular category take precedence in your life? How would you prioritize your goals from most important to least important?

You are an individual, and your priorities are unique to you. What may be top priority to someone else may not mean much to you, and vice versa. Set priorities that reflect your individual and present goals. Of course, you may often need to take the needs and desires of others into account when you set your priorities, if those people's lives are entangled with your own. For example, a parent will have the children's needs high on the priority list, and people in committed relationships will consider their partners. Even in the midst of the needs of others, though, never lose sight of what is most important to you. In being true to your priorities you are making the most of who you are.

Priority,
noun. Something that takes precedence in time or importance

Prioritize,
verb. To arrange items or tasks in order according to priority

Time Management

Don't forget to prioritize ... key to the next topic ... agement.

Time is one of your most va... you use or waste the time ... your goals in a steady, step-... successfully, you may find ... less time to accomplish ... tasks you have more time ... you have ever had before.

People have a variety ... es to time management; ... help you identify the p... rently use your time. Fc... *sequential learners* tend to organize ... within a framework of time. Because they stay aware of how long it takes them to do something or travel somewhere, they are usually prompt. *Intuitors* and *global* learners tend to miss the passing of time while they are busy thinking of something else. Because they focus on the big picture, they may neglect details such as structuring their activities within available time. They frequently lose track of time and can often be late without meaning to be.

Daily and Weekly Goal-setting

Time management on a daily and weekly basis is simply an extension of your goal-setting skills to even smaller increments of time. Daily and weekly goals are *short-term* goals. Each short-term goal should have its origin within one or more of your long-term goals; each is a link in a chain that enables you over time to attain those long-term goals. If one of your year's goals is to become more involved in your spiritual life, your weekly goal might be to attend services at a place of worship on the weekend, and your daily goal might be to set aside some meditation time for yourself. Even seemingly mundane daily goals such as eating breakfast or getting to class on time fit into the larger framework of goals to eat for health and succeed in school.

The process of choosing short-term goals that tie in to your long-term goals has multiple benefits. It gives meaning to your daily activities; it shapes your movement toward the achievement of your long-term goals; it gives you a sense of order and progress. This kind of control is a key ingredient in that all-important principle of taking responsibility for your life. When you select daily and weekly activities with larger purposes in mind, you establish that you are responsible for how you live.

To choose your activities rather than letting them control you can help you to avoid feeling as though your life is out of your hands. On any given day, you can either feel like everyone and everything jerks you around like a marionette, or you can realize that you choose each and every move. Dr. Covey says that if you accept the idea that you have no control, using language like "I have to" and "There's nothing I can do," you create that reality for yourself. However, if you realize your power to choose, using language like "I can take a different approach" and "I prefer," you become the master of your life. Late at night, an exhausted and resentful "I *have to* go to the store" can turn into "I *choose* to do my shopping now, even though I am tired, because it is important to me to have something to eat in the house tomorrow morning, and I actually have more time to do it now than I will have tomorrow." You are responsible.

Your Schedule

A schedule is a plan that allocates segments of time for the fulfillment of your daily, weekly, monthly, and more long-term goals. Because it serves as a concrete reminder of tasks, events, due dates, and deadlines, a schedule is one of the most useful tools for gaining control of your life. Few moments are more stressful than suddenly realizing you have forgotten to do something or be somewhere important. Scheduling can help you avoid that trauma.

Gather the tools of the trade: a pen or pencil and a *date book*. Some of you have probably kept date books for years; others may have never gotten into it. Even if you don't feel you are the type of person who would use one, give it a try. A date book is indispensable for keeping track of your time. Paul Timm says that "most time management experts agree that rule number one in a thoughtful planning process is: *Use some form of a planner where you can write things down.*"

There are two major types of planners: The day-at-a-glance version devotes a page to each day. This type gives you ample space to write the day's activities, but makes it more difficult to see what's coming up. The week-at-a-glance book gives you a good view of the week's plans, but has less room to write per day. If you like detail, you might be happier with a lot of room to write per day; if you prefer to more easily remind yourself of plans ahead of time, try the book that shows you a week's schedule all at once. It may be useful to you if your date book contains additional sections that allow you to note plans and goals for the year as a whole and for each month. You can also create your own sheets for yearly and monthly notations on a notepad section, if your book has one, or on plain paper that you insert into the book on your own.

Start by listing your long-term goals as they fit into the picture of your year, your semester, and your month. Then, each week and daily, write down what short-term goals you need to accomplish in order to stay on track toward the long-term goals. Here is how you might map out two different goals throughout your year.

This year: Complete enough courses to graduate
   Pump up my physical fitness

This semester: Complete my accounting class with a B average or higher
   Lose 15 pounds and exercise regularly

This month: Set up study group schedule to coincide with quizzes
   Begin regular running and weight lifting

This week: Meet with study group; go over material for Friday's quiz
   Run 7 miles total; go to weight room three days

Today: Go over chapter 3 in accounting text
   Run 2 miles

Now that you know *what* to write down, turn to your knowledge of priorities for help with how to *organize* those goals and tasks. Prioritizing enables you to use your date book with maximum efficiency. On any given day, your goals will have varying degrees of importance. Write them down first, and then indicate their different priority levels using three categories: *Essential*, *regular*, and *if-there's-time*.

Essentials are activities you must take care of no matter what; examples could be going to work, attending class, keeping a medical appointment, picking up a child from day care, putting gas in the car, and paying bills.

Regular tasks are what you normally do daily or a few days per week; for example, preparing meals, working out, doing homework, participating in a carpool, or taking out the garbage. Regular tasks are important, but offer more flexibility in terms of scheduling than essential tasks. Some regular tasks such as laundry, grocery shopping, or a weekend dinner with the extended family are often performed weekly.

The *if-there's-time* category includes activities you would like to do but can reschedule without much sacrifice. Examples might be a trip to the mall, a visit to a friend, a social phone call, a sports event, a movie, or a hair appointment. As much as you want to get to them, you don't consider them urgent. Many people wait to enter these kinds of tasks and goals in their date books until they determine if they have enough time left over after assigning time to higher priorities.

Use a **code** to categorize your tasks; choose your coding system according to what makes the most sense to you. Suggestions include highlighting tasks and goals using different colors for each category, writing an A, B, or C next to essentials, regulars, and if-there's-times respectively, or using symbols such as a star for essentials, a dot for regulars, and a question mark for if-there's-times.

Your date book also enables you to schedule events. Rather than thinking of events as separate from goals, tie them in with your long-term goals just as you would your other tasks. For example, attending a wedding in a few months contributes to your commitment to spending time with your family. Quiz dates, due dates for assignments, and meeting dates all fall in with your goals to achieve in school and become involved. Noting events in your date book where a quick look will remind you of them will enable you to stay on course. Indicate event dates wherever they apply, in your daily, weekly, monthly, and even yearly sections, so that you see where they fit in the context of many different time frames. Among the events worth noting in your date book are

- Due dates for papers, projects, presentations, and tests.

- Birthdays, anniversaries, and other special occasions.

- Benchmarks for steps toward a goal, such as due dates for sections of a project, a deadline for losing five pounds, or a date on which you need to contact someone.

- Important meetings, medical appointments, or due dates for bill payments.

Scheduling takes thought and energy. Here are some helpful hints.

1. **Take time to think about time.** Mr. Timm recommends that you devote a minimum of 10-15 minutes a day to planning your schedule. Although making a schedule takes time, it can mean hours of saved time later on. What if you forgot that you had two errands to run, both on the other side of town? Not planning a schedule could mean driving across town twice in one day. That's far more time than it would have taken to review your day's activities.

2. **Refer to your schedule.** Taking time to look at the schedule you have planned is the most important key to successfully following it. Many people make detailed schedules only to forget to look at them. Have your date book accessible at all times. Find one small enough to fit into your briefcase, bag, or even your pocket. Check it throughout the day to make sure you are on track.

3. **Categorize a week's worth of hours.** Estimate the number of hours you spend in each of the following activities in a week: School, Work, Homework, Family Time, Chores, Sleep, and Travel/Commuting. Assign what remains to Down Time/Relaxation, Meals, and Entertainment. Seeing how you spend your time may suggest possible changes in your schedule. Figure 3-1 shows one student's typical time allotments.

64
MAPPING YOUR COURSE: GOALS, PRIORITIES, AND TIME MANAGEMENT

4. Schedule down time. Life tends to blur when you have too many things to do. Schedule yourself some "down time" every day if you can; even just a half an hour can refresh you and revive your perspective. Fill the time with whatever relaxes you—enjoying a cool drink, reading, watching TV, playing a game or sport, writing, or just doing nothing at all. Make down time a priority.

To-Do Lists

To-do lists are just that—lists of things to do. Making to-do lists can serve you in a number of different ways.

Organizing your daily and weekly schedule. It may help you to use a to-do list as a reference for writing in daily and weekly schedule items. If you generate your daily or weekly to-do list on a separate piece of paper, you can look at everything you have to do all at once and make decisions about time frames and priorities. You might want to prioritize that separate list and then transfer prioritized tasks to appropriate days and weeks. Some people create their daily to-do list right on the date book page for that day if they have enough room to write.

A SAMPLE STUDENT'S WEEK

	Sleep	School	Work	Homework	Family/Meals/R&R	Chores	Travel/Commute	TOTALS
Monday	6.5	6	6	1	2	1	1.5	24
Tuesday	8	9	0	2.5	2.5	.5	1.5	24
Wednesday	7.5	0	9	3	3.5	0	1	24
Thursday	5.5	9	0	3.5	2.5	2	1.5	24
Friday	7	6	4	2	2	1.5	1.5	24
Saturday	9	0	6	3	3	3	1	24
Sunday	8	0	0	7	5	3	0	24
TOTALS	51.5	30	25	22	20.5	11	8	168

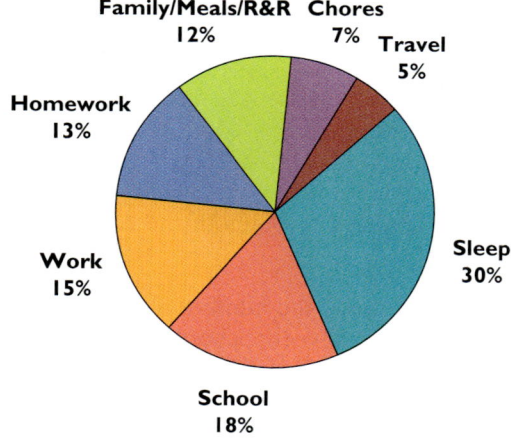

FIGURE 3-1

Keeping track of if-there's-time tasks. If you noted every task in your date book, it might get a little crowded. You can keep a list of if-there's-time tasks in a separate place in your date book so that it is handy when you have an unexpected pocket of free time. Keep this list current by crossing off items as you accomplish them and writing in new items as soon as you think of them. Rewrite the list as it becomes messy or worn. A sample of this kind of list follows:

- Fix screen on door.
- Sort old clothes for donating to charity.
- Buy extra greeting cards.
- Put photos in album.
- Sort through videotapes and alphabetize.
- Find wedding gift for Maggie and Mike.

Maintaining your focus during a busy period. You might want to tailor a to-do list to an important week such as exam week, a business trip or vacation, or an especially busy day or event such as a party or a presentation day at school. Keeping this kind of specific to-do list with you can help you prioritize and accomplish an unusually large task load.

Staying on course long-term. When you make your original list of long-term goals for the year or the next few years, keep it with you. Sometimes you can lose track of them in the haze of daily tasks. If it is easy to refer to, you can remind yourself at a glance of the path you are trying to travel. Then you can revamp your short-term goals to get yourself back on track if need be. In addition, your list is there for you to adjust if your goals and priorities shift.

Procrastination and other Time Traps

How many times have you said to yourself, "Oh, I'll take care of that later?" Sometimes you have a good reason to put something off; however, **procrastination** occurs when you habitually postpone unpleasant or burdensome tasks. Procrastination is often deliberate, especially when you are facing something that scares you. You can find lots of little projects you "have to take care of" when the important item overwhelms you. The energy and creativity you put into avoiding a task might just as well be used to get the task completed.

The fear that underlies procrastination is normal and has many sources. People project goals too far into the future, set unrealistic goals that are too frustrating to reach, or have no goals at all. People procrastinate because they don't believe in their ability to actually complete a task, don't believe in themselves in general, or are convinced they will fail. If continued over a period of time, procrastination can develop into a habit that will dominate a person's behavior.

Strategies to Fight Procrastination

1. **Weigh the benefits to you and others of completing the task versus the effects of procrastinating.** What will happen if you get it done? What will happen if you continue to put it off? Which situation is better? Chances are you will benefit more in the long term from facing the task head-on.

Fight Procrastination

2. **Ask for help with tasks and projects at school, work, and home.** You don't always have to go it alone. Instructors, supervisors, and family members can lend support, helping you to more comfortably complete a dreaded task. For example, if you have put off an intimidating assignment, ask your instructor for guidance. If you avoid a project because you dislike the employee with whom you have to work, talk to your supervisor about adjusting the assignment of tasks or personnel. Once you identify the fear, see who can help you face it.

3. **Don't expect perfection of yourself.** No one is perfect. It's better to do your best, whatever that may be, than to do nothing at all.

4. **Set reasonable goals.** Allow enough time to complete them. Write your goals where you can refer to them, on a list or on index cards.

5. **Talk to yourself positively.** Tell yourself, "I am OK. I have the ability to do this. I am a competent, valuable person who can complete this task."

6. **Get started.** Going from doing nothing to doing something is often the hardest part. You might want to use the motivation techniques from Chapter 8 to help you take the first step. Once you start, you may find it easier to continue.

7. **Consider the benefits of completing the task.** What rewards lie ahead? A burden off your shoulders? A more pleasant task? Some free time? Advancement? Pondering the reward may inspire you to get in gear.

8. **Analyze your task.** If it seems overwhelming, look at the task in terms of its parts. How can you approach it step by step? If you can concentrate on achieving one small goal at a time, the task may become less of a burden.

Other "Time Traps" to Avoid

1. **Saying "yes" when you really don't have the time.** Many people, in their efforts to please others, agree to help with tasks they can't easily fit into their schedule. It's great to be reliable, but not at your own

expense. Think over any potential addition to your schedule. Will it fit comfortably? Will it disrupt essential activities? Will it cause you to miss important events or risk being unprepared for tasks? If it will cause you more trouble than it seems to be worth, say "no" graciously.

2. **Studying at a bad time of day for you.** At what point in the day do you have the most energy? Is that when you study? If not, you may be wasting time. Fatigue may be preventing you from making the most of your studying. If you study when you are most alert, you will be able to take in more information in less time.

3. **Studying in a distracting location.** Consider your ideal study environment. If you need to be alone to concentrate, for example, studying near family members or roommates might be too distracting. Find a quiet corner or study room in your library where you can use your time efficiently. Conversely, people who require a busier environment to stay alert might do fine in a more active setting.

4. **Not thinking ahead.** Forgetting important things is a big time drain. One book left at home can cost you extra time going back and forth; one forgotten phone call can mean you have to do what you wanted to ask someone else to do. Five minutes of scheduling in the morning can save you hours. You may prefer to plan your day the night before. Assemble the clothes you will wear and place items you need to take with you by the door or wherever you are sure to notice them.

5. **Not curbing your social time.** Fun has a way of eating up time. You plan to make a quick telephone call and the next thing you know you've been talking for an hour, losing time you could have used for studying or sleep. Don't cut out all socializing, but wear a watch and stay aware of the time. If friends invite you for dinner, consider joining them later for coffee and dessert. Don't consume alcoholic beverages if you have more studying to do later on. Don't give in to peer pressure: "You're not leaving already?!! You don't really have work to do, do you?" Your friends will respect your persistence in the long run, and you will respect yourself when you see the rewards.

6. **Not delegating.** No one can take a test, read a chapter, or eat a meal for you, but you can delegate some tasks to other people. A relative might be able to take your car in for repair. A friend going to the post office could pick up some stamps for you. Another day-care parent might be able to pick up your child on a day when your time runs short. Check into those possibilities, and don't forget to return the favor.

HANDLING CHANGE

Even the most carefully constructed goal systems fall prey to life's constant shifts. As your needs, desires, and environment change, you need to adjust your goals, priorities, and schedules to fit those changes.

Reevaluating and Modifying Your Goals

Why might you need to adjust your goals? People don't always set the best goals for themselves. Some turn out to be unreachable; some may not pose enough of a challenge; others may be unhealthy for the goal-setter or harmful to others. Even more common are goal shifts that go along with your changing life. Accept your changes, and step back from your path often to evaluate how you may need to adjust goals accordingly.

Real World Perspective

Q Jonathan Early, student at the DeVry Institute of Technology in Atlanta, Georgia

I went to college right after high school. I started out as a psychology major because I had a good teacher in high school who really got me interested. Medicine also seemed really fascinating to me, and I planned to go to medical school after college. But for whatever reason I eventually lost interest, and somehow I knew I couldn't do that kind of work as a professional. I skipped lots of classes and it got to the point where I didn't want to be there at all. My grades got pretty bad too, but my biggest problem was not going to class. Eventually I made a choice to leave school. It was a really tough decision, especially since my family really wanted me to stay, but I felt like I was wasting money.

Even though I worried about how to make a living outside of school, I dropped out for four years. During that time I became interested in computers, and now I'm back in school studying computer science. I like it a lot, but how can I be sure that this is the right choice? Where can I find support for my decision to change my goals, and what resources will help me stick to my objective this time?

A Susan H. Chin, Professor and Language Arts Chair at DeVry Institute of Technology in Atlanta, Georgia

I am glad that you made the decision to return to college, and I applaud your interest in computer science, an area of dynamic growth. Among grads with technical degrees, those in computer-related fields are in highest demand. Job opportunities include business applications programming, computer-related sales and sales support, data base applications, software support and maintenance, technical documentation, and LAN and network support. According to a survey of career counseling offices at 365 colleges and universities by the National Association of Colleges and Employers, salary offers for computer science majors have averaged $33,813, a 6.4 percent increase from 1994.

Research computer companies, so you know what technical knowledge and skills are most in demand. Check with your college Graduate Placement Office and look in the classified section of your newspaper to learn about employment opportunities. Read the college catalogue descriptions of the courses you will have to take to earn your degree. All of this will help you determine if computer science is the right choice for you.

The power to attain objectives doesn't come from outside resources; it stems from your own motivation and your own commitment. Verbalize your short- and long-term objectives and then write them out. Writing out your objectives is an important step because then you can see more clearly what you need to do to attain these objectives, and you have a plan of action.

Step One: Reevaluate

Before making changes, take time to reevaluate two things: your goals and your progress toward them.

The goals. First, determine if your goals still fit the person you have become in the past week, or month, or year. Circumstances can change quickly. An unexpected pregnancy might cause a woman to postpone starting a course of study. An engaged couple in the market for a used car may discover their combined income enables them to buy a new car. Sometimes achieving your goals conflicts with someone else's goals. Your spouse may want to move to a larger apartment, but the rent increase would prevent you from finishing required coursework.

Your progress. If you feel like you haven't gotten far, determine if the goal is out of your range or simply requires more stamina than you had anticipated. Don't rush to let yourself off the hook—you may risk letting an important goal slip away. As you work toward any goal you will experience periods of progress and stagnation. Sticking with a tough goal may be the hardest thing you'll ever do, but the payoff will be worth it. On the other hand, if after your best efforts it becomes clear that a goal is out of reach, don't feel you have failed. An adjustment may bring success. Perhaps the goal doesn't suit you; for example, an active, global learner might become frustrated while pursuing a detail-oriented, sedentary career such as accounting.

Step Two: Modify

Based on your reevaluation, you can modify a goal in two ways: (a) adjust the existing goal or (b) replace it with a different, more compatible goal. For example, the woman with an unexpected pregnancy could adopt a goal of taking three credit hours at a time in night school, gradually earning her a degree, or she could postpone her coursework until the baby is older. You and your spouse could put some money into fixing up your current living space and the rest toward classes, or postpone the goal of moving until you finish school. You never stop changing; make sure your goals keep up with you.

Shifting your Priorities

Priorities can change instantaneously, from day to day, year to year, and situation to situation. The changes in your needs and wants affect how you prioritize your goals. If you can adjust your priorities to fit the changes, you will be more able to handle life's unexpected complications. Here are some examples of where those changes can happen.

- *Family situation.* If you get married, have children, take a relative into your home, or divorce, your obligations change radically.

- *Residence.* A home owner has to care for the yard; moving to an apartment erases that priority.

- *Finances.* Schooling, additional mouths to feed, and car loans increase your need to come up with sources of income.

- *Work situation.* Losing a job makes finding another a priority; taking on a new job forces you to prioritize other goals differently in the remaining available time.

- *Time of year.* Extra money for gifts is a priority around the holidays; finding a vacation opportunity might be a priority during the summer.

- *Stage of life.* What is important to you at eighteen years old can be radically different from your priorities at forty.

- *Time of day, day of the week.* Work and child care take priority each day, but washing your car may only become important on weekends when you have extra time.

- *State of mind.* If you're in a mood to deal with all of the little things you've been ignoring, they may take priority over regular tasks. If you are driven to focus on one major priority, other tasks may take a back seat.

- *Emergencies.* A medical, financial, or family emergency can take precedence over all other priorities in a hurry.

Adjusting your Schedule

Since priorities determine the map of your day, week, month, or year, any priority shift can wreak havoc with your schedule. Be ready to reschedule your tasks as your needs change. On Monday, paying a certain bill might be an if-there's-time; by Saturday, it could become an essential if you haven't yet gotten to it. Some days a surprise essential will pop up and take priority over everything else, such as a medical emergency or a family situation that demands your involvement. Some days you will have a cancellation and find yourself with lots of time on your hands. Go with the flow of the day as best you can.

As tightly as you may schedule your life, something will inevitably come along from time to time that will destroy your plan. Try to expect the unexpected, keeping some flex-time in your schedule in case you have to shift tasks around. If a child becomes ill and you have to miss a class or a meeting to take her to the urgent care center, you have rescheduled according to a new priority. On the other hand, if you have to suddenly stay late at school or work and you miss an event with your child, again, you have chosen what was most important at the time.

Summing Up

Goal-setting turns your dreams into real plans. Once you establish your personal mission, you can work your way through smaller and smaller increments of time, translating your long-term goals into monthly, weekly, and daily tasks and events. Prioritizing gives you the power to decide what is most important to you at any given time, and to focus your energy on those priorities. Effective time management gives meaning to your life, enabling you to map out your goals so that you can see how each day takes you further toward your larger purpose. As you manage change in goals, priorities, and scheduling, watching for procrastination and other time traps, you will realize the rewards you have earned by taking responsibility for how you live your life.

CHAPTER 3: APPLICATIONS

Keys for your Key Chain: Skills Worth Keeping

List here what to you are the five most important keys, or skills, you have learned from reading this chapter.

1. _____
2. _____
3. _____
4. _____
5. _____

Key Into Your Life: Opportunities to Apply What You Learn

Exercise 1 Your Personal Mission Statement

Using the examples in the chapter as a guide, and considering what you want out of the different areas of your life, create your own personal mission statement. You can write it in paragraph form, in a list of long-term goals, or in the form of a Think Link. Take as much time as you need; make sure that what you end up with covers everything you want your life to be, in general terms. Write a draft on a separate sheet of paper and give yourself a chance to revise it a few times before you write the final version here. If you have created a personal mission Think Link, attach it separately.

_____
_____
_____
_____
_____
_____
_____
_____
_____
_____

Exercise 2 Establishing and Tracking Long-term Goals

In each of the five categories of goal types, name one of your most important long-term goals. Imagining that you were to start working toward each goal tomorrow, map out the course of your activity. Indicate the steps that will comprise your pursuit of each of those goals in the next year, the next six months, the next month, the next week, and tomorrow.

Your Goal	One Year	Six Months	Month	Week	Day
Example: I want to develop a better relationship with my father.	Instead of moving, I will complete my course of study at a college near my parents' home.	I will seek a better understanding of our relationship by looking into how the school counseling center can help.	I will see my counselor every two weeks and make sure that I schedule at least one get-together with my father.	I will see if my father needs help with anything around the house this weekend.	I will call my dad just to talk.
Personal					
Family					
School/Career					
Financial					
Lifestyle					

Exercise 3 Short-term scheduling

Get yourself a clean new date book and look at your calendar. What is coming up for you next month? On the calendar layout that follows, fill in the name of the month and appropriate numbers for the days. Record important events and tasks on the calendar, remembering to take into account your goals from the previous exercise. Include the following:

❏ Due dates for papers, projects, presentations, and tests.

❏ Birthdays, anniversaries, or other special occasions.

❏ Key steps toward long-term goals.

❏ Important meetings, medical appointments, or due dates for bill payments.

After you have completed this chart, recreate your entries in your date book so that you have them at your fingertips. Map out each month in your date book using a similar chart.

Month of _____

Sunday	Monday	Tuesday	Wednesday	Thursday	Friday	Saturday

Mapping Your Course: Goals, Priorities, and Time Management

Exercise 4 Discover How You Spend Your Time

Start with an estimate. In the first chart, enter the total time you think you spend per week on each activity.

Activity	Time in Hours
Class	
Work	
Family time/child care	
Studying	
Sleeping	
Eating	
Commuting/Traveling	
Personal business (shopping, medical visits, etc.)	
Household maintenance	
Telephone time	
Leisure	
Religious activities	
TOTAL	

Subtract the total number of hours you estimate you spend on these activities from 168 (the number of hours in a week).

168

minus Total _____

Unscheduled time _____

Now, spend a week recording the actual amount of time you spend on these activities. Tally the hours in the boxes in the table using straight tally marks; round off to half hours and use dots for half-hour increments.

Activity	Mon	Tue	Wed	Thu	Fri	Sat	Sun
Class							
Work							
Family/child care							
Studying							
Sleeping							
Eating							
Commute/Travel							
Personal business							
Household maintenance							
Telephone							
Leisure							
Religious activities							
TOTALS							

Add your totals to find your GRAND TOTAL: _____

Does this total match your estimate? If not, where are the differences? What has surprised you about how you actually spend your time?

_____

_____

What changes do you think you need to make in your time allotments?

_____

_____

_____

Fill in one more chart with the schedule you hope to attain. Refer to it as a weekly planning guide.

Activity	Time in Hours
Class	
Work	
Family time/child care	
Studying	
Sleeping	
Eating	
Commuting/Traveling	
Personal business (shopping, medical visits, etc.)	
Household maintenance	
Telephone time	
Leisure	
Religious activities	
TOTAL	

Exercise 5 To-Do Lists

Make a to-do list for what you have to do tomorrow. Include all tasks and events—essentials, regulars, and if-there's-times.

TOMORROW'S DATE:

1. _____
2. _____
3. _____
4. _____
5. _____
6. _____

7. _____

8. _____

9. _____

10. _____

11. _____

12. _____

Use a coding system of your choice to indicate which tasks or events are essential, which regular, and which if-there's-time. Place a check by the items that are important enough to note in your date book. Use this list to make your schedule for tomorrow in the date book. At the end of the day, briefly note here how things went. Did the to-do list help you? How did it make a difference?

_____

_____

_____

_____

Exercise 6 Your Procrastination Techniques

What are your habitual excuses for avoiding something you don't want to do? Name your top three.

1. _____

2. _____

3. _____

What are the positive effects, if any, of this behavior?

_____

_____

_____

_____

What problems does procrastinating cause for you? Describe a specific incident in which you procrastinated. What happened?

_____

_____

_____

_____

Choose one of your procrastination techniques to drop from your repertory. Since procrastination is a habit, use the habit-breaking techniques you explored in Chapter 2. The first time you are able to avoid procrastinating, describe what happened and how the change felt.

___

Key to Cooperative Learning: Building Teamwork Skills

Individual Priorities

In a group of three or four people, brainstorm a list of priorities. From the list that develops, pick out the ten that seem to be the most common. Group members then should take five minutes to themselves to evaluate the relative importance of the ten priorities and then rank them in the order that they prefer. Display the rankings of each group member side by side. How many different orders are there? Discuss why each person has a different set of priorities. What factors in different peoples' lives have caused them to select particular rankings? If you have time, discuss how priorities have changed for each group member over the course of a year, perhaps by having each person re-rank the priorities according to their needs a year ago. You may also want to project how priorities may change again in the future.

Key to Self-Expression: Discovery through Journal Writing

Personal time

Think over the last two weeks. When did you take personal time for yourself? What did you do? How did it make you feel? If you haven't had personal time in a while, make an effort to schedule some in the next couple of days and discuss the effect it had on you. Describe in a few sentences your idea of a perfect day spent alone—what you would do, where you would go, what state of mind you would hope to reach.

___

Key to Your Personal Portfolio:
Your Paper Trail to Success

Your Mission, Goals, and Priorities

Looking again at the five goal categories, Personal, Family, School/Career, Financial, and Lifestyle, select and write down five long-term goals for each. Use a separate sheet of paper for each category. Rewrite your goals again on the bottom half of each sheet, ranking them in order of priority with the most important first.

On another sheet of paper, rewrite all twenty-five goals together in one list; then use your chosen coding system to prioritize them. Both kinds of goal sheets illustrate what is important to you; one shows you what is most important within particular categories, and the other shows you what takes priority when all goals are considered at the same time.

Recopy your mission statement onto another separate sheet of paper, allowing yourself to make any edits that occur to you.

Keep your goal/priority sheets and your mission statement in your portfolio. Every few weeks, take them out to see if you need to make any changes. Your instructor may assign mission statement revisions from time to time. By the end of this course, your mission statement may have changed as a result of what you have learned about yourself.

C R E A T

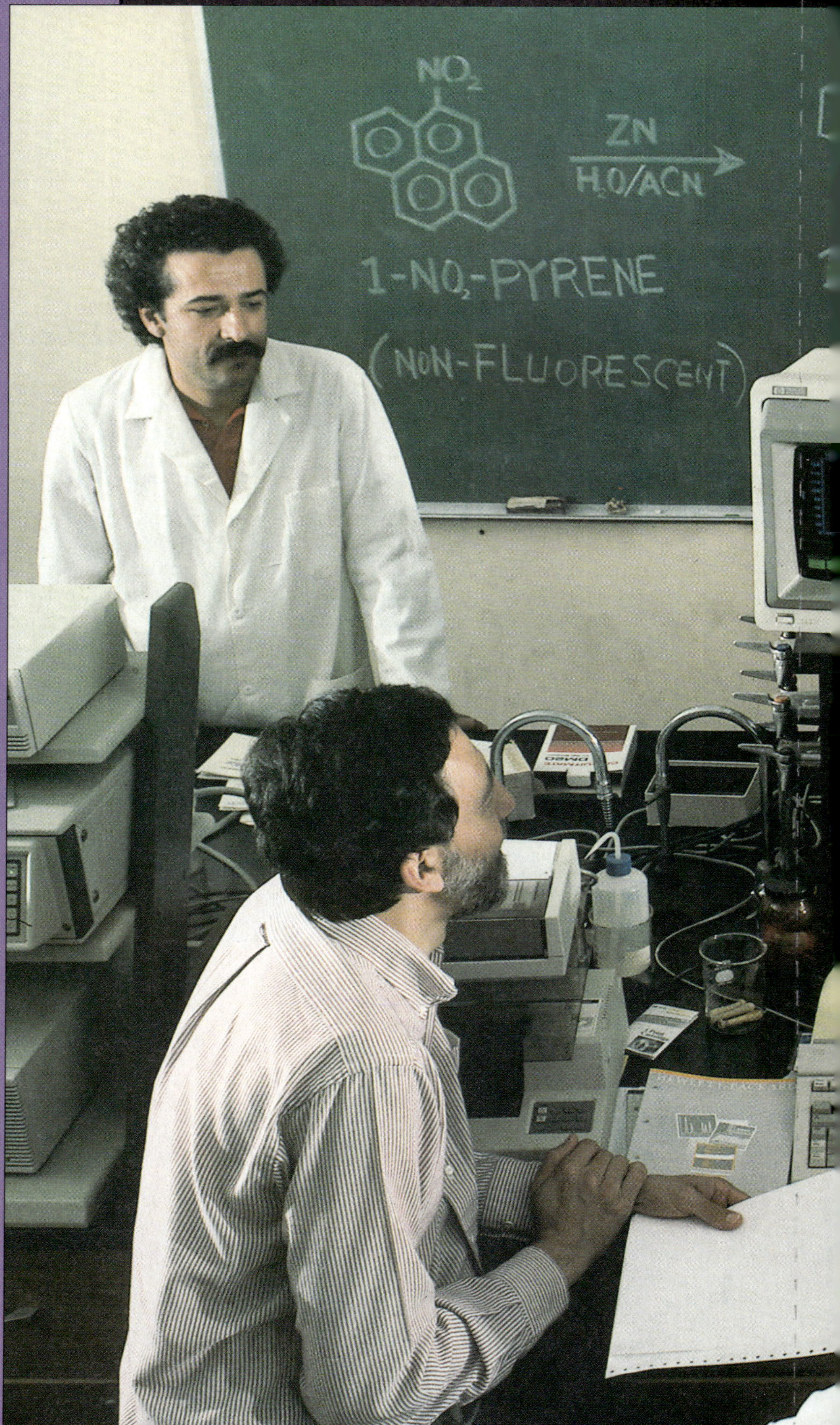

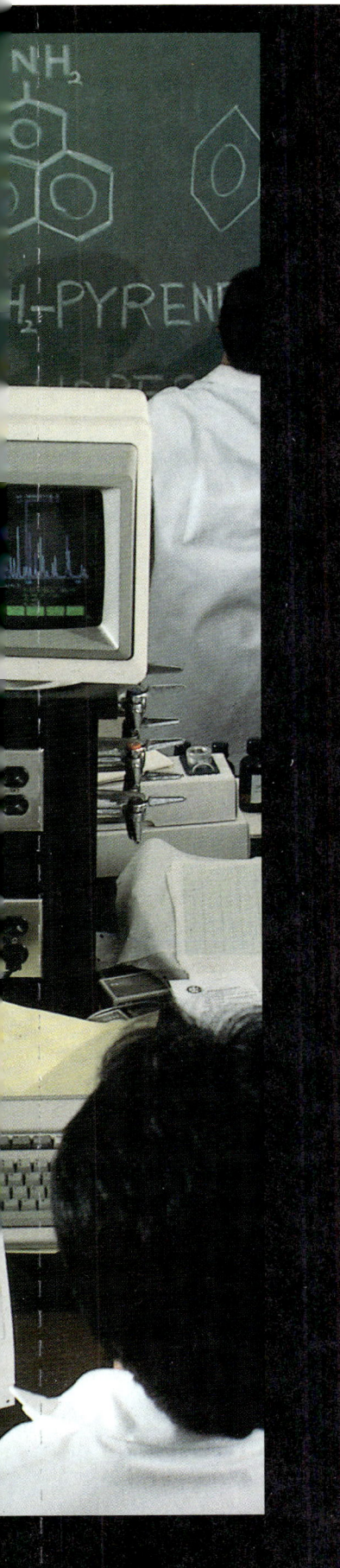

4

Opening Doors: Thinking Critically and Creatively

What comes into your mind when you consider the words *critical thinking*? Does the word *critical* give you a sense of something negative, tense, or harsh? What about the word *creative*? Does it sound mushy? These interpretations are common. However, whether or not you think about it on a regular basis, you use critical thinking every day of your life, and creativity more than you realize. Critical and creative thinking enable you to solve problems and make decisions. Your goal in this chapter is to increase your awareness of what they are and to further develop your ability to use them. The more efficient and flexible your thinking, the more effective you will be both in school and on the job, able to tackle any project, task, or situation with confidence.

This chapter explores the process of **critical thinking**, in part by introducing a system that identifies seven mind actions within the critical thinking process. You will learn that your mind uses *four major processes: creating and innovating, inquiring, problem solving,* and *decision making*. Finally, you will study *two important door keys* that help diversify and boost your thinking power: *intuition* and *perspective*.

CRITICAL THINKING

There are worlds of meaning in a chosen word. What something is called can in large part determine how you feel about it. A *friend* is a far cry from a *girlfriend* or *boyfriend* for someone who wonders where a relationship is going. A *misstep* or a *setback* feels more hopeful and less serious than a *failure* or a *disaster*. Words have a great deal of power over the mind. Use them to your advantage. Start by erasing any negative associations you may have with the term *critical thinking*. One of the dictionary definitions for *critical* is "indispensable, important." Critical thinking is important thinking.

Critical thinking goes beyond the simplest observation and recall. Through careful analysis of facts, situations, events, and ideas, it produces rather than reproduces. For example, you have spent the day working and you go out to your car to drive to your night classes about fifteen miles away. You get in, turn the key, and the engine gives only a weak sputter. Your initial observation is: "My car won't start." Your subsequent thoughts on what follows are examples of critical thinking.

❏ The car started this morning; I put some gas in at noon.

❏ This is just like last month when I couldn't get it to turn over.

❏ Last month when it wouldn't turn over it was out of gas, but I know I have half a tank.

❏ This is going to make me miss my class if I don't figure something out within a half-hour.

❏ It's been too long since the last tune-up—maybe this is telling me something. I know that the engine has been knocking a lot lately.

❏ Have gas, isn't too cold outside, haven't tuned up, heard knocking. Maybe this is happening because of a problem with my starter or fuel line.

❏ This is a problem because I don't know if I have the money to repair this right now. Plus I'll have to pay for towing if it absolutely won't start. At least I don't have any tests today. If I have to miss some of the class, I can ask someone to help me get the information I missed.

In processing those thoughts, including the initial observation, your mind has just gone through seven different moves, or primary actions, within which you can categorize almost any thought you have. Studying these seven actions will further your knowledge of how your mind works.

How You Think

The continual improvement of thinking skills that will bring you success both in school and on the job depends on a thorough understanding of the daily workings of your mind. Like anything else, it's tough to develop a skill unless you understand the basics of the task. You can identify your mind's actions using a system called the Thinktrix, developed by educators Frank Lyman, Arlene Mindus, and Charlene Lopez in 1979 in Howard County, Maryland. "In a responsive, cooperative, and thinking classroom, everyone should know how the mind works," says Dr. Lyman in *Enhancing Thinking Through Cooperative Learning*, edited by Neil Davidson and Toni Worsham. "The Thinktrix consists of seven fundamental thinking processes...[that] represent the ways [students] think all the time."

The Thinktrix names and explains those seven mind actions. You can learn them in the context of your thoughts as the owner of the sputtering car. After the name of each mind action, in italics, are words that describe the focus of that action.

Recall: *Facts, sequence, and description.* This is the simplest action; it builds on the most basic observation by describing facts or events or by putting them into sequence. "The car started this morning; I put some gas in at noon." You have recalled the recent events of your car's history in sequence.

Similarity: *Analogy, likeness.* With this action you look at what is similar about one or more things, comparing them to one another. You might compare situations, ideas, people, appearances—anything at all. "This is just like last month when I couldn't get it to turn over." You have found what is alike in two situations: the current car trouble, and last month's incident.

Difference: *Distinction, contrast.* This action deals with what is different about one or more things; you contrast them with one another. "Last month when it wouldn't turn over it was out of gas, but I know I have half a tank." You have contrasted the present with last month and found that there is at least one difference—the amount of gas in the tank.

Cause and effect: *Consequence, prediction.* Using this action, you look at what causes have led (or could lead) to what effects, or what effects trace back to what causes. You are looking at the consequences of an event or fact. "This is going to make me miss my class if I don't figure something out within a half-hour." The car problem could be the cause of missing class, which is the predicted effect, if you don't figure something out.

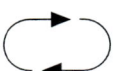

Example to Idea: *Generalization, classification.* From one or more facts or events, you develop a general idea. You classify one or more facts or events, or you find a pattern and generalize about several of them. "Have gas, isn't too cold outside, haven't tuned up, heard knocking. Maybe this is happening because of a problem with my starter or fuel line." In this case, from the facts or events you come up with an idea of what is causing the problem.

Idea to Example: *Categorization, substantiation.* In a reverse of the previous action, you see an idea and think of events or facts that back up that idea. "It's been too long since the last tune-up—maybe this is telling me something. I know that the engine has been knocking a lot lately." You have the idea that something is wrong with your car, and you have found facts that support your idea (the time since the last tune-up, the knocking you have heard).

Evaluation: *Value, judgment, rating.* Here you judge whether something is right or wrong, good or bad, identifying and weighing its positive and negative effects (pros and cons). "This is a problem because I don't know if I have the money to repair this right now. Plus I'll have to pay for towing if it absolutely won't start. At least I don't have any tests today. If I have to miss some of the class, I can ask someone to help me get the information I missed." With the facts you have gathered, you determine the value of your situation in terms of both the effects you have predicted and your own needs. Cause and effect analysis always accompanies evaluation.

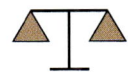

You use critical thinking mind actions in your daily life as well as in each exercise you have completed in this book. In this and following chapters, you will notice *icons*—the symbols above that correspond to each of the seven actions—next to some of the exercises. They will help you consider how your mind is working by indicating the one or two primary actions that the exercise requires. Often you will see more than one action for a given exercise.

The Value of Critical Thinking

Why is it helpful to understand how your mind works?

- *You can use it more deliberately.* When you encounter a question or problem and you have command over your thought process, you will waste less time haphazardly trying out various ideas only to realize none of them are quite right. By analyzing how your mind has to work through a difficult question or problem, you can more successfully pick your way through to the answer or solution.

- *You can master its actions.* Just like anything else, your mind gets better at what it does the more you use it. When you know how the mind works, you can focus your energy on improving your thinking and learning skills.

- *You can increase your success in school and maximize your value and promotability on the job.* The better you think, the less likely you are to be the sort of employee who does the bare minimum, over and over, without any change or improvement. Your mind can do far more than just reproduce on a daily basis according to your assigned tasks. You can produce by creating ideas, asking questions, solving problems, and making decisions; what you produce moves you ahead and, if you are at work, benefits your employer. If people recognize your critical thinking ability, they may encourage you to apply it to more and more challenging opportunities. Your mind only increases in power with more conscious and focused use.

> "The Thinktrix actions are tools to grant you, as a student, ownership of your thinking process. You have the power to be in charge of your own thinking."
>
> Frank Lyman, Ph.D., Professional Development School Center Coordinator for the University of Maryland/Howard County Schools

Your Mind's Four Major Processes

Your mind uses four major processes: creating and innovating, inquiring, problem solving, and decision making. Each of these processes uses combinations of critical thinking actions. If you are skilled at using them, they will keep you continually at the forefront of both your studies and your chosen career field.

Creating and Innovating

Creative, adjective.
1. having the ability or power to create
2. displaying productive originality

Everyone is creative in some form or fashion. Some people assume that the word creative refers primarily to visual and performing artists, writers, designers, musicians, and others who work in fields whose creative aspects are obvious. That's a pretty limited perspective. Creativity is inside everyone and exists, to some extent, in every field.

Creativity is the power to create *anything*, whether it is a solution, a tangible product, a work of art, idea, system, program, format—anything at all. Creativity means thinking in fresh new ways that increase productivity in whatever you do. Thomas Jefferson creatively designed the University of Virginia's original structures such that the students could learn about different kinds of architecture from the buildings in which they lived and studied. Stevie Wonder continues to pull a multitude of songs from his creative mind. City planner and architect James Rouse created a design for the city of Columbia, Maryland that would give residents easy access to schools, nature, and facilities while promoting community interaction. Ruth Bader Ginsburg, Supreme Court Justice, taps into her creativity as she searches for new ways to interpret the long-standing amendments of the Constitution.

You can be creative anytime if you let your mind explore changes and new territory. The safety and comfort of your standard ways of behaving, dressing, communicating, or scheduling can inhibit your creativity. Deciding to explore new ideas and solutions doesn't mean you were backwards to start with. It just means you can adjust to change in your needs, your workplace and educational arena, and your family and home environment. Change will always happen; opening yourself to different ideas about how to handle it spurs your creative spirit.

Expert on creativity Roger van Oech, in his book on the creative process *A Kick in the Seat of the Pants*, highlights this kind of flexibility in the face of change. "I've found that the hallmark of creative people is their mental flexibility," he says. "Like race-car drivers who shift in and out of different gears depending on where they are on the course, creative people are able to shift in and out of different types of thinking depending on the needs of the situation at hand. Sometimes they're open and probing, at others they're playful and off-the-wall. At still other times, they're critical and fault-finding. And finally, they're doggedly persistent in striving to reach their goals."

Children often have the kind of creative freedom that adults have put aside. Remember the games you used to make up, the outfits you would wear, the ideas you had about things when you didn't know the facts? You frequently came up with new thoughts or unusual observations, and you never worried whether they were helpful or useless. See if you can retrieve some of that creative freedom from your childhood.

Critical thinking and creativity are closely connected. Much critical thinking is creative, because it requires you to come up with original ideas and solutions to problems. For example, if you want to explore what's behind a certain effect, you think creatively about the variety of causes that may be involved. If you were brainstorming about what causes your fatigue in afternoon classes, you might realize that your diet and your heavy caffeine intake in the morning could play a role. Then you may decide to cut out caffeine altogether and make sure to eat some source of protein at breakfast every morning. Through your consideration of causes and solutions, you have been thinking both creatively and critically. The more complex mind actions that you use when thinking critically often engage your creativity at the same time.

Creativity plays a crucial role in resolving and preventing conflict, because discovering the causes of a conflict and formulating a solution requires a free, creative mind. The two mind processes that focus on conflict resolution—problem-solving and decision-making—demand creative thinking. As you go through these processes, thinking creatively leads you to solutions or decisions. Creativity also allows you to make the probing inquiries you need to get to the heart of the matter.

What are some problems and conflicts that require creative thinking?

❏ Figuring out how to get to school when your babysitter unexpectedly cancels on you.

❏ Planning a shopping list so that you end up with a variety of meals for the week.

❏ Deciding on a budget so that you can come up with the down payment for a car.

❏ Reorganizing a jumbled closet.

❏ Fitting homework into a tight schedule.

❏ Dealing with a discriminatory situation at work.

❏ Juggling work, home life, chores, fun time, and school.

❏ Finding an alternate route to school/work that avoids long-term construction.

❏ Putting together old items of clothing in a new way, creating an updated look.

Innovating is part of the creative process and most commonly refers to the creation of new ideas or things. When you do something innovative, not only have you created something, you have put together an idea, system, format, or tangible product that to your knowledge hasn't been seen or used before. Innovative students or employees who come up with productive, positive ideas can greatly improve the effectiveness of the work environment.

Brainstorming is a great way to generate creative and innovative ideas. You've already completed brainstorming exercises in which you've had to come up with lists or examples of situations. Brainstorming means letting ideas flow freely from your mind without immediate judgment. When you evaluate your ideas too quickly, you run the risk of abandoning them before you have let them develop or have predicted their effects. Write down your ideas so that you remember all of them. Then consider each one individually later on, after you have given them a chance to sink in. Brainstorming works well in groups because group members can become inspired by, and make creative use of, one another's ideas.

At the heart of creativity and innovation is trust. You must trust yourself to fall off the edge of tradition when you explore your creativity. Sometimes the craziest ideas end up being the most productive, positive, workable solutions around. Trust yourself; don't dismiss those far-out ideas too quickly. van Oech suggests that you come up with as many ideas as you can, being careful not to limit yourself. There are no "right

Brainstorming

answers"—just answers that may or may not be right for the given situation. The more ideas you generate, the better a chance that one may be just right.

Here are a few additional creativity tips to consider; they derive from van Oech's list of "mental blocks" to avoid that he discusses in *A Whack on the Side of the Head*.

Don't get hooked on finding the one right answer. There can be lots of "right answers" to any question, depending on your point of view. Shift your perspective and come up with a few. The more you generate, the better your chance of finding the best one.

Don't always be logical. Following strict logic may cause you to ignore your intuitive hunches.

Break the rules sometimes. All kinds of creative breakthroughs have occurred because someone bypassed the rules. Women and minorities can vote and hold jobs because someone broke a rule many years ago. Challenge rules with creative ideas.

Be impractical. Use your imagination to consider what would happen if you did something that didn't follow the regular practical pattern. Practicality can narrow the scope of your ideas.

Let yourself play. People often hit upon their most creative ideas when they aren't trying to think about anything at all—when they are exercising, socializing, playing around, or just relaxing. Often when your mind switches into play mode, it can more freely generate new thoughts.

Let yourself be foolish. It's easy to fall into the trap of conforming to peer pressure, doing whatever everyone else is doing. Although you may feel foolish doing something completely different, that independence could lead to some incredibly unique ideas. After all, the idea for Velcro came from examining how a burr sticks to clothing. What seems like a crazy idea at first can be a brilliant discovery.

Let yourself fail. If you try to only produce right answers, you may miss out on the creative process that takes you down a lane paved with failures on the way to the best possible solution. Failure opens your mind to possibilities; you may discover something unexpected on the way to where you thought you wanted to be.

Always consider yourself creative. Use your positive self-talk. What you tell yourself you are can become a self-fulfilling prophecy. If you think you are creative, you will be creative.

Inquiring

Answers fuel progress, and the route to answers is inquiry.

Whether you ask questions of yourself, people, or other resources, you have everything to gain from the process of inquiring. You know yourself and your needs; if you can ask the kinds of questions that lead you to the specific answers you seek, you will save yourself time and trouble. Being inquisitive brings growth.

Asking questions earns you respect because it shows an instructor or supervisor that you care enough to make sure you are on the right track. It paints a picture of a

Inquire, *verb. To seek information by asking questions*

concerned and conscientious person. The person who opens up to learning through inquiry will move far ahead of the person who refuses to ask questions. Smart, confident people aren't threatened by the fact that they don't know everything; they realize that no one can experience everything the world has to offer. If you seek answers from others, you have the opportunity to share and benefit from what they have learned.

Here's a hint about how to spur your inquisitive spirit: Find something that you are truly curious about. It doesn't have to have anything to do with what you study or what you do at work. What have you always wondered about? Is it recording music, making pastries, psychological disorders, snakes, types of flowers, 1960s Mustangs? Take some time to explore your area of interest. Notice your stepped-up level of energy and your heightened interest as you delve into new information. If you seek out interesting information in all kinds of different areas of study, work, and life, you may be able to spark that same kind of energy in yourself and in others.

Problem Solving

Your critical thinking strategies go into high gear when you're confronted with a problem. You solve problems of various levels of complexity every day; for example, figuring out how to get to work when the bus isn't running, considering how to handle a racist comment from another student, or managing your study time. If you use this lineup of steps, your problem-solving process will become more complete and efficient.

1. **Analyze the problem.** What are the facts? Here you *recall* the details of the situation: What is happening that needs changing? State the problem clearly, without the causes. Then explore why is it a problem for you. What effects does it have? Finally, ask yourself what caused the problem. In other words, look at the *causes and effects* that surround the problem.

2. **Brainstorm possible solutions.** Be creative. Think of *examples* of other problems that are *similar* and come up with a solution that might fit them all. How is this problem *similar* to other problems? What did you do about them? How is the problem *different* from other problems? What requires a different strategy?

3. **Explore each solution.** Why might it work? Why not? Why might it work partially? *Evaluate* the pros and cons, or the positive and negative effects, of each idea.

4. **Choose, execute, and evaluate the solution you decide is best.** Carry out your chosen solution and then look at the *effects* of your decision. What are the positive and negative effects of what you did? Was it, in terms of your needs, a good or bad solution? Would you do the same again or not?

Figure 4-1 demonstrates a way to turn the problem-solving process into a visual Think Link. Adopt this process and you will be able to solve personal, educational, and workplace problems in the most efficient way possible.

Decision Making

Decisions come up daily, hourly, even every few minutes. Do you turn left here? Do you ask someone out? Do you drop a course? Before you begin the decision-making process, evaluate what kind of decision it is. Do you have to decide what to have for lunch (usually a minor issue), or whether to separate from a spouse (most often a major life change)? Some decisions are little, day-to-day considerations that you can take care of quickly on your own. Others require thoughtful evaluation, time, and perhaps the input of others you trust. The following is a list of steps to take when using critical thinking to make an important decision.

PROBLEM-SOLVING MODEL

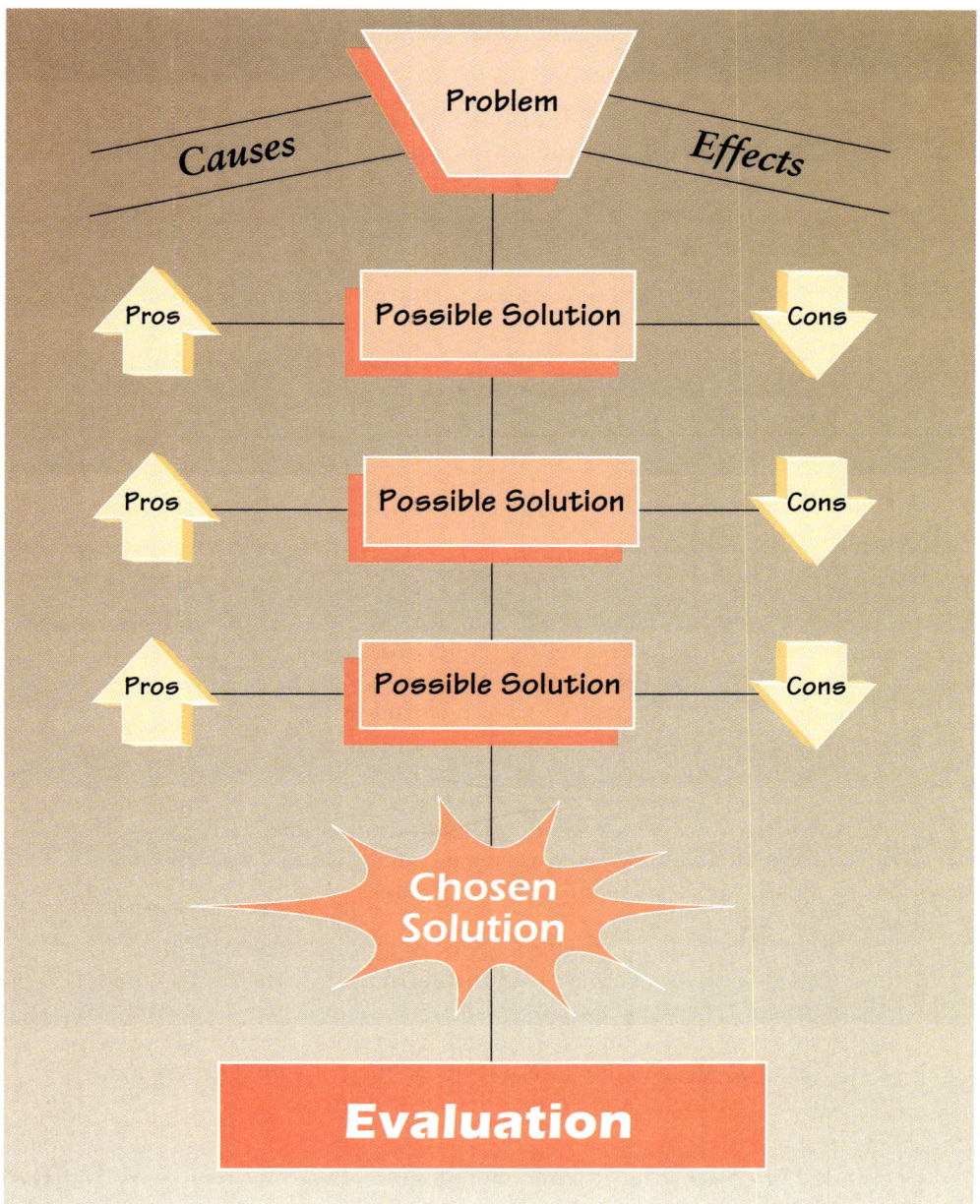

Source: Adapted from an organizer developed by Frank T. Lyman Jr., Ph.D., University of Maryland, 1983.

FIGURE 4-1

1. **Decide on a goal.** What do you want to come out of this decision? Considering the *effects* you want can help you formulate your goal.

2. **Establish needs.** *Recall* the needs of everyone (or everything) involved in the decision.

3. **Name, investigate, and evaluate available options.** Brainstorm decisions, and then look at the facts surrounding each. *Evaluate* the good and bad

effects of each possibility. Weigh these effects and judge which is the better course of action.

4. **Decide on a plan of action and pursue it to the goal.** Make a choice based on your evaluation, and act on your choice.

5. **Evaluate the result.** Was it positive? Negative? Some of both? What were the *effects*? *Judge* how everything turned out.

Here's an example of how a student might work through one kind of decision.

Goal: To decide where to attend school for my junior year. My father got laid off and my parents can't afford to continue to pay private college tuition.

Needs: I need to complete my education. I need to continue with my studies toward an undergraduate degree in nursing. My parents need to reduce the amount of money they spend on my college. I need to be able to transfer credits.

Options:

❏ *Continue at my current college*. Positive effects: I wouldn't have to adjust to a new place or people. I could continue my course work as planned. Negative effects: I would have to find a way to finance most of my tuition and costs on my own, whether through loans, grants, or work. I'm not sure that I could find time to work as much as I would need to, and I don't know if I would qualify for as much aid as I now need.

❏ *Transfer to the state college*. Positive effects: I could reconnect with people there that I know from high school. Tuition and room costs would be cheaper than at my current school. I could transfer credits. Negative effects: I would still have to work some or find minimal financial aid. The nursing program is small and not very strong.

❏ *Transfer to the community college*. Positive effects: They have many of the courses I need to continue with the nursing curriculum. The school is twenty minutes from my parents' house so I could live at home and avoid paying room costs. Credits will transfer. The tuition is extremely reasonable. Negative effects: I don't know anyone there. I would be less independent. The school doesn't offer a bachelor degree.

Decision: I'm going to go to the community college for two years and then transfer back to a four-year school to finish my bachelor's degree. Although I will lose some of my independence and my day-to-day contacts with my friends, the amount of money saved is so substantial that it is worth it. Plus, I won't have to work, so I can spend time concentrating on my studies. That should help me keep my grades up which will help me stay on schedule and transfer again later.

Evaluation: I'm pretty happy with the decision. It has been a little hard being back at home, but we talked it over and my parents are trying to let me set my own schedule. Since I am living under their roof, I am also trying to respect them and to understand how they worry. I make an effort to let them know where I am going, and they try to let me make my own decisions. I actually have fewer social distractions, so I'm getting more work done. My parents are grateful for the financial help and my father has some prospects for a new job.

Making decisions can take time. When you can work through a decision quickly and thoroughly, you will improve your efficiency. Acting on what you have decided as soon as possible allows you to benefit from your decision right away.

Two Important Door Keys

Intuition

Have you ever had that sinking feeling in the pit of your stomach when you think you might be making a poor choice? That's your intuition talking. Not only will it let you know when you're on the wrong track, it can also suggest a course of action.

Intuition—sometimes called a "hunch" or a "gut feeling"—can serve you as an inner advisor on such subjects as career paths, relationships, study environments, child-rearing, and more. At times your intuitive notions might contradict the voice of reason; however, the more you know yourself, the more you will be able to trust your intuition and what it reveals to you.

You may need to train yourself to tune in to your intuition. Your awareness of yourself and what you have learned through your life experiences will help. Intuition stems in large part from patterns that arise from the buildup of experience-based knowledge. When a current reality clashes with or is similar to a pattern, your intuition may try to let you know. For example, you may have had in your past problematic friendships with a couple of different people who share a similar personality type. If you meet another person who fits into the same category, your intuition may warn you to stay away. On the other hand, if you meet a person whose personality seems similar to people with whom you have always gotten along, you may feel intuitively receptive to that person.

The positive and negative effects of any solution should be weighed carefully. Ask yourself, what would happen if you followed a course of action that came to you in an intuitive flash? What would happen if you acted according to general practice and reason? Where do your intuition and reason agree and where do they differ? Compare the effects of each course of action. Which way will you and others benefit most? Will anyone be hurt? Make your decision after considering all the possibilities.

> **Intuition,** noun. The act of sensing or knowing something without the apparent help of rational processes; perceptive insight

Perspective

There are many people who may share with you a certain point of view in any one specific area. However, your particular world view is unlike anyone else's, because you are a unique combination of genetic heritage and environment. Each of the billions of people on this planet has his or her own unique view of the world. Call this world view perspective with a capital *P*. Some generalized examples of this kind of Perspective are an environmentalist who views the world in terms of how animals, plants, and ecosystems can be protected and supported, a parent who views the world in terms of how to make a better life for the children, and a disabled person who views the world in terms of what is accessible and who is accommodating to special needs.

Within this Perspective are many smaller perspectives with a small *p*, or views on specific topics. Sharing and adjusting perspectives is at the heart of any successful enterprise or relationship. For example, at a meeting with an instructor, you may express your perspective that the homework assignments are too much to handle, and the instructor may offer the perspective that they are an appropriate challenge. Through your discussion you may each adjust your perspectives from what you learn from the other person. In some cases you may even emerge with a common perspective. Think back to the sputtering car at the beginning of the chapter; whereas one person might see the experience as a trauma, another who has been dying for an excuse to buy a new car might see it as a blessing.

> **Perspective,** noun.
> 1. A general point of view or outlook
> 2. The ability to perceive how things relate to each other and their comparative importance

Real World Perspective

Q Joubin Mortazavi, student at the University of Southern California in Los Angeles, California

My family and I immigrated from Iran in 1979. Because of my parents' language restraints, I have to do a lot of work in the family business. My family runs a video game retail store. If my brother and I didn't work, my parents wouldn't be able to pull it off. I do mostly managerial work, buying and dealing with companies, overlooking employees, and doing paperwork. I cram school in Monday through Thursday and work Friday, Saturday, and Sunday. I do most of my studying on Sunday night, but I'm sacrificing the social side of college life. For about the whole month of December I have to do extra work along with finals and end-of-the-semester projects. These are the longest and hardest weeks for me.

Most people aren't fortunate enough to go to college without working. It seems that the more you work, the more you want to work to satisfy and support yourself, and you can risk sacrificing your education. The time that work takes up can really take a toll on your grades. What can I do to stay involved at work while maintaining my dedication to school?

A Jack Wilson, career transition specialist and principal of Career Sciences in Danbury Connecticut

First, you are to be congratulated on your decision to sustain your family's business while enhancing your career potential through education. The fact that you are doing work while going to school is a plus in the eyes of future employers. In today's world, employers place a high value on the various kinds of contingent work—part-time, temporary, co-ops, internships—that students do in addition to their studies.

The demands of being a working student cannot be avoided. To ease your mind about the hardship of working while in school, consider how your progress in your studies should increase your value in the workplace; perhaps you may eventually have an opportunity to take a higher-paying job and could hire a less experienced young person to replace you in the video game store. Or if you take any classes directed towards retail commerce, you may be able to take advantage of your new knowledge to expand your family's business. In either case, your education is a definite benefit.

Like many other students who are balancing family, work, and school, you are having to make sacrifices during this period of your life. Keeping it all in perspective is the key to success and positive thinking. If you see it as a developmental experience, a phase of your career that is helping you build your skills, knowledge, and competence in preparation for a brighter, rewarding future, you will be able to recognize that your sacrifices are worth the trouble. It seems from your dedication that your intuition has already told you this is true. Keep listening to its messages.

It's human to believe that your way is the best way. However, if you can make the effort to see the world through the perspectives of others, you may find yourself willing to adjust your own. You already have extensive practice in picking up new perspectives. You adopt them from your family, friends, experiences, and the media. Once you explore a new perspective thoroughly, you can make an educated decision to accept or reject it.

How does perspective help you think critically? Growth as a student and as a working person stems from change and evolution. If you continually strive to explore new perspectives, you will expand the base of knowledge upon which you draw when working through problems and decisions. In addition, you'll be helping those around you feel more positive about interacting with you. There's nothing that kills a classroom discussion or a meeting faster than a person who won't consider a new perspective. On the other hand, there's nothing that energizes more than a person who can continually say, "I'd like to consider your point of view. How do *you* feel on this issue? What do *you* think would be best?" Everyone wants that person to stick around. Be that person.

Summing Up

Ideas are a product of freedom plus preparedness; the freedom is the creativity you allow yourself to explore, and the preparedness is the skill you develop using critical thinking. Creativity allows you to explore new ground, and critical thinking focuses and structures creativity so that flashes of inspiration become workable and practical. Together, they can help you snare the productive, innovative thoughts that stir inside you and deal with any problem or decision that comes your way. Listening to your intuition will help you make the right decisions for your needs; understanding and continually adjusting your perspective will give you the knowledge you need to assure that your decisions are intelligent and well-founded. Knowing your mind's power gives you the opportunity to make the most of it.

CHAPTER 4: APPLICATIONS

Keys for your Key Chain: Skills Worth Keeping

List here what to you are the five most important keys, or skills, you have learned from reading this chapter.

1. _____
2. _____
3. _____
4. _____
5. _____

Key Into Your Life: Opportunities to Apply What You Learn
Exercise 1 Making a Decision

In this series of exercises you will make a personal decision using the seven mind actions and the decision-making steps described in this chapter. Before you proceed through each of the steps, write here an important personal decision you have to make.

_____
_____
_____

Step 1 Name Your Goal

Be specific: What do you want from this decision? What goal, or desired effects, do you seek? For example, if your decision is a choice between two jobs, the effects you want might be financial security, convenience, experience, or anything else that is a priority to you. It could also be a combination of these effects. Write down the desired effects that together make up your goal. Note priorities by ranking the effects in order of importance.

1. _____
2. _____
3. _____

Step 2 Establish Needs

Think about who and what will be affected by your decision. If you are deciding how to finance your education and you have a family to support, you must take into consideration their financial needs as well as your own when exploring options.

List here the people/things/situations that will be affected by your decision and indicate how each will be affected.

1. _____
   _____

2. _____
   _____

3. _____
   _____

Step 3 Check Out Your Options

Look closely at possible options. Some decisions only have two options (to move to a new apartment or not, to get married or not); others have a wider selection of choices. For example, you are a full-time student and the parent of a young child. You must coordinate your class schedule with your child's needs. Consider your options: (1) put your child in a day-care, (2) ask a relative to care for him, (3) hire a full-time nanny, or (4) arrange your schedule so that you can balance the duties with another parent.

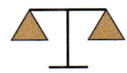

List the possible options for your own personal decision. Evaluate the good and bad effects of each.

Option 1 _____

Good effects _____

Bad effects _____

Option 2 _____

Good effects _____

Bad effects _____

Option 3 _____

Good effects _____

Bad effects _____

Option 4 _____

Good effects _____

Bad effects _____

If you are having trouble generating choices, try to recall if you ever made a decision similar to the one you are about to make. If so, describe it.

_____
_____
_____

What were your options at the time?

1. _____
2. _____
3. _____

Does that experience give you ideas for options with this decision? If so, what are they?

_____
_____

Step 4 Make Your Decision and Pursue It to the Goal

Taking your entire analysis into account, decide what to do. Write your decision here.

_____
_____

Next is perhaps the most important step: *Act* on your decision.

Step 5 Evaluate the Result

After you have acted on your decision, evaluate how everything turned out. What were the effects on you? On others? On the situation? To what extent were they positive, negative, or some of both?

List four effects here. Name each effect, circle Positive or Negative, and explain that evaluation.

Effect 1 _____

Positive   Negative

Why? _____

Effect 2 _____

Positive   Negative

Why? _____

Effect 3 _____

Positive   Negative

Why? _____

Effect 4 _____

Positive   Negative

Why? _____

Final evaluation: Write one statement in reaction to the decision you made. Indicate whether you feel you made a good decision, and why.

Exercise 2 The Idea Wheel

Your mind has a way of intuitively coming up with solutions to problems when you least expect it. Many people report having unexpected brainstorms while exercising, driving, showering, upon waking, even sleeping. When the pressure is off, the mind is often more free to roam through uncharted territory and can bring back treasures.

In order to make the most of this mind-float, you have to grab ideas right when they surface. If you don't, they sink back into your subconscious as if on a wheel. Since you never know how big the wheel is, you can't be sure when that particular idea will roll around to the top again. That's why writers carry notebooks—they want to make sure to jot down a thought when its spot on the wheel comes to the top.

Name five problems large or small to which you haven't yet found a satisfactory solution. Let them sit, but be on the lookout for ideas coming to the top of your wheel. The minute it happens, grab this book and write your idea next to the problem. Take a look at your ideas later and see how your intuition may have pointed you toward some intelligent and creative solutions.

EX →

Problem	Solution Ideas
1.	1. 2. 3.
2.	1. 2. 3.
3.	1. 2. 3.
4.	1. 2. 3.
5.	1. 2. 3.

Key to Cooperative Learning: Building Teamwork Skills

Group Problem Solving

As a class, brainstorm a list of common problems in your lives. Write the problems on the board or on a large piece of paper attached to an easel. Include anything that is an issue; for example, money, grades, family, job stress, discrimination, cars. Divide into groups of two to four; each group will choose or be assigned one problem to work on.

1. **Identify the problem.** As a group, state your problem and look at the causes and effects that surround it. Record the effects that the problem has on your lives. List what causes the problem. Remember to look for "hidden" causes (you may perceive that traffic makes you late to school, but the hidden cause might be that you don't get up early enough to have adequate commuting time in the morning).

2. **Brainstorm possible solutions.** Determine the most likely causes of the problem and then brainstorm possible solutions. Record all of the ideas that group members offer. After ten minutes or so, each group member should choose one possible solution to explore.

3. **Explore each solution.** In thinking independently through the assigned solution, each group member should (a) weigh the positive and negative effects, (b) consider similar problems, (c) determine whether the problem requires a different strategy from other problems like it, and (d) describe how the solution affects the causes of the problem. Evaluate your assigned solution. Is it a good one? Will it work?

4. **Choose your top solution(s).** Regroup. Take turns sharing your observations and recommendations. Then take a vote. Which solution is the best? You may have a tie; that's fine. Different solutions suit different people and situations.

5. **Evaluate the solution you decide is best.** When you decide on your top solution or solutions, discuss what would happen if you went through with it. What are the positive and negative effects of what you would do? Would it turn out to truly be a good solution for everyone? Would you do the same again or not?

Key to Self-Expression: Discovery through Journal Writing

Intuition

Recall a situation in which your intuition helped you solve a problem. Describe the situation. It could be having a hunch about what major to declare, getting a feeling about how to progress in a friendship or romantic relationship, a sudden decision about how to react when you or someone you care about was in danger, or any other situation where your intuition came into play. Were you willing to follow the directives of your intuition, or did you try to ignore it? What was the outcome of the situation?

_____

_____

_____

_____

KEY TO YOUR PERSONAL PORTFOLIO:
YOUR PAPER TRAIL TO SUCCESS

A Critical Evaluation of your Habits

You studied habits and how to change them in Chapter 2. Evaluate your habits now using your critical thinking skills and decide what changes you want to make.

- ❏ Your first step is to recall your list of habits. They can be work-related, school-related, family-related, personal—anything at all. Don't censor; write down good and bad habits alike.

- ❏ Rewrite your list, dividing the habits into two columns: Helpful (good) and Harmful (bad).

- ❏ Evaluate your habits: reorder your two lists of habits according to how strong a hold they have on you, with the best first in the Helpful list and the worst first in the Harmful list. In terms of their effects, which are the two most helpful and two most harmful? Circle them.

- ❏ Start a new page for each of the four habits you circled. For each, answer these questions:

What circumstances have caused this habit to emerge?

What effects, positive or negative, does this habit have on your life? What rewards or consequences come about because of it?

Do you want to keep or to change/stop this habit?

- ❏ For each habit you want to change, use your problem-solving skills to build a habit-altering solution to the problems that the habit causes. Create a problem-solving plan or Think Link. You may want to include a plan for developing a new habit in its place.

- ❏ Record your habit-changing progress on the page you have devoted to that habit. You can list events as they occur or make a calendar in which you mark days that you avoided or changed habitual behavior. Make a tangible record of your work on the habit.

Keep your habit lists and your four habit-evaluation pages in your portfolio. As you gradually make changes, update your lists. If you successfully change a harmful habit, cross it off, circle the habit that you now consider the worst, and set to work on it. Slow and steady wins the race.

U N D E R S T A

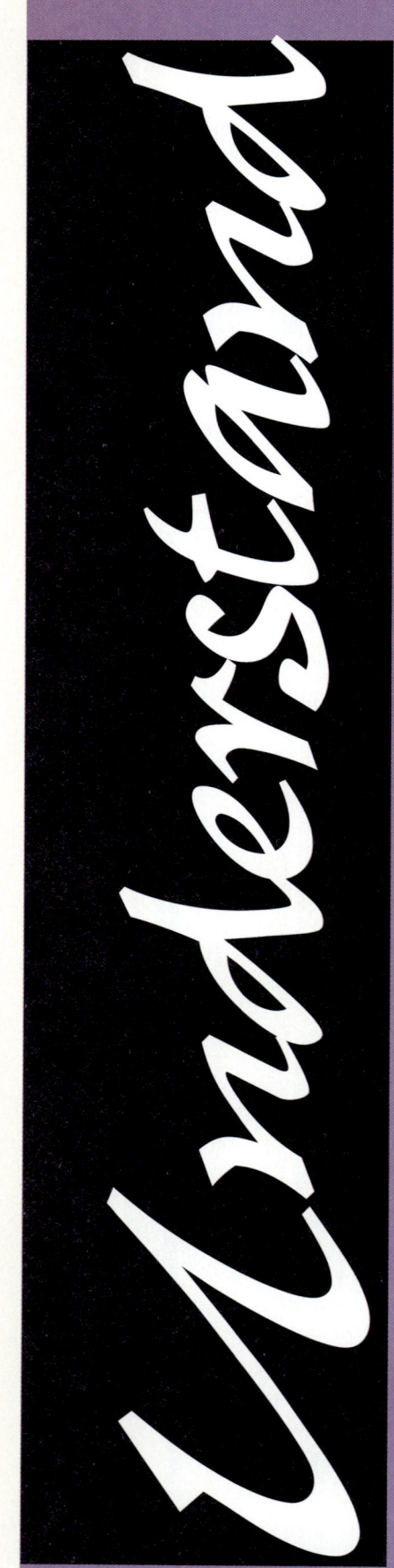

5

Word Keys: Communicating Through Writing

Think about the keys that you keep on a ring in your pocket or your handbag. You use them to get in and out of your house or apartment, your car, mailbox, place of work, maybe even your parents' house or a friend's place. If you have ever lost or misplaced them, you know the feeling—you're stuck. You can't go anywhere or do anything until you find them. If you are on a tight time schedule, panic may set in. When you find them, however, a load lifts from your shoulders, and you can freely get on with your activities.

Basic skills have the same effect on your life. They are the keys that allow you to *take in, retain*, and *pass on information*, the processes by which you build your knowledge and grow. When you don't have them, doors are shut to you, halting your forward progress. However, if you develop and master them, you free up a world of opportunity for yourself. Basic skills open the doors that lead to the chance to learn, grow, and succeed at school and on the job.

In this chapter, you will focus on language-centered keys: ***reading, writing***, and ***note-taking***. For each of these basic skills, you will explore strategies that will help you make the most of your abilities.

Reading

Words are everywhere; through reading, you take in the information they offer you. Whether you're reading school materials, newspapers, signs, package directions, letters, books, or instructions for filling out a form, your daily life depends on words. Even the most accomplished readers continue to build reading skills and vocabulary throughout their lives. As with so many other skills, practice pays off. The more you read, the more you learn about both the subject matter and about language and writing in general.

Reading skills are essential to school and workplace success. For career areas such as word processing, that need seems obvious. Words, though, come into play in any occupation. As the workplace gradually shifts from industry to digital and computer-oriented technology, and as society becomes more "information-driven" (focused on the knowledge and distribution of written information through the media, the internet, and other sources), you will need increased aptitude in reading to stay afloat. On the job you will need to be able to read instructions about how to use machines, directions to locations, notes from co-workers and supervisors, books and other materials for further skill development, company rules and regulations, and applications and tax forms, among other materials.

> A note for those of you who didn't grow up reading and speaking English: English is the business language of the United States. Your job success depends upon your ability to read and speak it well. Your native language also has value on the job; for example, when you need to communicate with customers, clients, or co-workers who speak that language more fluently than English. Treat both languages as equally important tools.

As a student, you often have a great deal of reading to do. Instructors assign textbook chapters, articles in newspapers or magazines, photocopied handouts, and various forms of literature. You also read research books and other materials as you work on specific projects. Reading often dominates your studies. Following are a few strategies that can help you make the most of your time and efforts.

Make Reading a Part of Your Life

Your day is full of many different activities, each one a result of a decision you make. You decide to get up in the morning, to go to class, to wash the dishes, to call someone. Make a decision to read, and stick to it. Reading for school comes first, of course; you won't always be able to make room in your busy schedule for pleasure reading. However, if you make a conscious effort to find time to read and find material you like to read, your skills and knowledge will continually expand.

1. **Find a time to read.** The time you choose may change from day to day as your schedule changes. Be flexible; try reading at any of the following times:

   ❏ During breakfast or lunch.

   ❏ Before bed.

   ❏ During your bus or train commute.

   ❏ At the laundromat.

   ❏ As your child naps.

   ❏ Between classes.

Never Leave Home Without Something To Read

❏ Instead of watching TV.

❏ While riding your exercise bike.

Never leave home without something to read. You never know when you'll have an unexpected wait in a line, at a public transportation station, or at a doctor's office. Reading is a wonderful way to pass the time.

2. **Find material to read.** Make academic assignments a priority. Then decide what else you would really enjoy reading. Here are a few suggestions:

❏ Magazines.

❏ Novels and poetry.

❏ Newspapers.

❏ Nonfiction.

❏ Religious material.

- ❏ Self-help books.
- ❏ Sports books.
- ❏ Romances.

If you don't know where to begin, check the best-seller list on display in your local library or bookstore. Seeing what other people are excited about reading may give you some ideas.

Follow Specific Reading Techniques

For school or work text, using a technique called *Preview, Read, Analyze, Review* will enable you to make the most of what you read. In this context the word *text* refers to the principal matter on a printed or written page as distinguished from notes, headings, and illustrations. Therefore, text is not just a textbook; it is whatever written material you read.

Preview

Your first step is to *take in whatever clues the text offers you*. Every piece of reading material you pick up will be different, but most will have one or more of the following features (textbooks tend to have more than do other materials):

- ❏ Preface.
- ❏ Table of Contents.
- ❏ List of objectives.
- ❏ Section headings.
- ❏ Paragraph headings.
- ❏ Bold/italic words or phrases.
- ❏ Boxed or separated text.
- ❏ Study questions.

These features are designed to give you a general preview of the material and, if applicable, its chapters. Just as a road map helps you get organized before you explore a city, looking ahead at what you are about to read helps you process the information in a more organized fashion.

If the material you plan to read does contain listed objectives and/or study questions, or if your instructor has given you questions to answer or specific information to seek out, keep them in mind as you read. If you stay aware of what you are looking for, you are more likely to notice answers when they appear. You can even keep objectives or questions nearby to make notes on as you read.

Read

Read through at your own comfortable pace. Use the following ideas to keep you on track.

- ❏ *Look for answers.* Keep in mind whatever objectives, key words, phrases or questions your preview reading pointed out to you. Look for them and for the information that explains them or provides answers. In critical thinking terms, keep ideas in mind and search for examples that support or explain them.

- ❏ *Reread.* Whenever you take a break from your reading, reread the last page or small section you completed before you continue on to new material. That brief bit of rereading will reorient your mind to the subject matter.

- ❏ *Highlight and write.* If you own the material you are reading, or if you have permission to make marks on it, you may find it helpful to highlight important words, concepts, information, or answers. Marking text with a bright-colored highlighter is often more helpful than underlining. When you underline, you add ink to the lines of text, and the "busyness" may confuse your eye. Write notes or ideas in the margin to tie your thoughts to specific parts of the reading (again, only do so if you own the material or are permitted). You can also write in a notebook assigned to reading notes, or on Post-It notes that you stick in the pages of the book.

- ❏ *See it.* Make an effort to visualize concepts in your mind as you read. Visualization often helps you remember what you have read, especially if you are a visual learner.

Analyze

When you've completed your reading, *take another look at the chapter objectives, review questions, key terms, and assignments*. Ask yourself these questions: **Do I understand these concepts? Does the material make sense to me? Can I answer the review questions?** If you answer yes to all three questions, go ahead and apply your learning to whatever exercises you need to complete. If your analysis tells you that you didn't get enough out of the reading, reread the material. This time, look more carefully for the specific answers and information you need.

Review

The more often you review, and the sooner after your first reading, the more you retain. Review both on your own and in study sessions with one or more other people. Even if one of those environments suits you better, the variety of doing both may result in greater retention.

Reviewing alone. Evaluate your retention; decide what information you know well and what you still don't quite grasp. Then, after briefly rereading what you understand, concentrate more fully on problem areas. Use some or all of the following techniques.

- ❏ Reread the preface, headings, summary.

- ❏ Reread the chapter.

- ❏ Review the parts you highlighted.

- ❏ Review your notes.

- ❏ Recite important concepts to yourself.

- ❏ Make flash cards with a word on one side and a definition or related information on the other. Test yourself.

- ❏ Think critically: come up with ideas from examples or examples from ideas, consider similar or different concepts, recall important terms, evaluate ideas, explore causes and effects.

- ❏ Make a Think Link that displays how important concepts relate to one another.

- ❏ Read all of the important information into a tape recorder and play it on your Walkman in your spare time. This especially helps verbal and global learners.

Reviewing with others. Different people remember different kinds of information. You can learn new concepts or refresh forgotten ones by reviewing with a partner or in a group. Some suggestions for group study follow.

- Have each person talk through their own summary of the chapter material.

- Take turns reading notes aloud, inviting others to raise a hand and offer additional information when they feel something important has been skipped.

- Read each other's notes to see if you missed anything.

- Make up study questions for each other.

- Have each person make up a quiz question; compile the questions into a quiz that all group members take. Discuss the answers.

Being an *active reader* means working through these four steps thoroughly. Active reading has the power to continuously improve your knowledge. Active readers interact with what they read rather than just sifting through it passively. If you preview, read, analyze, and review, you will interact with your reading at every turn. Think of reading material as a person with whom to have an exchange of ideas. That will encourage your mind to engage energetically in the reading process.

Note Taking

As a student, you need solid note-taking skills. However, the need to take down information skillfully doesn't end when you receive your diploma. Taking good notes is extremely important on the job—at meetings, when learning how to operate equipment, when taking phone messages, and in many other situations. Good note-taking involves *taking in the information, using good habits, evaluating what to write, organizing the information,* and *reviewing.*

Take in information

The key is to listen. You can't write what you don't hear. Active listening will enable you to hear it all; only then can you begin to use the rest of your note-taking techniques.

Form good habits

These basic habits will keep your notes clean and your note-taking as trouble-free as possible.

- Be well rested for class. This is ideal, of course, but not always possible. On the days when you just haven't had enough sleep, you might want to get yourself a drink to sip to help you stay alert (provided you are permitted to bring beverages into the classroom).

- Sit where you can see and hear well.

- Write legibly.

- ❏ Make sure you have working pens and/or sharpened pencils.
- ❏ Date each page or section of notes.
- ❏ Avoid mixing up notes from different classes. Use a different section in your notebook for each class.
- ❏ Keep a bigger notebook, with more paper, than you think you'll need. Plan ahead.
- ❏ Take notes during class instead of after. The sooner after you hear the information, the better.
- ❏ If you have trouble understanding something, ask the instructor (either during class or shortly afterwards) to clarify it.

Write down only what you decide is important

Many instructors talk rapidly. Even if you know shorthand, you won't be able to take down every word. As you take in information, use the following strategies to summarize and analyze as you go, selecting what seems important to remember.

- ❏ Follow the leader. Write down whatever the instructor emphasizes, writes on the board, repeats, or says will be on a test.
- ❏ Note significant words.
- ❏ Summarize by putting down key ideas.
- ❏ Skip articles and connecting words like *the* and *and*.
- ❏ Use abbreviations to save time. Abbreviate such items as states (AZ for Arizona), countries (Fr. for France), proper names after you have written the name in full once (N. for Napoleon), scientific terms (H_2O for water), literary works, organizations, or events using acronyms (WWII for World War II), and words you use often (ex. for *example*, esp. for *especially*, yr. for *year*).

Organize your notes

Only by taking notes according to a structure will you be able to make the most of what you write. "Whatever style of note-taking you use, format is extremely important," say William H. Armstrong and M. Willard Lampe II in *Barron's Pocket Guide to Study Tips*. "Consistency is also important. If you use the same system of indicating importance, such as indenting, spacing, or underlining on each page of your notes, your mind will perceive the key information with a minimum of effort." The two systems described in this section use the principle of structuring words and phrases by organizing concepts and subconcepts and connecting them to related information.

The first method, the standard outline, uses a system of indentation and alternating Roman numerals, Arabic numerals, and letters to indicate main ideas and the facts and examples that support or relate to them. Often there is further information to support the supporting information. Information is presented in levels, with each succeeding level indented from the level before it. Subtopics are designated in the following order, after the upper-case Roman numeral for main topics: upper case letters, Arabic numerals, lower-case letters, Arabic numerals in parentheses, and lower-case letters in parentheses. Never indicate a subtopic unless there are two or more of them. Figure 5-1 is one example of an outline.

SAMPLE OUTLINE

Civil Rights

I. Post-Civil War Era, 1860's
    A. Fourteenth Amendment, 1868: equal protection of the law for all citizens
    B. Fifteenth Amendment, 1870: constitutional rights of citizens regardless of race, color, or previous servitude

II. African-American Civil Rights Movement of the 1960's
    A. National Association for the Advancement of Colored People (NAACP)
        1. Established in 1910 by W.E.B. DuBois and others
        2. Legal Defense and Education fund fought school segregation
    B. Martin Luther King Jr., charismatic minister, champion of nonviolent civil rights action
        1. Led bus boycott 1955-1956
        2. Marched on Washington, D.C. in 1963
        3. Awarded Nobel Peace Prize in 1964
        4. Led voter registration drive in Selma, Alabama in 1965
    C. Civil Rights Act of 1964 prohibited discrimination in voting, education, employment, and public facilities
    D. Voting Rights Act of 1965 gave the government power to enforce desegregation
    E. Civil Rights Act of 1968 prohibited discrimination against African-Americans in the sale or rental of housing

III. Other developments
    A. Women
        1. Nineteenth Amendment (1920) granted women the right to vote
        2. Equal Rights Amendment (prohibiting discrimination on the basis of sex) passed Congress but failed to be ratified by required minimum of 38 states
    B. Affirmative Action
        1. Aims to give minorities and women preference in certain hiring situations to balance out previous inequities
        2. Required since the early 1970's
        3. Enforced by the 1972 Equal Employment Opportunity Act
    C. 1990: Americans with Disabilities Act prohibits discrimination against the disabled

FIGURE 5-1.

Some suggestions for outline organization offered by Armstrong and Lampe are chronological order (such as for a course of events), numerical order (size or number), alphabetical order, or place order. "The arrangement of ideas is a personal matter. The important thing is to have a sensible reason for the arrangement". It can be hard to stick exactly to outline form during a fast lecture or when the speaker doesn't organize the information in a way that would fit the form; do what you can to maintain a standard of organization. The key is that the logic you use makes sense to you.

The second method of organizing notes goes by a number of names such as "mind-map," "web," and visual organizer. One version, developed in Lexington, Massachusetts in 1965 by educator Dr. Frank Lyman, is called a Think Link. It is a creative map-like way of tying related ideas, examples, and other supporting information together, using geometric shapes and lines drawn to connect them. You can construct a Think Link in any form that makes sense for what you are mapping. Some examples are a sun shape with a central idea and facts radiating out from that center, a central idea with attached "satellite" ideas and their connected facts, steps showing connected ideas that build toward a conclusion, or a tree shape with roots as causes and branches as effects. Two samples are shown in Figure 5-2. Using a Think Link may help you see the connections between ideas more clearly, especially if you are a visual learner.

This too may be difficult to construct during a fast lecture. You may be more successful constructing a Think Link on a large sheet of paper after class. That way, you'll be organizing your notes and reviewing at the same time.

Review

Give your memory a boost. Regular review helps to assure that the information you take in and write down stays with you.

The sooner you review notes after you have taken them, the more you will be able to retain. Vary your reviewing techniques to increase your retention. Just reading over notes on your own can get dull, and when you lose interest, you can have trouble paying attention.

Follow these suggestions for varying your routine.

❏ Read over notes the night or day after you write them.

❏ Rewrite notes to improve sloppiness, clarify important concepts, connect information.

❏ Highlight your notes with a fluorescent highlighter to further pinpoint crucial words or phrases.

❏ Rewrite your notes in outline or Think Link form.

❏ Compare notes with a classmate to see if either of you are missing anything important.

❏ Meet with a few classmates for a review session where everyone talks over important concepts together.

❏ Meet with an instructor to make sure your notes cover everything they should.

❏ Color code your notes with highlighters or pens. For example, you might highlight in yellow everything related to a certain topic, or you could assign a highlighter color to each of a few different sets of related causes and effects.

SAMPLE THINK LINKS

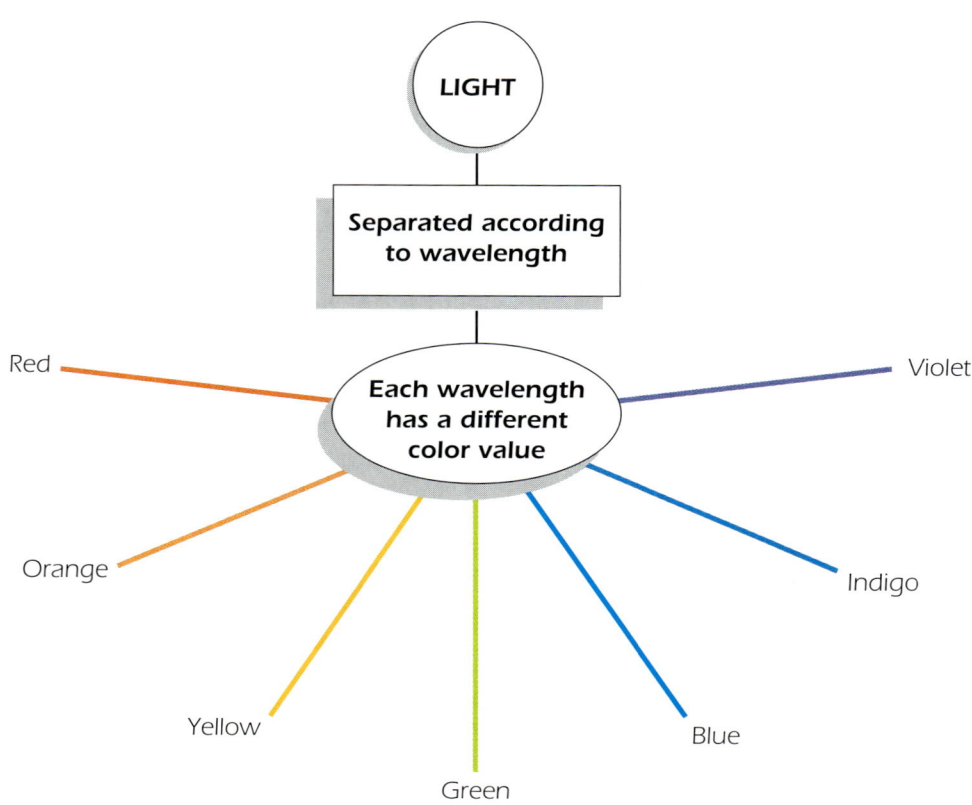

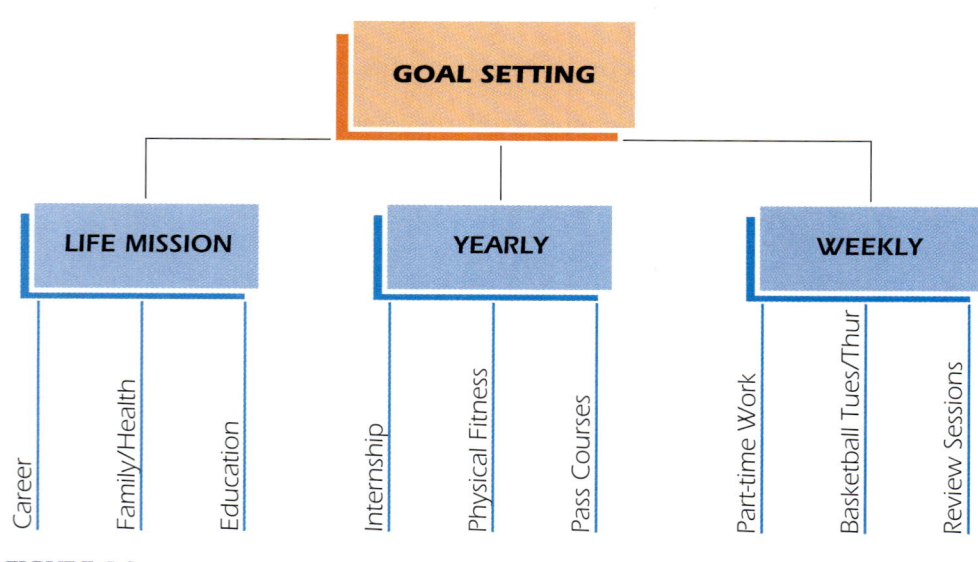

FIGURE 5-2

WRITING

Why is writing important? Depending on where you are in your college career and what you are studying, you may or may not be required to write often. Whether or not you write much right now, you will eventually need good writing skills to apply for, win, and keep a job in your chosen career area. The ability to communicate effectively in writing is considered a vital skill in any career field or line of business. Written communication—reports, letters, order forms, phone messages—is what powers the business world.

Professor, author, and language specialist Lynn Troyka, in her *Handbook for Writers,* defines four general purposes for writing: to *express yourself,* to *provide information for a reader,* to *persuade a reader,* and to *create a literary work.* For your academic and working life, however, she feels that two in particular are of most use to you.

1. **To provide information for a reader.** This kind of writing communicates ideas and facts. It shows up in business reports, minutes of meetings, informational memos, telephone messages, anytime you write down information so that the reader will know about it too. Informational writing primarily requires recall. A primarily informative note to an instructor might read, "I have been absent from class for three weeks due to a case of mononucleosis. I have been receiving copies of assignments and notes from a classmate. I anticipate returning to class next week and will turn in the mid-semester project on the 9th, with your permission."

2. **To persuade a reader.** This kind of writing takes an opinion and tries to convince the reader to adopt it. It is frequently used in letters, fliers, or pamphlets to convince people to buy something or vote for someone. You might use persuasive writing in a memo to your boss to argue for a raise, a cover letter to a prospective employer, in a product review—anytime you need to express an opinion in writing. You probably use all of the Thinktrix mind actions when writing persuasively. A more persuasive note to the same instructor might read, "Please excuse my absence from class due to illness. As I have been receiving copies of notes from a classmate and know the assignments that have been given, I feel that I have made as much of an effort to keep up as I could. Please note that my attendance record for your class prior to this illness was perfect. I would like to turn in the mid-semester project three weeks late and I hope you will not penalize me for my absences."

Effective writing is a twofold communication tool; it connects reader and writer in an exchange of ideas and thoughts. To the reader, it is a source of ideas. Through reading the written word, the reader takes in new ideas and concepts communicated by the writer. To the writer, writing is a tool that can help you organize and introduce thoughts. Elements such as structure, form, length, word choice, style, and voice give you a chance to craft your message according to what you want to say.

Not writing clearly could interfere with your success. Miscommunication can occur through the written word as easily as through the spoken word. Imagine what might happen if the date of an important meeting were incorrect, an unintentional insult turned up in a letter, or a phone number were one digit off. Good writing will help you avoid problems.

At times you will write to inform; at other times to persuade. Sometimes you will do both. The following strategies will help you write effectively, whatever your purpose.

Think about your audience

An important suggestion from Ms. Troyka is to think about who will be reading what you write before you start. Use your sense of empathy; make an effort to understand the situation from the other person's perspective. Think about how the person would like to receive the information you need to communicate. The more empathetic your communication, the more open the reader will be to receiving it.

When deciding how to construct your message, consider how you would speak to the person whom you are addressing. How you speak to a customer is different from how you speak to a supervisor, and how you address a co-worker is different from both of those. How you would express bad news differs from how you would express good news. The same principle applies to writing. Being sensitive to your audience will enable you to more easily get your point across.

> *"In an open society, everyone is free to write and thereby to create reading for other people. For that freedom to be exercised, however, the ability to write cannot be concentrated in a few people. All of us need access to the power of the written word."*
>
> Lynn Quitman Troyka, Professor, of English at Queensborough Community College, The City University of New York

❑ *Who they are* refers to the age, gender, ethnic background, beliefs (religious or political), values, roles (parent, employee, student), perspective, and/or interests of your audience. You might write a casual message to a friendly student, whereas you would pay more attention to grammar, gender sensitivity, and general appeal in a letter to an instructor.

❑ *What they know* can involve educational level, amount of knowledge on your topic, and any preconceptions. You might use a lot more technical language when writing a memo to a supervisor, someone who knows a lot about what you do, than you would when writing advertising copy for the general public to read.

Be legible

It doesn't matter how perfectly you have constructed your writing if the reader cannot read it. Using a typewriter or computer eliminates the problem. If and when you do write by hand, do it clearly.

Test your handwriting by writing something and asking one or more people to read it back to you. If they read it incorrectly, take a look at the trouble spots and rewrite them. Ask them to read it again to make sure it comes across correctly. Sometimes you will be required to use a certain handwriting style, but if you have the freedom to write in any style you choose, stick to your preference (print, cursive, all caps). Often people write most neatly in the style they feel most comfortable with.

Remember the Three Cs

Put them to use before you even pick up a pen—then they will seem more natural to you when you write. *Clear, concise, concrete* thinking equals clear, concise, concrete writing.

C is for CLEAR. Write only what you need to say;
connect ideas to useful examples.
C is for CONCISE. Use as few words as possible.
C is for CONCRETE. Keep it basic, simple and understandable.

For example, here is a memo before and after a Three C makeover:

Before: **There will be a meeting on October 5, at 6 P.M. for all those who might have an interest in participating in the volunteer group this fall. If you want to participate but you can't make the meeting, please let Mel McFadden at** *the Community Center Clearinghouse know and he will get in touch with you later. Leave him a note detailing your class schedule and other conflicts so that he can see if you will be available for the scheduled activities. We will be in the West Wing of the library, Room 2E, and we need to finish by 7 so that the next group can use the room. Thanks—see you soon.*

After: *There will be a Volunteer Group meeting held on 10/5 from 6 - 7 P.M. in the library West Wing Room 2E. The topic is fall community activities. If you want to participate but cannot attend, please post a note for Mel McFadden at the Community Center Clearinghouse; include your name, telephone number, and all schedule conflicts.*

The second message uses fewer words, simpler sentences, and nothing extra, leaving out unnecessary causes and effects. The reader gets the picture much more quickly and easily if you use the three Cs.

Read

Reading and writing affect each other because they are two sides to the same skill—steady reading develops better writing, and careful writing encourages better reading. As what you read sinks into your mind, you improve your knowledge about the selection and combination of words. That knowledge improves your writing no matter how proficient you may be. Everyone who writes will benefit from reading as often as possible.

Find opportunities to write

Life is hectic, and it can be difficult to find time to write. However, many tasks you already need to complete involve writing. Practice improving your writing skills in the following ways:

- *Personal letters*—to family, friends, publications, pen pals.

- *Professional letters*—cover letters, post-interview acknowledgments, recommendations for friends.

- *Journaling.* Keep a record of happenings, thoughts, and emotions. Be ambitious—try to write daily. You may find that if you aim to write every day, you will write a few times a week.

- *Cards and Thank You Notes*—for gifts, occasions, holidays.

Writing responds well to practice just like any athletic skill or artistic ability. The more you write, the more proficient you will become. You discover what works and what doesn't work about writing as you go, and thoughts will become more clear to you because you think critically about them as you write.

Proofread

What you write is of no use to a reader who cannot clearly understand the message. Proofreading involves rereading for the purpose of detecting errors and making

Real World Perspective

Q **Corey Anderson, student at Tennessee Technological University in Rogersville, Tennessee**

It takes a very, very long time for me to write papers. Most people can do a three- to five-page paper in four or five hours, whereas it would take me four or five days. I have the hardest time getting started, but even after I finish, I end up changing every little thing a million times. One big problem is finding the right tone. My style is very personal, and it doesn't sound professional enough.

Many of my teachers can tell which papers are mine without looking at the name. My grades haven't suffered because of this, but a few of my teachers have remarked that my papers are unprofessional. I usually end up rewriting the whole paper, sometimes more than once. I do well in writing classes, but only because I spend so much extra time. I love to write, but it's blood, sweat, and tears. How can I make things easier for myself?

A **Barbara Cox, Instructional Designer, Laguna Niguel, California**

Let's begin by clarifying a common misperception: Most people do *not* write an acceptable three-to-five page paper in four or five hours, unless they have already gathered and organized both the information they need and their comments about it. Every writer develops a strategy, whether consciously or not, that works for that individual writer. Stop comparing yourself to others; it will only increase your anxiety. Many writers suffer the frustrations you are experiencing. Here are a few ideas that may help.

Getting started. Writers often start writing before they are ready. Ask yourself these questions. Do I have all the information I need, including information about my reader(s)? Have I listed points I want to make? Have I decided what order to present these in? Do I know which information to use with each point? When the answers to these questions are "yes," you will be ready to write your first draft.

Editing. Students often try to improve too many things at once or overedit their writing out of a lack of confidence. Many writers overcome these difficulties by using a three-step process that should be done *in order*. (1) Edit for *content*; ask whether any important information has been left out or any irrelevant information included. Edit for organization of ideas; ask whether paragraphs and sentences are in a logical order. (2) Edit for *tone* and *clarity*, focusing on word choice and sentence structure. Eliminate or replace words and phrases that are too formal or informal or that contribute to wordiness. For instance, "end up changing" could be "change," or "until such time as" could be "when." The main sentence structure problem students have is l o o o n g (and often loose) sentences. Use this rule: Check all sentences that contain 30 words or more. (3) *Grammar, punctuation, spelling* and *formatting* should round out your work. If these are not among your strengths, ask an instructor or friend to review these aspects of your paper with you.

"Unprofessional" writing. You cannot correct your writing until you know what is unprofessional about it. Is the content weak or the organization confusing? Is your language too informal? Are your grammar and punctuation poor? Ask your instructors for more feedback on your writing. Engage yourself in basic writing improvements—and then lighten up. If writing is always blood, sweat, and tears, you won't love it for long.

changes. It enables you to get your point across accurately. Is your main point clear, concise, and concrete? Have you misspelled anything? Everything that you write matters; proofread everything. Some hints for proofreading follow:

- ❏ *Put it away for a moment.* Give yourself a rest before proofreading—a day, hour, or even a few minutes—so that you can see what you have written with a fresh perspective. Pretend you are another person who has never seen this material. Do you understand what you wrote? Be objective, and then make any necessary changes.

- ❏ *Pay attention to detail.* An incorrect phone number means no communication. Mistakes in dollar amounts, item numbers, addresses, or name spellings can cause problems and create uncomfortable situations. Check and double check information, punctuation, spelling, and numbers for accuracy.

- ❏ *Proofread for different purposes at different times.* Read once for details, then go back again and read for clarity, idea-example connections, and precise wording. It can be difficult to look for everything at once.

- ❏ *Have someone else proofread.* Another person's perspective can produce valuable advice and suggestions. Ask others to check for errors and to indicate what seems to come across clearly and what causes confusion. Take whatever advice you feel will improve your writing and put it into action.

Never underestimate the power of writing in your life. "Writing ability is needed by educated people," says Ms. Troyka. "Your skill with writing is often considered to reflect your level of education. College work demands that you write many different types of assignments. Most jobs in today's technological society require writing skill for preparing documents ranging from letters and memos to formal reports. Indeed, throughout your life, your writing will reveal your ability to think clearly and to use language effectively."

ESSAYS AND PAPERS

Essays and papers are among the more complex writing projects you will undertake. However, you don't have to let their complexity create anxiety for you. If you go one step at a time, taking advantage of what you know about thinking and writing, you will be able to organize and express your thoughts successfully.

This section is only a brief overview of the writing process; there are many full-length books on the subject. Good writing flows from clear thinking and takes hard work and consideration to create. You are not alone if you feel that you have to put a great deal of time and concentration into your writing. Beyond what you study here, you will benefit from taking your writing and composition classes seriously, reading other materials on writing (a few appear in the listed resources at the end of this book), and giving yourself enough time to think through your work clearly and comprehensively. You will use your writing skills often, in many different situations. If you continually work to improve them, they will serve you well.

When writing any essay or paper, working through the following steps will allow you to control the process and finish with a carefully crafted product: *establish the subject, specify the topic, gather information, plan the construction, write a first draft, revise and revise again,* and *finalize.*

Establish the Subject

Sometimes your instructor will give you a subject or a number of them from which to choose. Sometimes you will just have a general subject to work from. Sometimes you will have the freedom to choose your own. No matter what the source of your subject, two strategies can help you generate ideas about which to write: Brainstorming and freewriting.

You are already familiar with *brainstorming*, in which you list everything that comes to mind on a particular topic. *Freewriting* is a form of brainstorming in which you take a few minutes to write, without stopping, whatever thoughts come into your head. This kind of writing results in a stream-of-consciousness flow of thoughts from which you may be able to extract some useful ideas. When brainstorming or freewriting, avoid judging your thoughts. Let them flow out of the pen without your stopping to consider whether they will work or not.

Specify the Topic

After you generate a jumble of ideas, you need to narrow down your topic to one workable, interesting thought. Explore your lists and freewriting, noting what catches your attention. If your instructor has placed a restriction on topics (a certain subject, era of history, kind of thought process such as a comparison), be sure to honor it. Make sure you strike a balance between a topic that is too broad to cover adequately and one that is too narrow to allow for much exploration and argument. For example, "The Plays of Shakespeare," and "Shakespeare's use of the circle in Act IV, scene vii of *King Lear*," are on either side of the range; "Shakespeare's circle imagery in *King Lear*," may be just right.

Turn your topic into a *thesis statement* to be proven in the course of the paper. A thesis statement both gives you a goal and gives your paper a sense of motion toward that goal. Ask yourself two questions: What do I intend to prove? What is significant about what I intend to prove? Together, those two questions can help you arrive at a comprehensive statement. In the above example, proving that Shakespeare uses a lot of circle imagery in *King Lear* is only half the battle. The other half is to express what is significant or illuminating about that imagery. "Shakespeare, in his *King Lear*, uses the image of the circle to highlight the cyclical path of life and death."

Gather Information

Now that you know what you want to write about, *research* your topic. Use available resources from your library, your class materials, current news, the Internet, or any other source of information. Researching allows you to gather the raw material from which you will construct your paper.

Plan the Construction

Any solid structure starts with a comprehensive plan. Using the ideas from your initial brainstorming, the facts and thoughts from your research, and any new ideas that your research has generated create a plan of your paper in either *outline* or *Think Link* form. Don't worry about being neat or formal; this outline is purely to help you organize the flow of facts and ideas.

In the outline or Think Link, start with your central thesis and work forward from there, generating supporting ideas and putting them in a logical order. Exercise your critical thinking skills—connect examples to the ideas that they support, list effects that result from causes, compare and contrast. Give yourself the freedom to change and reorganize your plan as you work through the process of deciding how to structure your paper. One way to do that is to use small Post-it Notes as outline entries or Think Link boxes, and switch them around until their configuration makes sense.

Write a First Draft

Focus on the big picture as you write. Avoid getting bogged down in punctuation, spelling, sentence style, or other details at this point. Your intent in writing a first draft is to get your ideas down on paper in whatever condition they emerge; later you can refine, reorganize, cut, add, and edit. You may want to keep your resources, outlines, and Think Links near you as you work so that you can refer to them. On the other hand, you may also want to try working without them; Lynn Troyka suggests writing a *discovery draft*, where you set aside your materials and write strictly from the ideas that form in your mind.

Writing doesn't always flow; you may experience "writer's block." If you get stuck, take that feeling as a cue to switch gears. Stop writing and take a break. Write a different section of the paper. Freewrite or brainstorm for a while. Listen to some music. Let your writer's block guide you into a new, fresh perspective.

Paragraphs are the building blocks of your work. Make them solid by introducing or concluding each with a sentence that indicates the topic and tone of the paragraph. In the body of the paragraph, discuss examples and ideas that expand upon and support the topic.

Revise and Revise Again

You have generated many ideas; now, work to mold them into a coherent whole. Shift yourself from the freedom of the first draft to a more painstaking, detail-oriented approach. In *Quick Access Reference for Writers*, Ms. Troyka lists some questions for a writer to ask him or herself when revising. These questions include the following:

- ❏ Is your topic appropriate and narrow enough, and does it convey your purpose?

- ❏ Does your essay take into consideration your audience and their level of awareness?

- ❏ Are points and paragraphs arranged logically?

- ❏ If some material strays from the topic, have you cut it?

- ❏ Do paragraphs each have a topic sentence followed by supporting information?

- ❏ Do you conclude effectively, tying everything together?

Revision is a positive, important process. Give yourself time to revise more than once if you can. Don't imagine that the best writers create perfect papers right from the start; actually, a good writer values the refining process of revision. When you take the opportunity to look at your work anew, you will find that both your message and how you can best express it will become more clear to you. Also, don't hesitate to enlist another reader—often another person will note problems that you wouldn't have seen on your own.

Finalize

Read your work one more time in order to edit; check for proper grammar and sentence structure, punctuation, spelling, and usage of other tools such as capitalization and abbreviation. Then, type a final draft on a typewriter or computer according to the guidelines your instructor has set for you (single- or double-spaced, bound or unbound, cover page or no cover page, name and other information in the proper location). Finally, proofread your final copy, carefully and slowly checking for errors. Correct any you find. Errors can make a bad impression with even the most inventive and intelligent of papers. Hand in a piece of work that you feel proud to have created.

Summing Up

Your ideas may go to waste unless you can express yourself clearly. No matter what major and career path you choose, command of the language will give you a distinct advantage. Use the techniques you have learned in this chapter for active reading, organized note taking, and clear, inventive writing to get you to your goal.

CHAPTER 5: APPLICATIONS

Keys for your Key Chain: Skills Worth Keeping

List here what to you are the five most important keys, or skills, you have learned from reading this chapter.

1. _____
2. _____
3. _____
4. _____
5. _____

Key Into Your Life: Opportunities to Apply What You Learn
Exercise 1 Your Reading Preferences

What do you read, and how often?

Material	Daily	Weekly	Sometimes	Never
Major daily newspaper				
Weekly paper or Sunday paper				
Magazines				
Novels				
Poems				
Romances				
Sports books				
Non-fiction				
Letters				
Essays				
Children's schoolwork				
Plays				
Religious writings				
Short stories				

Exercise 2 Branching Out

Choose three items from the preceding list that you read the most. For each, indicate the specific titles of the materials that you read. What draws you to each piece of material?

1. _____
   _____
   _____

2. _____
   _____
   _____

3. _____
   _____
   _____

Choose two items from the list that you would be least likely to read. For each, discuss what discourages you from reading that type of material. Have you ever tried it? What happened? How might reading this material benefit you?

1. _____
   _____
   _____

2. _____
   _____
   _____

Choose one kind of material that you never read and read it sometime in the next week. What did you read? What new ideas did you pick up from your reading? Will you do it again? Why or why not?

_____
_____
_____
_____
_____
_____
_____
_____

Exercise 3 Your Writing Has Purpose

You are campaigning for a promotion at your job. You feel strongly that you deserve the position. You have the following facts to show you have proven yourself worthy:

- You are always on time to work.

- You follow instructions well.

- The soon-to-be-vacated position is held by a supervisor of yours with whom you have worked closely.

- You complete work early and seek out other projects or help co-workers.

- You intend to stay with the company.

Write two short paragraphs, one that *informs* by stating the facts, and one that *persuades* your boss that you deserve the promotion. Then combine them into one memo to send to the boss. Use your knowledge of causes and effects, showing what causes you to deserve the promotion and what the positive effects will be if you do receive it.

MEMO

To: _____

From: _____

Re: _____

Exercise 4 Know Your Audience

Create a memo regarding a meeting of an organization that you know of at school. For this exercise, you will write three different versions, tailoring the memo to different people, or "audiences." Using the same set of made-up facts about the meeting (time, place, subject matter), write a memo to each of the following:

❏ A member who is a good friend of yours

❏ A Dean who will be a guest at the meeting

❏ Someone whom you don't know who is thinking about joining the organization

_____
_____
_____
_____
_____
_____
_____
_____
_____
_____
_____
_____
_____
_____
_____
_____
_____
_____
_____
_____

Exercise 5 Notes on Notes

Reread the section on Note Taking. Then, take notes on it. Your notes may be in whatever form you prefer—outline, Think Link, or a combination. Use highlighters, all caps, or page positioning to emphasize important concepts in your notes. Use this blank space to record your notes, or use a separate sheet of paper if you need more room.

Indicate here, for review, what four terms characterize the kind of learner you are (see Chapter 2).

_____

What note-taking techniques work best for you? What strategies and conditions help someone with your learning style take notes and retain the information most efficiently?

_____
_____
_____
_____

Key to Cooperative Learning: Building Teamwork Skills

Reviewing

Divide up into groups of three or four and make up a quiz together. Choose a chapter of this book—this one or any of the chapters that you have already covered—and assign each person a section about which to make up a question. One person should create an essay question that requires evaluation; another should ask a similarity-or-difference question; a third person should create an idea-to-example or example-to-idea question; and a fourth person, if you have one, should write a recall question.

Your question:

_____
_____
_____
_____
_____
_____

Next, choose one person to put the quiz together and type it. Make photocopies, or have your instructor do so, and take the quiz.

Lastly, discuss the answers to the quiz together. Your instructor may even want to assign a different chapter to each group and then have the whole class try each quiz; that way, you will review every chapter you have covered so far.

Key to Self-Expression: Discovery through Journal Writing

Words

Some people love to work with words—writing them, reading them, speaking them—while others would rather do anything else. Where are you on the continuum? Did you enjoy your English classes in high school? Which area of study did you prefer—literature, grammar, or creative writing? Does your ideal job have you working with words or not, and if so, how?

_____
_____
_____
_____
_____
_____
_____
_____
_____
_____
_____
_____
_____

KEY TO YOUR PERSONAL PORTFOLIO: YOUR PAPER TRAIL TO SUCCESS

Writing Sample

Any job you take will require some level of writing skill. Write a one-page, three-paragraph cover letter to a prospective employer. Get creative—you may use fictitious names but select a career field of interest to you. Use the following format:

- ❏ *First paragraph*: A statement telling the reader what kind of job you seek, how you found out there was a job available (or how you decided to write to that particular person), and one general statement about your qualifications.

- ❏ *Second paragraph*: A brief discussion about why you want the job and a more detailed description of what you have to offer. What would you want a prospective employer to know first about your experience, skills, and qualities? Choose facts that would make the reader want to look at your résumé.

- ❏ *Final paragraph*: A mention of any enclosures (such as an application and/or résumé), a polite request for an interview, and an expectation of a response.

Exchange your first draft with that of a classmate. Read each other's letters and make notes in the margins. Discuss each of the letters with each other, considering and approving corrections and changes together. Create a final draft for your portfolio.

F O C U

Focus

6

Mind Keys: Retaining What You Learn

As easy as it is to dwell on the importance of successfully completing exams, assignments, papers, and projects, your grades aren't the bottom line. Have you ever done well on a test only to realize a week later that you could hardly remember what it was all about? It's possible to successfully survive all kinds of rigorous academic experiences without being able to keep what you learned for very long. However, one of the purposes of pursuing an education is to develop brain power that you can use in the future. Good grades might get you in the career door, but they won't help you stay there unless you prove that you have the knowledge and skills to back up your record. College is a small fraction of your life. Work to keep what you learn; you have a lot of opportunities to use it ahead of you.

The mind keys you will explore in this chapter will help you boost your ability to retain what you learn. Improving your *listening* and *concentration* will enable you to take in as much of the information presented to you as you can. Fine-tuning your *memory* and your *test-taking* abilities will help you work on keeping information with you for further use. In addition, taking a fresh approach to *working with numbers* will help you combat math anxiety and see how your math skills benefit you in and outside of class.

Listening

It has been said that people have two ears and one mouth because listening is more important than talking. Listening brings you the world, whether you are a hearing person or a deaf person who "listens" by reading sign language. In your student life, many class formats rely on listening as the primary means of taking in information. For example, in a large lecture format class, you might not even be able to see well what your instructor writes on the board; your primary task is to listen to what is said. On the other end of the scale, you may have small group classes that focus on discussion and exchange of opinion, little or none of which is noted in writing.

The ability to listen is one of the most important and valued skills you can possess. Because everyone wants to be understood, people value a listener who makes the effort to clearly comprehend what is heard. In the workplace, the success of any endeavor depends on good communication. Poor listening means communication breakdown and mistakes; good listening means that things get done as planned.

Although they are closely related, *listening* and *hearing* are two distinct activities. Hearing, like breathing, is something people take for granted. It happens automatically; you hear many sounds without conscious effort on your part. However, hearing doesn't automatically result in the retention of what you have heard; listening, when done properly, usually does. Listening starts with hearing and adds effort and focus. It is an intentional action; call it *active listening*.

Imagine yourself in line in a crowded cafeteria. You are trying to choose a drink, the cashier is waiting to ring you up, and a friend is talking to you about a conflict that arose with someone you both know well. Chances are, not enough of what your friend says will reach your brain. As an active listener, you might suggest that your friend hold off on the conversation for a moment and meet you at an empty table. Then, after you get your drink, pay the cashier, find the table, and pull up a chair, you can take a deep breath, look your friend in the eye and say, "OK, start over."

Increase your listening efficiency through practicing the following aspects of active listening.

Stop what you are doing In a hurried world you can easily make a habit of doing many things at once, but listening skills can suffer when you do. If you are running a machine and taking a phone call when a co-worker tries to talk to you, you might not hear correctly. If a friend is whispering to you in class, you will miss either the lecture or the whispered message; you may receive parts of both, making neither comprehensible. When you need to hear something, the computer, telephone, cash register, copy machine, or other conversation will have to wait.

Don't overlap listening and responding People often stifle their listening abilities by formulating responses, or actually responding, while still listening to what is being said. If you react too quickly, you will not receive all the information you need to make an appropriate response. Listen to everything before responding. You can't stop thoughts from forming in your head; however, you can delay your expression of them until you've heard all of the information and had time to consider it. If you have ever gotten angry at someone before you heard the whole story, you know what kind of damage an early response can do. Hold off; you never know if perhaps "you failed the test," could be followed by, "but so did everyone else, so I'm tossing out this grade and giving a new test next week."

Stay receptive and nonjudgmental Sometimes a reaction to the person speaking, especially when negative, can distract you from what they actually say. As normal as it is to act on personal bias, it doesn't always benefit you. Rein in your personal judgments and stay open to what you hear; it may surprise you. A parent who often frustrates you might be offering a veiled apology; a supervisor may follow criticism with praise. Give others the chance to express themselves before you make your conclusions. Even if you do hear what you had imagined you would, you will know that your response is honestly based on a full understanding of what was said to you.

Pay attention   Use your eyes and your mind in addition to your ears. Letting your mind wander or turning your eyes away will prevent you from receiving the entire message; however, a simple visual and mental focus can vastly improve the quality of your listening. Focusing your eyes on the person speaking guides your energy toward that source, helping you to take in information. Concentrating your mental energy will help you shut out distractions.

You can even extend your focus to your body. Facing the speaker and adopting a relaxed, open facial expression will show your interest and encourage the speaker to open up and speak comfortably. Have you ever tried to speak to someone who doesn't look at you, doesn't turn toward you, or doesn't stop what he or she is doing while you talk? Even if the person did hear what you have to say, you might cut off your communication because the person's lack of focus indicates disinterest. You will hear more by paying attention; it shows that you value the information you receive.

Repeat   After you have received information from someone, take a minute to repeat the message to see if you have heard it correctly. Repeating offers three benefits:

- You assure the speaker that you are listening attentively.
- You reinforce what you heard by saying it out loud.
- The speaker has a chance to correct any misunderstandings.

Repeating can be especially useful when taking in important information such as deadlines, rules, test dates, and any changes or corrections to your schedule. When you repeat the information and hear it confirmed or corrected in return, it solidifies your comprehension of the information. There's a big difference between "The meeting is canceled" and "The meeting is rescheduled." Repeating will help you get it right.

CONCENTRATION

Concentration lends power to your thoughts and attention in two ways:

It focuses them on a subject of your choosing.

It increases their intensity and strength.

You only have a certain amount of brain power available to you at any given time. If you have three or four other things on your mind when in class, for example, you will devote probably less than 50 percent of your energy to the class. That means you will receive less than 50 percent of the benefit available to you. Just as a concentrated cleaner has the power to do more work with less fluid, a concentrated mind can handle more difficult jobs with less effort and frustration.

What helps you develop and maintain concentration?

- *Be Present.* Bring your mind to wherever your body is—that way you can take advantage of the increased efficiency that results when they work

Real World Perspective

Q **Adam Bachelder, student at the University of Minnesota in Minneapolis, Minnesota**

I have a friend who was kind of neurotic about his grades. He was a real studying machine. His GPA was almost perfect, and he was involved in all kinds of honorary societies. He was under a lot of pressure from his parents, but he was also putting a lot of pressure on himself. He was planning to go to law school, and when it came time for him to take the LSAT, he wanted to be the first person to get a perfect score. He studied like crazy, took courses on the LSAT test, and spent an incredible amount of money on books.

Finally the pressure was too much. About a week before the test, he became physically ill and had to be hospitalized. He was about 6'3" and weighed only about 140 pounds at test time. He couldn't take the test because he was in the hospital being treated for a mild psychological disorder. He was so weak, both physically and emotionally, and had a really tough time dealing with this test. This is an extreme case, but most students, including myself, can relate to this kind of test anxiety. There have been plenty of times when the pressure I put on myself to succeed has done more harm than good. How can I make the most of tests instead of letting them get the better of me?

A **Jenny Robbins, Executive Director of Development, The Princeton Review**

Much of the stress that students experience over standardized tests can be alleviated through proper planning and gathering of information. Investigate the average test score/GPA of students admitted to the programs in which you are interested (admissions offices and/or school guide books can provide this information). Gather information from the test companies about the exam (request a current Registration Bulletin by phone). Take a practice test to explore strengths and weaknesses (often included in registration booklets; you can also order practice exams from the test company or buy a book of simulated tests from the book-store). Find out when to take the test (your advisor can help you decide or refer you to someone who can give you more details).

This student, or any student, could take steps to relieve some of the pressure. First, you can postpone the test in a case of illness. If you are not feeling well it may be best not to take the exam at your registered time. If your application deadlines are not immediate, call the testing company and change your registration to the next test date. If you plan ahead, you can have more than one opportunity to take an exam, should you need it. Next, try to take the exam when your schedule allows for time to devote your attention to preparing for it. Also, set a reasonable goal. A perfect score on an exam won't guarantee acceptance to a program and a low score won't necessarily prevent admittance.

The "more is better" mode of test preparation used by this student is not recommended. Instead, select one good book or course (ask friends/advisors for recommendation) and focus your efforts on it. Methods and strategies may differ from book to book and from course to course, making your preparation more stressful. Include lots of practice with sample exams. And don't forget to consider the big picture. Admissions committees will be considering college grades and extracurricular activities as well as your personal statement. You are more than just a test score.

together. When in class, concentrate on class. When at work, focus on your tasks. When having a conversation, pay attention to what is being said.

❏ *Be Current.* Recall what you read in the first chapter about the advantages of focusing on the present. Thinking about what happened in the past or what you plan for the future takes you away from what deserves your attention right now. The more energy you expend processing information when it is first presented, the less time you will spend trying to reconstruct it later.

❏ *Breathe.* A few minutes of slow, calm, deep breathing can help you clear your mind and prepare it for concentration. Imagine that you exhale your busy brain activity along with the air you blow out, taking in clarity as you breathe in. Close your eyes to shut out any visual distractions. After a minute or two, you should feel more calm, clear-headed, and ready to focus.

❏ *Focus your eyes.* As with listening, a visual focus can help you pay attention. Looking at something specific, whether it's an instructor, a written page, or an image, can help you to concentrate.

❏ *Find a relaxing environment.* Some locations hinder concentration. Think about what distractions bother you. If an environment makes it difficult for you to concentrate, for example, a busy family room with kids watching TV, change it (turn the TV off and ask the kids to play somewhere else) or move to a different location (relocate to the kitchen). Distractions vary for different people; some have trouble concentrating in a busy, noisy area, while for others the silence of a completely quiet room is distracting. Find what environment helps you maximize the strong points of your learning style.

❏ *Take time out for a break.* The energy that concentration demands can wear you out. After a long study session, you might feel as tired as you would be if you had gone for a long bike ride. Instead of forcing yourself to push ahead without a break, take time out every once in a while to do something relaxing and completely different. When you absolutely cannot concentrate anymore, that's a signal to change gears. Take a nap, exercise, read, go for a walk, have lunch, or do anything else that takes your mind off your work. When you return to work, you will be refreshed and ready to go.

Memory

Learning is built upon memory because you can't have truly learned something unless you remember it. A capable memory increases your efficiency; learning once and working to retain that information beats learning and relearning over and over again. Plus, the better your memory, the more time you save yourself at school and at work. When you can remember information and procedures, you avoid having to hunt down the information yourself or ask someone else to take time to help you.

You take in immense amounts of information every day. The scope of the media has increased dramatically in recent years; people are bombarded each day by information and opinions from network and cable television, advertising, radio, books, and a horde of newspapers, journals, and magazines. The development of electronic mail and the Internet has opened up another whole world of information to the public. Plus, information travels fast. In a few minutes you can send something by fax or electronic mail that not too long ago would have taken days. Although memory lapses are often attributed to old age, it's no wonder people of all ages have trouble recalling information. Our culture is overwhelmed with it.

Alvin and Heidi Toffler, long recognized as influential social thinkers, say that information and knowledge have become a resource more important than money, labor, or land. "We are creating new networks of knowledge. [...] Businesses, governments, and individuals are collecting and storing more sheer data than any previous generation in history," they report in *Creating A New Civilization: The Politics of the Third Wave*. "Because it reduces the need for raw materials, labor, time, space, capital and other inputs, knowledge becomes the ultimate substitute—the central resource of an advanced economy. And as this happens, its value soars." As you become more adept at processing, storing, and retrieving knowledge, your increased value in the workplace will bring you increased success.

It takes some effort to work with such an abundance of information. Memory expert Harry Lorayne, in his book *Super Memory—Super Student*, identifies memory as what lies in the gap between the location of information you need and the understanding and application of that information. The two keys to filling that gap are the *efficient gathering* and the *organized storage* of knowledge and information.

Gather efficiently   Lorayne emphasizes how strongly memory, knowledge, and thinking are linked. "*Memory is knowledge*; those are two magnets that cannot be separated. I'm not suggesting that memory is a substitute for understanding, application, or experience. But it sure is the most direct avenue to those desirable conditions and surely is the most important part of them." Knowledge is the resource with which you perform all of your other thought actions. What can help you gather it efficiently?

- *Listen and Concentrate.* Your eyes and ears are the primary "intake valves" for the most important information you receive. If you practice active listening and concentrate, you will be more likely to receive all the information coming your way.

- *Repeat.* When you repeat, you increase your intake efficiency; the physical action of speaking or writing solidifies the information in your memory. Furthermore, repeat as soon after you take in the information as possible. You will tend to forget most rapidly during the short period right after exposure to information; you lose less information as time goes by. For example, when you have an interesting dream, you will usually forget most of it unless you talk about or write down what happened immediately after you wake up. That principle applies to any knowledge. Solidify your knowledge by reviewing immediately after learning it and then continuing to review on a regular basis.

Organize your storage   Once you take in the knowledge, you need to store it in ways that will enable you to retain it and to quickly retrieve it when you need it.

- *Associate.* Your mind remembers new information by linking it in some way to something that you already know or remember. One way to have information available to you is to consciously associate it with other more familiar or simpler information. Putting something new in the context of something you already know helps you relate to it more easily. Meeting new people is one chance to associate. Say you meet a thin person named Sharon Lean. You can remember her name because of how she looks. Maybe she happens to look like your best friend Karen, which rhymes with Sharon.

- *Write.* Beyond helping you retain information, writing helps you recall it later, analyze it, and develop new ideas about it. Write down daily to-do lists, important phone numbers, points brought up in a meeting with a supervisor, the objectives for a class, or the names of group members at a meeting. Rewrite notes you took, reorganizing them logically and emphasizing the key points you want to remember. The more you write, the more things stick.

❑ *Group and sequence.* When you have to memorize a number of things at once, any patterns you can create will help you. Group items according to similarities. Keep groups to around 10 items; it's hard to memorize more than that at one time. Sequence items according to whatever pattern applies—priority, chronological or alphabetical order, number, or category. For example, if you had to remember the names of seven authors, you might organize them alphabetically by last name, chronologically by birthdate, categorically by what kind of literature each wrote, or by priority, considering how important each was to what you were studying.

❑ *Visualize.* Especially for the visual learner, turning information into mental pictures can help. You might visualize chemical formulas inside the matter that they represent (H_2O floating in water). You might see the names of architects plastered across the front of their most famous buildings. You might imagine related pieces of information tied to each other in ridiculous ways; if you needed to remember that Picasso painted "The Three Women," you might imagine the women in a circle dancing with a Spanish pig (pig-asso). Be creative, and don't reject outlandish images; as long as they are useful to you, that's what's important. "We usually forget mundane, everyday, ordinary things," says Lorayne. "The ridiculous-picture idea takes anything out of the mundane. Forming a logical picture takes too little thought—Making the pictures ridiculous forces you to think of the items."

❑ *Use mnemonic devices.* Pronounced nehMAHNick, these devices are word tricks that help you to organize and categorize information in easy-to-recall structures. Mnemonics cannot go beyond aiding recall; they don't help you understand, process, or analyze the information. They help you dredge it up quickly, though, and that's an important first step. Following are descriptions of different types of mnemonics; you can choose which to use based on what helps you more or what suits a particular type of information.

> "Memory is the stepping-stone to thinking, because without remembering facts, you cannot think, conceptualize, reason, make decisions, create, or contribute. There is no learning without memory."
>
> Harry Lorayne, authority on memory training and author of *Super Memory—Super Student*

Acronyms are formed from taking the initial letters of a series of words and making a new word. Examples include NATO (<u>N</u>orth <u>A</u>merican <u>T</u>reaty <u>O</u>rganization) and sonar (<u>so</u>und <u>n</u>avigation <u>a</u>nd <u>r</u>anging). Don't restrict yourself to words that make sense; whatever you can remember easily is valid, whether it is a "real" word or not. Remember, sonar was accepted as part of the English language some time after it was created as an acronym. Trying to remember the first six U.S. presidents might lead you to construct an acronym such as WAJeMMA (George <u>W</u>ashington, John <u>A</u>dams, Thomas <u>J</u>efferson, James <u>M</u>adison, James <u>M</u>onroe and John Quincy <u>A</u>dams).

Creative rhymes, tunes, and phrases can jump-start your recall. If you've ever had a song stubbornly stick in your head despite all of your efforts to forget it, you will realize what power a rhythmic or rhyming turn of phrase can have. For example, the classic rhyme "Thirty days hath September, April, June, and November, all the rest have thirty-one, save February…" helps many people recall exactly how the months differ in length. You might link the title of a jazz tune to its rhythm and melody line; Miles Davis has a two-note repetitive musical phrase in "So What" that matches the title perfectly.

Special sentences help you recall pieces of information, often in a particular order. One oft-used way to remember biological classifications, from largest to smallest, is the sentence, "King Philip clomped on father's good shoes" (kingdom, phylum, class, order, family, genus, species).

TEST TAKING

Tests are often a source of anxiety. They can in large part determine whether you gain admission to a school, pass a class, graduate, or land a job. People who have the power to influence your success take test grades into account when making decisions. Whether they reflect an accurate measurement of your mastery of a particular subject or not, test grades will affect your success in school and beyond.

Maintaining a positive and appropriate attitude toward tests is the most important step you can take. Armstrong and Lampe, in the *Barron's Pocket Guide to Study Tips*, ask if you have ever thought of a test as a beneficial opportunity instead of a visitation of torture or a battle in which the instructor wants to beat you down. After all, your instructor doesn't spend many hours preparing and grading tests for his or her own personal gain. Look at a test as an opportunity to learn and to show what you can do. "Students who accept a test as a challenge to show the teacher the extent of their knowledge of the subject and to improve their grades are stimulated…This attitude requires the relationship between student and teacher, and question and answer, always to be one of cooperative production rather than competitive destruction."

Here are two more thoughts to keep in mind when developing a more realistic and positive perception of tests.

1. **Test grades don't necessarily indicate your level of learning.** For example, your grade may reflect only the situation surrounding one particular test—you could have been sick, preoccupied, or have had trouble finding time to study. Also, test anxiety can be a problematic factor. Someone who has studied hard but becomes anxious about tests could end up with a bad grade, while someone else who hasn't paid as much attention but isn't threatened by tests could pass with flying colors. If you feel your grades don't reflect your work, emphasize other positive points (experience, project successes, positive recommendations) when you speak with your instructor about a final grade or when you search for work.

2. **You are the one who is ultimately responsible for your grades.** Take control by preparing comprehensively for tests. While you shouldn't automatically accept test grades as an accurate evaluation of your proficiency level, try to develop your test-taking abilities so that they come to reflect your knowledge accurately. Don't give tests more power than they deserve, but do realize that the grade may stick with you.

Preparing for Tests

How can you prepare for tests, whether at school or when applying for a job, so that you will show what you can do?

Find out what you can about what will be on the test. Note carefully what you find out in class or from a photocopied handout about the test. Talk to your instructor, or interviewer if you are being tested while applying for a job, beforehand if you don't have a clear idea of exactly what material will be covered. Structure your studying accordingly.

Study practice tests or sample tests. These are available for certain specific classes. You might find them in the library or class test file. Your instructor may also keep them on hand.

Review regularly. If you review on a regular basis over time, you will have an easier time retaining information. Start as soon as you know the test schedule and test topics; if an instructor gives you a class synopsis on the first day that spells out the schedule for you, make a habit of reviewing your notes weekly, starting right away. Time away from the material can damage your retention; consistent review helps by limiting those periods of time away. If you can, always give yourself at least a week to review for a test.

Spread out your review periods. If you have one week and think you will have to study for ten hours to get through all the material, do one hour a day on the weekdays and two and three on Saturday and Sunday respectively instead of having a marathon study session on Sunday. The material will stay with you if you renew it periodically over a longer period of time.

Avoid cramming whenever possible. Remember, the point is to be able to retain information so that you can use it in your future work and life. At best, cramming will jam it into your short-term memory in time for you to recall it on the test, but chances are it will fade away soon after. In reality, many students find themselves in predicaments where they have no choice but to cram. If you end up there some night, try spreading out your review through whatever amount of time is available to you for studying. If you can work from 8 P.M. to 2 A.M., assign a different topic or chapter to each hour. Take a break every hour for ten minutes. Focus on the most crucial and general ideas and connected examples (facts and events) instead of trying to know it all. Take your time and relax so that any tension you feel doesn't eat up your energy. Then, after the test, remind yourself that you want to save yourself this kind of pain in the future, and vow to take responsibility for planning ahead next time.

Study in whatever kind of environment distracts you least. Distance yourself from conversation, the telephone, food, TV, and anything else that prevents you from concentrating. Whether you prefer your own room, the library, an empty classroom, or the outdoors, find a place that helps you focus.

Sleep well. If sleep falls by the wayside during intense periods of studying, get back on track in preparation for a test. Don't stay up all night studying for a 9 A.M. exam. Although pulling an "all-nighter" is rarely an ideal move, it can harm test performance more than other abilities. If you were to stay up to finish a paper, you could at least take breaks when you need to and get some rest as soon as you turn it in. Taking a test, however, requires an alert mind that can work efficiently and rapidly in a limited period of time. Studying all night tires out your brain as much as it does the rest of your body. Don't risk being sluggish; log as many hours of sleep as you can before test time. If you are well rested and alert, you will turn in your best performance.

Eat right. Food is fuel. Good fuel promotes good performance, and poor fuel hinders it. Sugar and caffeine can't replace a well-balanced meal. Trying to boost your energy level with sugar sends you way up only to quickly bring you way back down. If you try to wake yourself up with coffee or a caffeinated soda, you may find that you don't think as well on that sort of artificial energy source. In addition, some people experience anxiety and panic if they ingest any significant amount of caffeine, which can cause trouble when trying to calm down and think clearly at test time. Eat a good meal before a test—and if you find you don't have time, grab a granola or cereal bar for quick energy.

Answer the easiest test questions first

Taking Tests

Following are some ways to maximize your potential for success on test day.

Plan ahead. Make sure you know the date, time, and location of the test. Arrive early so that you have a few minutes to get settled and take a breath before you start. Bring any materials you will need, such as pens and pencils, paper, or an exam booklet. If it is an open-book test, don't forget your book.

Relax. Worrying takes a lot of energy and fragments your concentration. Train your focus on the test. Take a few long, slow, deep breaths before you start. Take your time. Tell yourself that you have what it takes to do well on the test. Stay in control.

Look over the test beforehand to get an idea of its scope and to decide approximately how much time you can spend on each question. Just as you save time in your day by scheduling tasks, planning out when and how you will answer test questions will save you from wasting time. Otherwise, you may take a half-hour to answer one of five questions and then realize that you have only twenty minutes to deal with the other four.

Read/listen to the directions before you start. Many mistakes occur when a tired student doesn't pay enough attention to the directions. What if you saw ten questions and didn't understand that you need only choose seven to answer? Directions save you time and trouble.

Answer the easiest questions first. Unless your test is on a computer, you don't have to do the questions in order. Working with the questions that feel most comfortable will both boost your confidence and give you more time to spend on the more difficult questions.

When in doubt, stick with your first guess. Your intuition fuels your guesses and is sometimes more accurate than the overthinking that might occur later.

Don't waste too much time pondering. If you're stuck, go on to another question and come back to it.

Leave time to check over your answers. It's easy to make careless errors. Don't change answers unless you are positive you made a mistake.

Be kind to yourself. Don't be too hard on yourself if you feel you didn't do well on a test. You did the best you could at that time. If you do receive disappointing results, take it easy. You are not a failure because you failed one test. Look at what went wrong—whether you got nervous or didn't know the material well enough—and think about how to succeed next time. Talk to your instructor; together you might be able to figure out where you fell short and how you can improve.

Types of Tests

Most tests fall into one of two categories: *objective* (true or false, multiple choice, fill-in-the-blank) and *subjective* (essay). Some tests may contain elements of each.

Objective Tests Objective questions test your ability to retain, recall, compare, and contrast information. When you have a test that combines objective and essay questions, work on the objective questions first—they usually require less analysis. Objective tests use three main types of questions: true or false, multiple choice, and fill-in-the-blank.

True or false

True or false: Many people in their forties and fifties are reentering the work force on a different career path than they followed before.

Nothing replaces solid knowledge of the subject, but if you have to guess, you have a fifty-fifty chance of getting these right. Read each sentence carefully; some longer sentences may combine true and untrue statements, making the final answer false. Watch for words that signal absolutes, such as *all, every, none, always,* or *never*. They are less often true than sentences with relative words such as *most, often, rarely, few,* or *usually*.

Multiple choice

An IRA account is: a. *A statement by an Irish militant group*
b. *A checking account*
c. *A retail credit account*
d. *An account for retirement savings*

Again, as with true or false, you're in the best shape if you have studied well and know the material enough to answer confidently. When that isn't the case, a few strategies can help you guess. It can be to your advantage to make a guess because a question left blank usually counts as a wrong answer. If you guess, you have at least a 20-25 percent chance of getting it right (if there are four or five answers to choose from).

Here are some additional hints. *Beware of absolute words;* opt for answers that have relative words instead. If two of the possible choices are *opposites* of each other, or if they are strikingly *similar,* one of them is probably the right one. Try *reading the question and answers quietly to yourself.* One of them may sound right to your ear.

Fill-in-the-blank

Water is a combination of two elements:_____ and _____.

There's not much room for guessing here—it's pure recall. You have to know your stuff, although some instructors will give you partial credit for partially correct answers. Even when you know the answer, make sure that it fits grammatically with the rest of the sentence. Check your answer for completeness and accuracy, making sure it matches exactly what the question asks.

Subjective Tests Essay questions demand the same information recall that objective questions do, but they ask more of you. They require organization, writing, knowledge of the given topic, and analysis of the subject of the question. For example:

COMMON ESSAY QUESTION WORDS

Analyze. Break into parts and discuss each part separately.
Compare. Discuss two things, focusing on similarities (can mention differences).
Contrast. Discuss two things, focusing on their differences.
Criticize. Judge what's good and bad about a concept.
Define. Give a brief statement of the meaning of a word/concept/item.
Describe. Tell or write about something in detail.
Discuss. Consider the pros and cons of an issue or idea.
Enumerate/List/Identify. Specify items in the form of a list.
Explain. Make an idea clear by providing examples.
Evaluate. Give your opinion about the value or worth of something.
ILLUSTRATE/SHOW. Give examples.
Interpret. Explain the meaning of a concept or idea, using examples.
OUTLINE. Organize the main points of an idea and discuss them.
Prove. Use facts to show that something is true.
Relate. Show how two ideas/events are associated.
State. Explain clearly and simply.
SUMMARIZE. Give the main points in brief.
Trace. Present a history of the way something developed.

FIGURE 6-1

Compare and contrast the House of Representatives and the Senate.

Read the question and any instructions carefully so that you know what the question asks of you. Certain words in the question can clue you in to what you need to do, so watch for them and know exactly what they mean. Figure 6-1 explains some commonly used words.

Be as concise as you would in any other piece of writing. Longer isn't necessarily better when it comes to essay questions. If you answer clearly and accurately, linking ideas to concrete examples, you will come out ahead of someone who hides the facts in a thick sea of words. Wandering off the subject or writing too much takes up a lot of your precious time.

When writing answers to essay questions, it is especially important to outline your answer before you start writing. Taking that extra minute to organize your thoughts will help you remember all the important points you want to make. In addition, pay attention to your handwriting, spelling, grammar, and neatness. It may not matter how brilliant your answer is if the person grading it is distracted by spelling mistakes and sloppy penmanship. Good mechanics will let your ideas shine through.

WORKING WITH NUMBERS

The ranks of students who are comfortable with math and science material seem to gradually narrow through high school and into college. Many perceive that working with numbers is something a person either has the knack for or can't understand, with no middle ground. However, your skills can improve with work and a little confidence. Although most people won't regularly be making complicated calculations in their chosen careers, nearly everyone will periodically need to add, subtract, multiply, and divide. Some will also calculate fractions, decimals, and percentages. Math skills help with spreadsheets, money earned or spent, petty cash, pricing, personal finances, and more.

"Math is about patterns that exist in the world—like the veins in leaves having order," says Marcia Learner, author of *The Princeton Review's Math Smart*. "When you see patterns in the world, you are understanding math." You are using mathematical skills when you double ingredient amounts for a recipe, figure out the tip on a restaurant check, or compare the mileage of two different routes to the same city.

The key to being at ease with numbers, and even interested in them, is to focus on how they serve you from day to day. Percentages can help you compare the financial benefits of different loan programs. Adding and subtracting will allow you to balance the checkbook, pay bills, and allocate funds to different accounts. Fractions will help you compare numbers at work if you evaluate salaries, gross and net income, bills, rent, insurance, and other costs in order to see if you're staying in the black. People are naturally less threatened by what they use in their everyday lives.

You won't always see a connection between what you have to do in class and what you think you will use later on in the real world. That's true of many subjects, not just math. You may not remember a principle from an obscure philosophy class or the last time you used a language that you have studied for years. However, you benefit in some way from every class you take. Beyond learning facts, figures, formulas and other information, different subjects help you to develop different kinds of thinking skills. The precise calculation and intricate problem solving involved in working with numbers helps you develop precision, a focus on detail, patience, and a sense of order.

Numbers also hone your critical thinking skills: you recall formulas, compare and contrast different equations and amounts, apply mathematical ideas to specific problem examples, and see what kinds of effects mathematical laws have on number patterns. From examples of how numbers behave in certain situations, you develop general ideas about how they work. You even apply formulas to problems and evaluate how well they help you arrive at a solution.

Dealing with classroom calculations can be difficult. Following are some strategies that may help you.

MIND KEYS: RETAINING WHAT YOU LEARN

❏ When taking notes in math classes or when working through problems, be sure to include every aspect of the formulas, rules and principles, and problems that you study. "Write everything down," says Lerner. "Writing everything down and making it visual are some ways to make math something you can do easily." Once you have written it, you can ponder it and refer to it. Then, if you have gone through a problem and reached an incorrect answer, you will be able to retrace your steps and figure out exactly where you made a mistake.

❏ Analyze problems carefully. Make sure you have all of the data you need and have taken every aspect of the problem into account.

❏ Break the calculation into the smallest possible pieces. If it doesn't make sense as a whole, go step by step and don't move on to the next step until you are clear on what you've done so far.

❏ Recall similar problems and how you solved them; you may also want to rework those problems. Past experience can give you valuable clues to how a particular problem can be handled. When you rework past problems, you reinforce what you learned from them, making that knowledge more accessible for application to a new problem.

❏ When available and appropriate, use a calculator, adding machine, or computer program that performs mathematical functions for you. There's no shame in it, especially on the job when you aren't being graded on the process by which you arrive at an answer. Most workplaces will encourage the use of machines for the sake of speed and accuracy. Check every step of your work as you go, and recalculate to confirm that you have reached the correct answer.

❏ Take your time. Precision and accuracy demand concentration and focus; haste makes waste when it comes to calculations. Even with a calculator it's easy to press a wrong key without realizing it, and one wrong key can make a world of difference when the final amount appears.

❏ If you have any doubts about your ability, ask someone to help you. It's better to get help than to make a mistake.

❏ Check your work as you go. If you have time, recalculate completely to confirm that you have reached the correct answer.

❏ Work backwards. If you are stumped and the answer is available to you, start from the answer and see if you can figure out step by step how to get back to the original question. Reversing the procedure may let you know where you may have made a mistake or skipped a step.

❏ Check your solution with the original goal. Does it make sense? For example, if you are adding ten different dollar amounts all over $100 and you end up with $935.23, something is wrong. Your mathematical intuition will help you confirm the accuracy of your work.

Summing Up

Your education opens the door to a vast resource of knowledge; with the aid of certain strategies, you will be able to gather maximum benefit from what you take in. As an active listener, you will hear important information. Through concentration, you will be able to focus your mental energies on the information as you learn. By honing your memory, you will retain information so that you can apply it to new situations in the future, and in improving your test-taking skills, you will be able to display your retention and command of knowledge and its applications. Even calculations won't worry you when you can confidently work with numbers. Knowledge is a gift; accepting it, retaining it, and putting it to use are skills you can master.

CHAPTER 6: APPLICATIONS

Keys for your Key Chain Skills Worth Keeping

List here what to you are the five most important keys, or skills, you have learned from reading this chapter.

1. _____
2. _____
3. _____
4. _____
5. _____

Key Into Your Life: Opportunities to Apply What You Learn
Exercise 1 Optimum Listening Conditions

Describe two situations that make it easy for you to listen.

1. Where are you? _____

   What time is it? _____

   Is anyone else there? Who? _____

   What other activity is happening, if any? _____
   _____

   Is there any background sound? If yes, what is it, and why does it help you?
   _____

2. Where are you? _____

   What time is it? _____

   Is anyone else there? Who? _____

What other activity is happening, if any? _____
_____

Is there any background sound? If yes, what is it, and why does it help you?
_____

From these two situations, name five listening conditions that you feel are crucial to your success.

1. _____
2. _____
3. _____
4. _____
5. _____

How can you create those conditions more often?
_____
_____

Exercise 2 Be Present

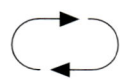

Take five minutes to list on a sheet of paper every worry or concern you have right now. Brainstorm; write down every one that comes into your mind in the space of five or ten minutes.

Now divide those concerns into three categories: What has already happened in the *past*, what is still to come in the *future*, and what you can take care of right *now*.

Past	Future	Now

Leave the past and future and concentrate on the present. Choose two of the concerns you have the power to address now. Indicate for each what causes the concern and what solution you propose to alleviate it.

1. Concern: _____

Causes: _____

_____

Solution: _____

_____

2. Concern: _____

Causes: _____

_____

Solution: _____

_____

Exercise 3 Create a Mnemonic Device

Take a look at all of the principles of good memory, whether they apply to how you take in information or how you store it. Make up a mnemonic device that allows you to remember them quickly. You can use a sentence, an acronym, or a rhyme.

_____

_____

_____

_____

Think of one other time when you have used a mnemonic device to remember something. What was the device? How did it help you?

_____

_____

_____

_____

Exercise 4 Boost Your Memory

What do you have the most trouble remembering? Is it names, phone numbers, tasks you need to accomplish in a day, birthdays, due dates for assignments? Write it here.

_____

Now spend a week concentrating on improving that particular part of your memory. For example, if you have trouble with names, ask for people's names as often as you need to. Repeat them in your mind and use them when you talk to the person; for example, "It's nice to meet you, Caroline." Write names down in a book. Associate names with other names, memorable characteristics, and anything else that helps information to stick.

Indicate your techniques here:

1 _____
_____

2 _____
_____

3 _____
_____

Did your skills improve? If so, what technique (or combination of techniques) helped the most? If you plan to make a habit of one or more techniques, which are they and why?

_____
_____
_____
_____

Exercise 5 Real Life Math

Do you experience math anxiety?   YES   NO

Try this exercise. Look at the last ten items in your checkbook—deposits, cash withdrawals, checks written. Write down the balance of your checking account as it stood before those ten items. Then compute the math by hand, adding deposits and subtracting debits from the starting amount. Take your time and work carefully.

Checking Account
Balance: $_____.__
       1. $_____.__
                $_____.__
       2. $_____.__
                $_____.__
       3. $_____.__
                $_____.__
       4. $_____.__
                $_____.__

5. $____.__
    $____.__
6. $____.__
    $____.__
7. $____.__
    $____.__
8. $____.__
    $____.__
9. $____.__
    $____.__
10. $____.__
TOTAL: $____.__

When you have completed the exercise, do it again using a calculator. Does your first answer match the calculator answer? If not, work the calculator again to make sure you have not made your error there. If you still don't have a match, go back and try your calculations by hand again. Note where along the line you made a mistake. Work backwards if that helps you. Slow, careful, precise calculations are excellent medicine for math anxiety. Taking your time will give you confidence.

Key to Cooperative Learning: Building Teamwork Skills

Hone Your Listening and Memory Skills

Improve listening and memory through teamwork. Divide into groups of six to play a game called Celebrity. Each group will have three teams of two. Using equally sized scraps of paper, each person must write down the names of five well-known people, one on each scrap. The well-known people may be living or dead and can have achieved celebrity status in any field—sports, entertainment, politics, arts and literature, science and medicine, etc. Each scrap of paper should be folded to conceal the name written on it. Put all of the scraps together in one container (there will be thirty in all). The only other equipment you need is a watch with a second hand.

The first stage of the game is as follows: Within each team of two, there is a giver and a receiver (team members switch roles every time they have a new turn). Teams take turns guessing. While all other teams watch and a member of a non-guessing team times the pair for one minute, the giver of the guessing team chooses a scrap of paper and describes the named celebrity to the receiver without saying any part of the person's name. The giver can use words, sounds, motion, singing, anything that will help the receiver. (For Michael Jordan: "Famous Chicago basketball player, retired and played baseball for a White Sox farm team and then went back to basketball, bald…" etc.) If and when the receiver guesses correctly, the giver keeps that scrap and chooses another, continuing to go through as many names as possible before the one minute is up. When time is called, the container of names (minus the names guessed) moves to the next team. (If a name remains unguessed when time is called, that scrap has to go back into the container without the giver revealing the name.) Play continues until all the names have been guessed. Each team counts their scraps, notes the score, and returns the scraps to the container, mixing them up again.

The second stage really tests your listening and memory. Play starts again, only this time, the giver may offer only one word to indicate the name on the scrap chosen. Usually that one word will be a summary or a memorable part of the clues used before for that name. Here you realize that you had to have listened carefully not only to your own clues, but to those of the other groups, because you will often choose scraps that weren't yours before. Timing is again one minute, and the collecting of scraps proceeds in exactly the same manner. Givers may repeat the one word over and over or use physical cues to help. The final score is the total of the first and second round scores.

Key to Self-Expression: Discovery through Journal Writing

Tests

Talk about how you feel about tests and how you generally perform. Answer the following: Do you experience test anxiety? Does your performance on tests accurately portray what you have learned or does it fall below your capability? Describe a study plan that would give you maximum confidence and preparation for an exam that will combine essay and objective questions. You have two days before the exam is to begin. What strategies or techniques do you use? Why?

Key to Your Personal Portfolio: Your Paper Trail to Success

Test-Taking and Memory

Test your test-taking skills and memory. After you have completed the following questions and checked your answers (making corrections if necessary), keep this in your portfolio.

1. Define these essay-question words and write an example question for each.

   Illustrate _____

   Question: _____

   Contrast _____

   Question: _____

   Analyze _____

   Question: _____

   Evaluate _____

   Question: _____

   Discuss _____

   Question: _____

   Trace _____

   Question: _____

2. What will help you guess on a multiple-choice question you don't know?

   Name three guessing strategies.

   _____
   _____
   _____

3. True or false: You should never cram for a test. _____

   Outline or map an essay before writing. _____

   You are in control of how well you do on the test. _____

   A quiet room is always best for studying. _____

Grades play a role in future success. _____

All-nighters give you momentum. _____

Your grades reflect your true abilities. _____

4. Which of these is not a basic test strategy?

   a. Leave time to check your answers.

   b. Read directions before beginning.

   c. When in doubt, change your answer.

   d. Complete easier questions first.

5. Name three test-preparation strategies:

   1. _____

   2. _____

   3. _____

What subject do you test best in? _____

Why do you think that is? _____
_____

What subject do you test worst in? _____

Which test-preparation strategies might help you improve in that subject, and why?

_____
_____
_____
_____

6. What are the two keys to a powerful memory?

   _____
   _____

CHAPTER 6:
APPLICATIONS

7. Name three memory-boosting strategies and give examples of each.

   Strategy:_____

Example:_____

   Strategy:_____

Example:_____

   Strategy:_____

Example:_____

E M P O W E

Empower

7

Maintaining the Essentials: Taking Care of Yourself

It's easy to think of your mind and body as two independent parts. You go to school for your mind; you exercise for your body. You eat right to improve your body; you read books to improve your mind. However, your body and mind are inextricably connected, interacting in many different ways. Your physical condition and mental state affect each other. After all, your brain is an organ and depends on the healthy operation of your body as do all of your other organs. You can reunite yourself by accepting that your beliefs and convictions play an important role in your physical health. If you pay as much attention to your thoughts as to your bones and muscles when choosing positive lifestyle changes, the combined efforts of mind and body will bring you health and success.

As you read this chapter you will explore the keys to *maintaining a healthy body*—exercising, eating properly, and getting enough sleep. You will discover ways of *maintaining a healthy mind* through methods of dealing with stress and depression. The section on *health traps* will present some facts and resources for thinking critically about the effects of alcohol, tobacco, drugs, and eating disorders, and *managing addiction* offers important coping techniques. Finally, you will focus on the mental and physical aspects of *sexual issues*.

Maintaining a Healthy Body

Your daily schedule frequently leaves too little time for you to take care of yourself. As you complete assignments for class, work for your boss, mail checks to creditors, keep your car running, take care of your family, call friends, and do chores, you may find yourself becoming strung out. It's time to turn your attention to you. The healthier you are, the more energy you'll have for both yourself and for those who share your life.

Eating Right

It's true that you are what you eat. From the day you were born, you have been building a body with the air you breathe and the food and drink you ingest as your only construction materials. If you eat well, you will build a strong and healthy body. If you take in an overabundance of fat, sugar, processed foods, and other less-than-nutritious substances, your body will operate at less than full power. It's like building a house with stones and mortar versus throwing together a shack with straw and mud.

The choice and the responsibility are yours. You are both the builder and the only full-time resident of the building.

The U.S. Departments of Agriculture and of Health and Human Services has developed a publication called Dietary Guidelines for Americans. In it they list seven important rules of healthy eating.

1. Eat a variety of foods.

2. Maintain healthy weight.

3. Choose a diet low in fat, saturated fat, and cholesterol.

4. Choose a diet with plenty of vegetables, fruits, and grain products.

5. Use sugars only in moderation.

6. Use salt and sodium only in moderation.

7. If you drink alcoholic beverages, do so in moderation.

Two themes stand out in this list—**balance** and **moderation**.
Balance. If you vary your diet with foods from the different food groups—meats and meat substitutes such as tofu, dairy, breads and grains, and fruits and vegetables—you are more likely to take in the different nutrients that your body needs. Nutritionists emphasize fruits and vegetables, recommending five servings from that group per day. If that sounds difficult, consider this easy five-a-day day: a banana or a glass of juice at breakfast, a salad at lunch (worth two veggies), an apple for a snack, and green beans with dinner. A good balance of foods will also help you stay away from overloading on fat, which is concentrated mostly in the meats and dairy groups.
Moderation. Exercise moderation in everything you eat, no matter how nutritious it seems to you. Eating too much of even the healthiest food still means more calories than one body needs, and can disrupt your digestive system. Conversely, in reasonably small amounts, sugars, salts, and fats won't harm you. Your body needs *some* fat and sodium to function properly. Portion control is the key. *The New Wellness Encyclopedia,* compiled by the editors at the University of California at Berkeley

Real World Perspective

Q — Michelle Renee Bologna, student at the University of California-Irvine in Redlands, California

In high school, I'd always been an overachiever, involved in everything. Although my friends and family supported me, I thought that approval wouldn't always be there when I went to college. So, in search of societal approval, I started to model. I even moved to Italy, but I quickly realized that the fast-paced and corrupt world of modeling wasn't for me. When I entered college, feeling empty after that experience, I threw myself into activities and academics, maintaining a high average and joining a sorority. Towards the end of the quarter I began to starve myself. People commented on my weight loss, giving me the attention I wanted. But I was so depressed that I thought I wanted to die. All I could think about was eating, and I became bulimic as well.

Over Christmas break, a friend from Italy visited me. Once fit and healthy, she now looked like a skeleton. She told me what was happening to her was happening to me too. We made a promise to each other to get help, and I started seeing a therapist. I began to realize that the food and weight issue is covering up the real problem—a fear of not being accepted. I quit school because I couldn't concentrate and continued therapy while working a job. I am back in school now, but some people hardly recognize me, and I take it personally because I am still very sensitive and in the early stages of my recovery. How can I cope with my problem and still make the most of my educational opportunity?

A — Nadja Daguillard, Vice President in the Emerging Markets division of Lehman Brothers in New York, New York

Your problem is not that others do not accept you, it is that you do not accept yourself. As a consequence, it's hard for you to realize that other people care for and respect you. Often we become overachievers in order to be so busy that bad feelings from the past don't surface. But when the gratification from being involved runs out, depression can surface, sometimes resulting in anorexia or bulimia. Your disorder serves two purposes: punishment, which is undeserved, and attention, so that someone can rescue you. You need to rescue *yourself*; the real work is opening your heart to feel the pain so that it can go away. Therapy and forgiveness can help you begin. Imagining that people around you love and accept you, and most important of all that you feel the same way, will help you to make that possibility more real.

Education can only add to the person you are. Look at school not as a solution to your problem but as a productive way to build the intellectual aspect of you while you work at healing the emotional aspect. It can serve as a necessary and interesting alternative to the immense psychological homework that you'll be doing. The world is lucky to have overachievers, for they possess a drive to build, grow, teach, and be role models for others. Words from another overachiever on the way to complete recovery: it does happen. After rain there is always sunshine. Enjoy a good meal, you deserve it.

Wellness Letter, advises you to moderate your amount of food intake according to one basic measure: **Don't eat more than your body can use.** Like any other machine, your body only uses the fuel it needs in any given day. Any extra fuel is stored as fat. To avoid packing on extra fat storage, try to tune in to what your body tells you about when you are hungry and when you have eaten enough. Eat slowly so that you don't miss the "stop" message when it comes.

Two more guidelines will round out a healthy eating plan.

When you eat is part of eating properly. Schedule your meals so that you spread your food intake out over the day. If you eat too much at one time, especially late at night, your meal will more likely tire you out than energize you. You're better off eating several small meals at regular intervals; your body draws energy more readily from small meals because they take less work to digest. This isn't easy to do when eating on the run, in a car, between classes, and after a late night at work. However, if you make it a priority, you can change. Take an extra fifteen minutes in the morning to fix yourself a healthy lunch instead of going for fast food. Find a reusable lunch bag with a cold pack inside to keep your food fresh. Make some tuna salad over the weekend to use for sandwiches all week. Vary breads and sandwich fixings so you don't get bored.

Maintain control over problematic substances—sugar, fats, salt, and caffeine. A splurge from time to time—a piece of cake, a great cup of coffee, or an order of French fries—can make life enjoyable. In large or constant doses, though, they have the potential to damage your health. Sugar gives you quick energy but lets you down fast; fats pile on extra pounds that overburden your system; too much salt can raise your blood pressure to dangerous levels; caffeine can make your heart and nervous system work overtime. Many people develop addictive behavior around these substances, especially sugar and caffeine. If you think you overdo any of these, try cutting way back for a week and evaluate how you feel (if you overdo fat, cut your fat intake and stick to unsaturated fats). If you feel better, keep it up or bring back the culprit in small, infrequent amounts.

Eating well allows your mind to focus on important tasks because it both reduces potential distractions and supplies good energy. It's tough to concentrate on your work when you are exhausted, hungry, jittery from sugar or caffeine, or ill from poor nutrition. A well-fed body frees the mind.

Exercise

If you don't use it, you can lose it. Like a car, your body can fall into disrepair unless you put it to work. Good physical fitness increases your energy efficiency. An efficient body system has more energy to direct toward the fulfillment of goals, thereby boosting mental health and self-esteem.

A fit body also helps the mind handle stress. Take a look at this evidence, from *The New Wellness Encyclopedia*. "In one study, two groups of college students—one that exercised and one that did not—were given a test consisting of problems, most of which could not be solved, and told that the test was a good indicator of how they were likely to perform in college. The nonexercising students showed increased blood pressure, muscle tension, and anxiety when told they did poorly on the test. The exercising group also showed increased muscle tension and anxiety over the poor test results, but not as much as the nonexercisers, and showed no increase in blood pressure." Exercise helps to release life's tensions, promoting a calm and rational focus on problem solving rather than a panicked and aimless worrying.

Staying in shape requires discipline. Exercise isn't a quick fix; in order to obtain maximum benefit, you need to make regular exercise a way of life. Always check with a physician before beginning any exercise program, and adjust your program to your physical type and fitness level. If you haven't been exercising regularly, start slowly. Walking is one of the most beneficial, least stressful forms of exercise. Try walking at a comfortable pace for 20 minutes at a time, three times a week. If you exercise frequently and are already relatively fit, you may prefer more of a more intense workout for a longer duration.

The type of exercise you choose depends on factors such as time available, physical limitations, preferences, available facilities, and level of fitness. For example, a person with persistent knee problems may choose to swim or bike and might want to avoid running due to the demands running places on the knee joint. Someone who wants to lose fat may walk for long periods of time; someone who wants to gain muscle may work out with weights three times a week. Biking, in-line skating, and skiing require equipment; running and dancing do not. You might need to gather a team together for softball, baseball, basketball, or volleyball; you can do yoga, a body-sculpting class, or an aerobics tape on your own.

Types of exercise fall into three main categories: *cardiovascular (heart and lung) training*, *strength training*, and *flexibility training*. Some exercises fall primarily in one category (working with weights is strength training; bicycling is mostly cardiovascular). Others combine elements of two or all three (astanga yoga requires constant movement for the cardiovascular system, stretching for flexibility, and the constant support of body weight for strength). For maximum benefit, *crosstrain*—combine elements from all three types in your exercise program and alternate your exercise choices. Crosstraining will help you avoid overworking certain muscles and will assure you a comprehensive workout. If you build your cardiovascular fitness with brisk walking a few times a week, alternate your walking days with yoga or body-sculpting for flexibility and strength. If you lift weights, you might ride a stationary bike or use a stairmaster on your off days for cardiovascular work.

How can you find time to make exercise a priority?

❏ Walk everywhere you can

❏ Use the stairs rather than the elevator or escalator

❏ Purchase exercise tapes for use at home

❏ Exercise with your children by taking a walk or playing outdoors

❏ Run to an errand

❏ Register for one of the many physical education courses offered by your school

❏ Do strenuous chores, if your doctor approves, such as shoveling snow, raking, or mowing the lawn

❏ Purchase a secondhand exercise bike or stairmaster for use at home

Exercise is a key component of both healthy mind and body. As a bonus, you'll look better too.

Sleep

You can't function well without adequate sleep. While you sleep, your body digests foods, repairs parts, replaces cells, and builds bones. Your mind, while in a state of rest, sorts through problems and questions. If you don't get enough sleep or sleep poorly, it shows. Lack of sleep causes poor concentration and irritability, which means a less-than-ideal performance at school and at work. Irritability can also put a strain on important personal relationships. If you try to make up for lost sleep with caffeine, its boost will wear off, perhaps leaving you more tired than before.

Gregg D. Jacobs, Ph.D., in *The Wellness Book*, says that different people need different amounts of sleep. "Adults average about seven to seven-and-one-half hours of sleep per night, and many individuals function effectively with four to six hours of sleep. In fact, 20 percent of the population (slightly more in men) sleep less than six hours per night." You can gauge your sleep needs by evaluating how you feel during the day. If you get less sleep than you think you need but aren't fatigued or irritable during the day, you may have slept adequately. Age also affects sleep patterns; as people grow older, they often sleep more lightly and require fewer hours of sleep.

Dr. Jacobs recommends the following steps to good "sleep hygiene."

Avoid or gradually taper off the use of sleeping pills. Physical and psychological dependence on sleeping aids can increase as dosage increases, often creating a need for larger doses, a hangover effect in the morning, and even greater insomnia if you stop using them abruptly.

Reduce consumption of alcohol and caffeine. Caffeine keeps you awake. Alcohol reduces your periods of deep sleep, causing you to benefit less from your sleep time.

Exercise regularly. Studies have shown that regular exercise, especially in the late afternoon or early evening, promotes good sleep because it raises body temperature and then allows it to fall. The lowering of body temperature can encourage sleep.

Complete tasks early in the evening. If you get your phone calls, planning, and chores over with early on, you can have a couple of hours to wind down and calm your brain activity before you turn in.

Set up a good sleeping environment. Little or no light usually facilitates sleep. Some people like to have complete quiet; some prefer the "white noise" of a fan or air conditioner; a few others like quiet music. Make sure the temperature is comfortable.

Reduce fluid intake after 8 P.M. Otherwise, you may wake up needing to make trips to the bathroom in the middle of the night.

Many things get in the way of finding time to sleep: a fussy baby or sick child, your own illness, late socializing, ingesting food and drink late at night, late-night telephone calls, and noises both outside and inside.

What is out of your control? The baby or child in need of attention, your own illness, and outside noise require you to cope as best you can. What can you control? Late nights out, food and drink, late-night telephone calls, and noise inside are within your power to change. Plan ahead. Don't stay out late the night before a big test. Ask your friends not to call after a certain hour. Don't have nachos at eleven o'clock the night before an important meeting. Respectfully ask the people in your living space to keep it down when you need to rest. Be willing to do the same for them.

Sleep well—you're not yourself without it.

Maintaining a Healthy Mind

Dealing with Stress

Stress, noun. A state of mental or physical urgency, pressure, or difficulty

No one is immune to stress. When you think of the word "stress," you probably have images of tension, hardship, problems, anger, and other negative thoughts and emotions. However, the dictionary definition shows that it doesn't always have to be bad.

Stress is primarily an effect of life change. Change, whether for the better or for the worse, demands an adjustment of priorities and a reallocation of energy. Those demands often result in stress. Therefore, a happy wedding or a move to a bigger and better home can cause as much stress as trouble with an instructor or an overload of tasks at work. Almost any change in your life can create some level of stress.

Although stress may have its origins in either positive or negative changes, your *response* to stress largely determines its effect on you. It's possible to experience a negative change as good stress, for example, through a positive response. If you are able to respond to the challenge of stress by stepping up your motivation, it can have a good effect. Perceiving stress as good encourages you, gives you a reason to act, and inspires you to push the boundaries of your abilities. If you bend under stress, feeling pressured, constricted, and anxious, stress can have a bad effect. Perceiving stress as bad can stall your forward progress, causing you to pour your energy into anxiety rather than into problem solving.

For example, the change of entering college brings the stress of having to gather funds for tuition and any other expenses. A student who responds positively might be encouraged to study harder in order to get his or her money's worth and to manage time more efficiently in order to be able to work part time. A student who responds negatively may become distracted and anxious and may take on too much outside work, potentially resulting in academic trouble. In the event of a death in the family, one person may withdraw and fall into a depression, whereas another may become inspired by thinking about the relative and draw strength from his or her example.

A negative response to stress may cause physical problems, strain on relationships, and interference with ability to work.

You can take one of two approaches to life changes that cause stress for you. You may either control the cause (adjust the life change) or control the effect (focus on effective stress management techniques).

Start with the cause and change what you can; if the cause lies beyond your control, then work on handling its *effect* on you. For example, if your grades are sliding because you've become distracted from your schoolwork, see how you can change your behavior. However, if a case of the flu keeps you in bed for a week, you can reduce any stress effect by make up the work as soon as you recover.

How can you adjust to changes that are at least partially in your control?

1. **Keep your promises.** Not doing something you are supposed to do, or not finishing it, can cause internal tension; you may feel guilty for not living up to your word. In addition, the pressure you put on yourself to finish in a hurry, or the anger of others who counted on you, can increase the stress. Do what you say you will do.

2. **Set reasonable, manageable goals.** Trying to achieve something that is out of your reach will cause more stress than success. Perform a small task well rather than a larger one that may trip you up.

3. **Break jobs into smaller tasks.** Just as with goals, tasks will appear more manageable when approached as a series of smaller steps. Analyze the task before you begin so you can progress in an orderly way.

4. **Don't procrastinate.** The longer you wait to do something, the more difficulty you will have doing it. However distasteful the task, it will be much worse when time runs short and the expectations of others hang over your head.

5. **Be thorough.** Loose ends can be irritating. Many people find that only when they finish something completely can they enjoy a feeling of accomplishment. Finish the job and move on with a clear conscience.

Break jobs into smaller pieces

What can help you cope with stress that is beyond your control?

1. **Exercise, eat right, and get adequate sleep.** One of the reasons a healthy body promotes a healthy mind is that physical health allows the mind to focus on problems clearly. If just getting through the day exhausts you, you won't have much energy left to deal with other issues. Physical activity also helps you release pent-up, stress-related emotions, calming and freeing your mind to consider other perspectives.

2. **Whatever relaxes you, do it.** All work and no play can cause stress. Take breaks regularly: play music, take a nap, read a book, go for a drive in the car, or see a movie. Recreation is just that: re-creating yourself by restoring your mind and refreshing your body. Jennifer Louden, in *The Woman's Comfort Book*, suggests you develop personal rituals that soothe your spirit. Design a ritual that means something to you, whether it is a candlelight bath, writing in a journal or reading from a certain book before you go to sleep, or listening to a particular selection of music in the dark. Be creative.

3. **Change your surroundings.** Getting away from situations and locations you associate with stress can lighten the effect it has on you. Natural settings such as a park, a riverbank, the mountains, or the beach are particularly effective for placing problems in perspective.

Respond to stress by thinking positively and making the necessary changes. When it demands your attention, fulfill the demand so that you can turn your attention to other things.

Depression

Although almost everyone has experienced feeling depressed from time to time, sometimes depression takes a stronger hold. As many as 10 percent of Americans will experience a major depression at some point in their lives. This kind of depression isn't the same as temporary blues. The sadness or melancholy that life's troubles can cause from time to time usually fades after a short period; depression lasts longer and is more severe.

Depression affects your mood, thinking, and behavior. You may feel constantly sad, worried, anxious, and sometimes irritable. You may lose your interest in activities or people that usually make you happy. You might be listless, having little energy, wanting to sleep a lot or sometimes having trouble sleeping at all. You could experience a loss of appetite or a desire to eat constantly. You may move through your normal activities on auto pilot or you may abandon many of them out of disinterest. You may cry a lot, feel hopeless and in despair, and even have thoughts of suicide.

Depression can stem from a variety of causes, and isn't always easy to explain. What is a minor setback for one person can throw another into deep despair. One factor is events; highly stressful changes such as financial trouble or the loss of a loved one can trigger depression. Some people may have inherited a genetic trait that makes them more disposed to depression than others. Doctors have also determined that depression sometimes has its origin in an imbalance of chemicals in the brain. Illnesses, injuries, and medications can also contribute to depression.

If you recognize yourself anywhere in this discussion of depression, realize that your condition is nothing to be ashamed of and that you don't have to suffer alone. The best thing you can do for yourself is to seek help from a qualified professional who can help you sort through the potential causes of your depression and choose the best treatment solution. Find a counselor at school or on the outside in whom you can confide. Some depression responds to therapy; some that involves chemical imbalance may require medication. As much despair as you may feel, have faith that there is a way out. If you know someone else who suffers from depression, your initiative in helping them to find treatment may save a life.

> *"Your success in making changes in your lifestyle, such as losing weight or stopping smoking, is directly related to your belief that you can make those changes and that they will positively affect your health and well-being."*

Herbert Benson, M.D., Associate Professor of Medicine at the Mind/Body Medical Institute of Harvard Medical School, and Eileen M. Stuart, R.N., M.S., Associate in Medicine, Harvard Medical School

HEALTH TRAPS

Alcohol, tobacco, and drug users come from all socio-economic levels, racial and cultural groups, genders, and areas of the country. The stereotypical homeless IV drug user or drunk comprises only a small percentage of substance users and abusers. Although some moderate users are fortunate enough to enjoy long lives, for many others substance abuse can cause financial struggles, emotional traumas, health problems, and even death. If you care about yourself and the people around you, carefully consider the positive and negative effects before using these substances. They can be traps that cause you to risk your health without realizing the consequences.

Why do people risk harmful addictions when the statistics are so grim? The trap lies in what the user perceives as the positive effects. Like any habit, alcohol, tobacco, and drugs seem to offer rewards.

- ❏ It's elegant/cool/fun.
- ❏ It helps me relax.
- ❏ It puts problems out of my mind.

❏ It helps me socialize.

❏ It's interesting.

As attractive as these rewards may seem, the fact remains that the abuse of alcohol, tobacco, and drugs can destroy lives. The fun of a night out drinking may fade quickly if an intoxicated driver causes an accident that results in severe injury or death. Take the time to make intelligent choices.

Alcohol

Alcohol is a social beverage and a drug. People receive mixed messages about it as they grow up: "Alcohol is fun." "Alcohol is dangerous." "Alcohol is cool." "Alcohol is for adults only." These conflicting ideas can make drinking appear more glamorous, secretive, and exciting than it really is.

The National Institute on Alcoholic Abuse and Alcoholism estimates that alcohol contributes to the deaths of 100,000 people every year through both alcohol-related illnesses and accidents involving drunk drivers. The National Council on Alcoholism and Drug Dependence reports that up to 40 percent of industrial fatalities are linked to alcohol consumption and alcoholism. Heavy drinking damages the liver and digestive system and kills brain cells. Alcohol impairs the ability of the central nervous system to function normally, often causing an inability to work in frequent users. Indeed, as *The New Wellness Encyclopedia* states, "chronic, excessive use of alcohol can seriously damage every function and organ of the body." Prolonged use also often develops a dependence in the user, making it seem impossibly painful to stop drinking regularly.

When used in moderation, alcohol doesn't have to be such a problem. Many people drink only now and then, on social occasions. The key lies in controlling when, where, and how much you drink; whether you have that control depends on why you drink. If you drink purely to be social or because you like the taste once in a while, you are far more likely to be able to control those factors than someone who drinks to escape responsibilities, forget problems, or fit in with others socially.

Tobacco

Some people choose to smoke because others around them do so. Others feel that it signifies maturity or like to have something to do with their hands. Still others like the mild stimulation and sense of alertness it gives them. Marc Alan Schuckit, M.D., in his book *Educating Yourself About Alcohol and Drugs: A People's Primer*, reports that 28 percent of the population chooses to smoke. He feels that number is surprisingly high considering the negative physical effects that nicotine, the drug in tobacco, can have.

Inhaling tobacco smoke damages the cells that line the air sacs of your lungs. This is true for smokers as well as for those breathing secondhand smoke. Smoking causes lung, throat, and mouth cancers, increases the risk for other cancers, causes heart disease and circulatory problems, and impairs the development of the fetus in the womb.

People have varying degrees of difficulty when quitting smoking. When asked how long it took to completely stop wanting a cigarette, one person who hadn't smoked in twenty years answered, "I'll let you know." That former smoker decided, however, that the payoff was worth it. Even if you have smoked regularly for years, quitting can allow your lungs to eventually rejuvenate, replacing damaged cells with a new structure of healthy ones. Increased life expectancy, greater lung capacity, and more energy—plus the savings of money formerly spent on cigarettes—may inspire any smoker to consider making a lifestyle change. Weigh your options and make a responsible choice.

Drugs

People use drugs for many different reasons, including curiosity, a need to be accepted by others, a desire to forget about problems and responsibilities, an escape from reality, and in cases of drug addiction, avoidance of the pain of withdrawal.

Many of these rewards are empty. Drug-using peers may accept you for your drug use and not for who you are; problems and responsibilities may return tenfold when you emerge from a high; the pain of withdrawal may not compare to the pain of the damage that long-term use of a drug can do to your body.

You are responsible for choosing what you want to introduce into your body. If you apply your critical thinking skills to the subject of drugs, you can draw your own conclusions about how the positive effects compare with the negatives ones. The more informed you are, the more you will able to make choices that benefit you and avoid choices that harm you. Take a look at Figure 7-1 to see the most commonly used drugs and their potential effects.

HOW DRUGS AFFECT YOU

Drug Category	Drug Types	How They Make You Feel	Physical Affects	Danger of Physical Dependence	Danger of Psychological Dependence
Stimulants	Cocaine, amphetamines	Alert, stimulated, excited	Nervousness, mood swings, depression, stroke or convulsions, psychoses, paranoia, coma at large doses	Relatively strong	Strong
Depressants	Alcohol, Valium-type drugs	Sedated, tired, high	Cirrhosis, impaired blood production, greater risk of cancer, heart attack, and stroke, impaired brain function	Strong	Strong
Opiates	Heroin, codeine, other pain pills	Drowsy, floating, without pain	Infection of organs, inflammation of the heart, hepatitis	Yes, with high dosage	Yes, with high dosage
Cannabinols	Marijuana, hashish	Euphoria, mellowness, little sensation of time	Impairment of judgment and coordination, bronchitis and asthma, lung and throat cancers, anxiety, lack of energy and motivation, reduced ability to produce hormones	Moderate	Relatively strong
Hallucinogens	LSD, mushrooms	Heightened sensual perception, hallucinations, confusion	Impairment of brain function, circulatory problems, agitation and confusion, flashbacks	Insubstantial	Insubstantial
Inhalants	Glue, aerosols	Giddiness, lightheadedness	Damage to brain, heart, liver, and kidneys	Insubstantial	Insubstantial

Source: Adapted from *Educating Yourself about Alcohol and Drugs: A People's Primer* by Marc Alan Schuckit, M.D., Plenum Press, 1995.

FIGURE 7-1

An additional negative effect of drug use is that it violates federal law. You can injure your reputation and employment possibilities if you are caught using drugs or if drug use impairs your performance in school or on the job. These days many companies test both employees and job applicants. You can't blame a company for wanting to make sure they get their money's worth when they hire someone; in 1988, alcoholism and drug use combined cost employers over $40 billion in reduced productivity. Employers don't want to take the risk that a drug user will have trouble working up to potential.

Eating Disorders

Weight control issues have different sources. Some people have inherited genes that predispose them to weight gain. Others suffer from medical conditions such as hypothyroid syndrome that affect their bodies' ability to process food efficiently, and weight gain results. Beyond these physical causes, anyone who eats large amounts of food or foods with a high fat content can gain weight. Being overweight isn't healthy for anyone. It forces your heart, lungs, and other organs to work overtime in order to carry extra weight around. It can also aggravate ailments and diseases such as digestive problems, arthritis, diabetes, and cancers.

Weight gain isn't always just a medical or chemical problem. Many people unknowingly demonstrate the mind-body connection by eating to find comfort and escape problems. Food can become an addiction as powerful as that to any alcohol or drug. Judith Linsey Palken, M.S., R.D., as quoted in *The Wellness Book*, suggests that people who seek solace in food dig down deep to find the real problem. "If you tend to make poor food choices, try to determine what triggers the problem. Only by understanding the emotions and situations that lead you to overeat can you begin to make changes." It's important to remind yourself that food cannot fill the gaps that problems in areas such as personal life, school, or work can leave.

Overeating

When people eat for reasons other than to supply their bodies with adequate fuel, they can become compulsive overeaters. Bob Schwartz, in *Diets Don't Work!*, discusses the choices overeaters can make when they turn to food for more than their basic needs. His list of why people eat includes the following:

❑ For comfort

❑ Out of boredom

❑ Because they feel compelled to finish what's on the plate

❑ Out of frustration

❑ Because it's cheap or free

❑ As a procrastination technique

❑ Because everyone else is eating

❑ Because it's a holiday tradition

❑ To please a family member

❑ Out of worry

❑ Unconsciously, often in front of the TV

Do you see yourself in some of these? If so, whether or not you would call yourself an overeater, you may benefit from examining your eating habits. "Everyone acts in ways that don't benefit them," says Mr. Schwartz to the overeater. "Yours just center around eating…You have the courage to examine those habits and tell the truth about them. After recognizing what they are, you can work to change them."

There are weight-loss programs and resources available to you if you decide to lose weight. The best among them combine a balanced, low-fat diet with an increase in exercise. Check some books on the subject out of your library, look in the yellow pages under Weight Control Services, or ask your counselor for advice. Different programs have different purposes. While a program like Weight Watchers lays out a specific diet plan, Overeaters Anonymous gives no diet advice, focusing solely on developing a healthier mental attitude toward food. Explore all of your options and choose one or more that serve your needs. Above all, don't forget to confer with a physician before starting any weight-loss program.

Anorexia Nervosa and Bulimia

Some people (mostly women) develop such a strong desire to be thin that it creates unnatural self-starvation or purging. A person who becomes dangerously thin through self-starvation has *anorexia nervosa*. A person who binges on excessive amounts of food, usually sweets and fattening foods, and then purges it through self-induced vomiting has *bulimia*. Both are serious medical disorders and require a doctor's care. Anorexia can result in death from starvation; bulimia can destroy the digestive tract and teeth with digestive acids. Neither indicate a healthy self-image. If you suffer from either, find help immediately. Anorexia nervosa often requires hospitalization due to extreme weakness and organ dysfunction. A counselor can help you find a hospital, an outpatient program, or a residential treatment center that will help.

Managing Addiction

Addiction is tangled up in life's stresses. People who have developed addictions are not terrible people—they are human beings who have let one aspect of their lives run out of their control. If you have an addiction, evaluate the facts of the situation. Compare the ways in which you are causing yourself pain to the rewards that you receive, and decide if what you are allowing to happen is worth it. Realize that you are responsible for what happens to you; your initiative to improve is the key to the solution.

Facing Addiction

Addiction is incredibly hard to beat alone. Because substances often bring about physical and chemical changes in your body, quitting is often more than a matter of will power; it can involve physically guiding your body through a painful withdrawal. Asking for help isn't an admission of failure, but an act of power and a courageous move to reclaim a troubled but valuable life. How can you tell if you need help? Listen to your body, your mind, and those who care about you. Look carefully at your behavior. Ask yourself these questions from a self-test.

Within the last year:

1. Have you tried to stop drinking or taking drugs but found that you couldn't for long?

2. Do you get tired of people telling you they're concerned about your drinking or drug use?

MAINTAINING THE ESSENTIALS: TAKING CARE OF YOURSELF

3. Have you felt guilty about your drinking or drug use?

4. Have you felt that you needed a drink or drugs in the morning—as an "eye-opener"—in order to improve a hangover?

5. Do you drink or use drugs alone?

6. Do you drink or use drugs every day?

7. Have you found yourself regularly thinking or saying, "I *need*" a drink or any type of drug?

8. Have you lied about or concealed your drinking or drug use?

9. Do you drink or use drugs to escape worries, problems, mistakes, or shyness?

10. Do you find you need increasingly larger amounts of drugs or alcohol in order to achieve a desired effect?

11. Have you found that the same amount of drugs or alcohol has less of an effect as time goes by?

12. Have you forgotten what happened while drinking or using drugs (had a blackout)?

13. Have you been surprised by how much you were using alcohol or drugs?

14. Have you spent a lot of time, energy, and/or money getting alcohol or drugs?

15. Has your drinking or drug use affected your friendships?

16. Have your drinking or drug use caused you to neglect your partner, children, or other family members, or caused other problems at home?

17. Have you gotten into an argument or a fight that was alcohol- or drug-related?

18. Has your drinking or drug use caused you to miss class or blow off schoolwork?

19. Have you failed a test/assignment due to alcohol or drug use?

20. Have you rejected planned social events in favor of drinking or using drugs?

21. Have you been choosing to drink or use drugs instead of other activities or hobbies you used to enjoy?

22. Has your drinking or drug use affected your efficiency on the job or caused you to fail to show up at work?

23. Have you continued to drink or use drugs despite any physical problems or health risks that your use has caused or made worse?

24. Have you driven a car or performed any other potentially dangerous tasks while under the influence of alcohol or drugs?

25. Have you had a drug- or alcohol-related legal problem or arrest (possession, use, disorderly conduct, driving while intoxicated, etc.)?

[Adapted from the Criteria for Substance Dependence and Criteria for Substance Abuse in the *Diagnostic and Statistical Manual of Mental Disorders, Fourth*

Edition, published by the American Psychiatric Association, Washington, D.C., and from materials entitled "Are You An Alcoholic?" developed by Johns Hopkins University.]

If you answered yes to one of these questions, you may want to evaluate your alcohol and/or drug use and to monitor it more carefully. If you answered yes to three or more questions, you may benefit from talking to a professional about your use and the problems it may be causing for you.

- ❏ **Counseling.** You can find help from private, government-sponsored, school-based, or workplace-sponsored counseling centers. Call your school's health center or a local hospital; if they don't have the appropriate program for you, they can refer you to one nearby. Check in the yellow pages under "Drug Abuse and Addictions" for listings of services in your area. Some programs are free; some that require payment may make allowances for financial limitations, charging you according to what you can pay.

- ❏ **Detox centers.** If you have a severe addiction, you may need a controlled environment in which to separate yourself completely from the substance that you abuse. Some you visit daily; some become your home for a while until you have gotten through the critical period of withdrawal.

- ❏ **Support groups.** You can derive a great deal of help and comfort from sharing your experiences and hearing about the trials of others who understand from experience what you are going through. Alcoholics Anonymous is the premier support group for alcoholics; it has helped a great number of people over many years and is based on a twelve-step program of recovery. Membership is essentially free; members contribute what they can when they attend meetings. AA has spawned many other support groups for addicts such as Overeaters Anonymous and Narcotics Anonymous. Other groups have different philosophies; try out a few different groups to see what suits you.

Instead of avoiding your problems through substance abuse, promise yourself that you'll begin to address them in a more direct, more effective way. You owe yourself that kind of health and respect.

Substance Abuse Affects Others

The pain and negative effects of substance abuse go beyond the body and mind of the abuser. Those involved in the abuser's life are often drawn into the addiction, becoming *enablers* or *codependents*. Melody Beattie, in the book that she wrote from her own experience, *Codependent No More*, defines codependents as "people whose lives had become unmanageable as a result of living in a committed relationship with an alcoholic." This definition holds true for any kind of addict; for example, replace the word *alcoholic* with *drug addict* or *compulsive overeater*.

A codependent spouse, parent, or child of an addict becomes overwhelmingly preoccupied with the happiness of that person. If the addict is sad, they are sad. If the addict is happy, they are happy. They blame themselves, believing that they are the cause of the problems that have driven the addict to abuse substances. They expend boundless energy caring for the addict in every possible way, pouring their love into a black hole and feeling more and more alone and drained as they wonder why nothing comes back to them in return. They overcommit and then feel responsible for everything over which they have assumed control, even other people's problems. They become so involved with the addict's life that they lose sight of their own, which results in low self-esteem and resentment. They rescue everyone but themselves.

Being a codependent can be as painful and as harmful to the psyche as being an addict. If you have an addict in your life and respond in a codependent way, your first step is to become aware of your behavior. Then, says Beattie, you have to detach yourself. "Detachment is not a cold, hostile withdrawal...Ideally, detachment is releasing, or detaching from, a person or problem *in love*...based on the premises that each person is responsible for himself, that we can't solve problems that aren't ours to solve, and that worrying doesn't help. We adopt a policy of keeping our hands off other people's responsibilities and tend to our own instead. If people have created some disasters for themselves, we allow them to face their own proverbial music. We allow people to be who they are. We give them the freedom to be responsible and to grow. And we give ourselves that same freedom."

This means that where a codependent husband might have called in sick and made excuses for his wife before, he will now let her take responsibility for her actions by explaining her behavior herself. A codependent parent might refuse to defend a child to a concerned teacher and might instead ask for the truth. A codependent child might stop cooking for and cleaning up after a parent whose abuse has caused an inability to fulfill basic needs. Most often, an addict will not take responsibility for changing his or her life until a codependent stops the kind of caretaking that covers up the problems that need to be addressed.

If you don't have an abuse problem but have a friend, significant other, child, or parent who does, think about how it affects you. Not everyone responds codependently, but if you feel you do, look into programs that can help you work through your feelings and your ineffectual reactions to the abuser in your life. Looking for help is a sign that you are ready to care for yourself instead of for everyone else. Al-Anon, Ala-Teen, Co-Dependents Anonymous and Adult Children Of Alcoholics (ACOA), all based on the AA model, focus on helping codependents reclaim their own lives. You will be doing yourself and the abuser in your life a favor.

Sexual Issues

Sexual relationships involve both body and mind on many different levels. The mental aspect, what sexuality means to you and the role it plays in your life, is your own private business. However, the physical aspect goes beyond the private realm. Individual sexual conduct can have consequences for all involved, consequences such as unexpected impregnation, the spread of the Human Immunodeficiency Virus (HIV) possibly leading to Acquired Immune Deficiency Syndrome (AIDS) virus, and the transmission of other sexually transmitted diseases (STDs). Your self-respect depends on your making choices that maintain your own health and safety as well as that of any person with whom you are involved. With sexual issues, as with so many other concerns, weigh the positive and negative effects of your options before making any decision.

Birth Control

If you opt for birth control, you have a number of choices. The following list describes the most established methods of birth control, with effectiveness percentages based on proper and regular use.

Condom (94% effective): fits over the penis and prevents sperm from entering the vagina. Use latex; natural skins are not effective in protection against STDs.

Diaphragm or cervical cap (85% effective): a bendable rubber cup that fits over the cervix and pelvic bone inside the vagina (the cervical cap is smaller and fits over the cervix only). Both must be fitted initially by a gynecologist and used with a spermicide.

The Pill (97% effective): a dosage of hormones taken daily by a woman, preventing the ovaries from releasing eggs. Side effects can include headaches, weight gain, and increased chances of blood clotting (women with circulatory diseases in their family history should avoid the pill). Must be prescribed by a gynecologist.

Spermicidal foams, jellies, or inserts (84% effective alone): usually used with diaphragms or condoms to enhance effectiveness, they have an ingredient that kills sperm cells. They stay effective for a limited period of time after insertion.

Intra-uterine device or IUD (94% effective): a small coil of wire inserted into the uterus by a gynecologist (who must also remove it). It prevents fertilized eggs from implanting in the uterine wall. Possible side effects include bleeding.

Norplant or Depo-Provera (nearly 100% effective): both introduce hormones into the body for extended periods of time. Norplant is a series of small tubes (up to five) implanted by a doctor into a woman's upper arm, preventing pregnancy for up to five years. Depo-Provera is an injection that a person must receive from a doctor every few months. Some women experience side effects similar to those caused by the pill.

Surgery (nearly 100% effective): surgical alteration of the male or female sexual organs to prevent pregnancy. Only recommended for those who have no desire for children or who have all the children that they want; reversing the procedure isn't always possible.

Abstinence (100% effective): just saying no. No intercourse means no risk of pregnancy; however, alternative modes of sexual activity may still spread STDs.

Rhythm method and withdrawal (variable effectiveness): not the most reliable protection. The rhythm method involves abstaining from sexual intercourse during ovulation (difficult to time accurately). Withdrawal means that the penis is pulled out of the vagina before ejaculation; however, sperm can escape in the fluid released prior to ejaculation.

Choose a method you and your partner can both use comfortably. If a partner refuses to honor your preference, reevaluate your relationship. It's important that your partner care enough to worry about your health and safety. Literature on this subject is plentiful; check your library or bookstore, talk to your doctor, or call a helpful organization such as Planned Parenthood. Make informed choices.

Sexually Transmitted Diseases

Sexually transmitted diseases all cause discomfort at some level, although some are worse than others. Even the less serious ones such as gonorrhea, chlamydia, herpes, and syphilis can cause lifelong physical problems and even severe illness if left untreated. Have a doctor examine any irregularity or discomfort; the sooner you treat one of these diseases, the less chance you have of suffering.

The most serious of the STDs is AIDS, brought on by the spread of the contagious Human Immunodeficiency Virus (HIV). Not everyone who tests positive for HIV will develop AIDS, but AIDS currently has no cure and will result in eventual death for anyone diagnosed with it. The spread of AIDS has been strong and steady over the last ten years and hasn't let up.

AIDS disarms the body's immune system, rendering it unable to fight viruses that it normally would kill. HIV can lie undetected in the body for up to ten years before surfacing, and a carrier can spread it during that time. Although AIDS was at first associated with male homosexuals, anyone can contract it. AIDS is growing fastest among heterosexual populations, especially women and children.

HIV is transmitted through two types of bodily fluids: fluids associated with sex (semen and vaginal fluids) and blood. People have been known to acquire HIV through sexual relations, sharing hypodermic needles for drug use, and receiving tainted blood transfusions. You cannot become infected with the virus unless one of those fluids is involved; therefore, it is unlikely you would contract HIV from toilet seats, hugging, kissing, or sharing a glass.

The best defense against AIDS is abstention from sex. The second best defense is the use of a latex condom. Natural skin condoms may let the virus pass through. Avoid using Vaseline or any other petroleum jelly as a lubricant, as it can destroy the latex in condoms and diaphragms. Although some people dislike using condoms, it's a small price to pay for preserving your life. Having an HIV test won't hurt either. If you have begun to date someone seriously, have a test done at your doctor's office or at a government-sponsored clinic. Check with your school's heath services department; they may be able to administer an HIV test there. Better safe than sorry. People have learned to live with HIV, but if you and a long-term partner are both HIV negative and committed to each other, you have a valuable gift of safety and security.

Sexual Harassment

Your sexuality is private. It is for you to express when, where, and to whom you choose. Sexual harassment occurs when someone violates that privacy or tries to interfere with or take away your choices. It also occurs when someone does, says or displays something sexual that is offensive to you.

Both men and women can be victims of sexual harassment, although the more common situation involves a woman subjected to harassment by a man. Sexual harassment covers a wide range of behavior that has been divided into two types. The first, quid pro quo harassment, refers to a request for some kind of sexual favor or activity in exchange for something else; it is a kind of bribe or threat ("If you don't do X for me, I will fail you/fire you/make your life miserable"). The second, hostile environment harassment, indicates any situation where sexually charged remarks, behavior, or displayed items in academic or work environments cause discomfort. Harassment of this type ranges from lewd conversation or jokes to pornography kept around.

Sexual harassment can be difficult to identify and monitor because it is so subjective. What offends one person may seem acceptable to another. If you take offense or feel degraded or exploited by anything that goes on at school or work, you have a right to speak up and address the problem with either the person harassing you or another authority who you believe can help you. Perhaps the person simply had no idea that his or her behavior could be perceived as offensive; on the other hand, the person may have dishonorable intentions toward you.

In the event that you feel you are the victim of sexual harassment, you must make a decision about how to act. Evaluate the positive and negative effects of your options. Some people fear that speaking up may cause them to lose their jobs or fail their classes. Some feel that no one will believe what they have to say. These are very real fears; however, remaining silent may have more deep-seated negative consequences. Not reporting the incident can damage your self-respect; when you neglect to stand up for your rights, you may be sending yourself a subtle message that you don't feel you are worth the trouble. Furthermore, staying in a class or at a job where you feel threatened may jar your confidence and have long-lasting effects on your mental stability.

Making the best decision is a delicate and personal process. Even if after you think it over you find that you cannot bring yourself to report the harassment, find someone to talk to—a counselor, an advisor, a mentor—who can help you work out your feelings about it. Bottling them all up inside of you will only compound the damage. If you do report it or even go on to take legal action, gather as many supportive people around you as you can. Remind yourself that no matter how difficult the road may be, you are worth the trouble.

Summing Up

Bringing your mind and body back into harmony takes constant effort. You need to eat properly and moderately, exercise regularly, and make sure that you sleep well and enough. You need to work through the changes that can cause stress by finding positive ways to respond to them; the more you can learn from stressful situations, the more able your mind will be to solve problems efficiently. You should watch for signs of depression; if you find them, you should seek help in order to bring your mind back into balance. Health traps such as alcohol, tobacco, drugs and eating disorders can split your mind and body and jeopardize your physical and mental health. Pull yourself back into center by managing addiction. The final mind-body connection involves sexual issues. Protect your safety and that of others by making smart decisions about your body. Make wellness something that reunites your mind and body and helps you become one.

MAINTAINING THE ESSENTIALS: TAKING CARE OF YOURSELF

CHAPTER 7: APPLICATIONS

Keys for your Key Chain Skills Worth Keeping

List here what to you are the five most important keys, or skills, you have learned from reading this chapter.

1. _____
2. _____
3. _____
4. _____
5. _____

Key Into Your Life: Opportunities to Apply What You Learn
Exercise 1 Food Log

Do you eat properly? Find out by keeping track of everything you eat for three typical mid-week days. Don't change your normal eating habits for this exercise. You want an honest assessment. Here, tally how many servings you eat each day from the four food groups, and indicate any sweets, caffeine, or high-fat foods you eat. As an extra exercise, you can write in detail everything you eat on a separate piece of paper, including amounts with the names of each food.

	BREADS	DAIRY	MEATS	FRUITS/VEG	SWEETS	CAFFEINE	HIGH-FAT
Day 1							
Day 2							
Day 3							

Did you overdo it anywhere? If so, name the category: _____

Did you not eat enough of any of the four groups? If so, which one?: _____

Choose one change that you want to make in your eating habits. Name it here.
_____

Using your problem-solving plan, draw a Think Link on a separate piece of paper (see Chapter 5) to explore how you plan to change.

CHAPTER 7:
APPLICATIONS

Exercise 2 Exercise Log

Log your exercise over a two-week period. Don't forget to include exercise such as climbing stairs, walking when your ride didn't show up, or cleaning your floors.

DAY	TYPE OF EXERCISE	DURATION OF EXERCISE
1		
2		
3		
4		
5		
6		
7		
8		
9		
10		
11		
12		
13		
14		

From a look at this table, evaluate your fitness profile.

_____
_____
_____
_____

If you had to make one change in your physical activity, what would it be?

_____
_____

Make the change as soon as possible. Evaluate the change. How did it make you feel? Do you sense any change in your energy level or strength?

_____
_____
_____
_____

Exercise 3 Sleep Log

For a week, log exactly how many hours you sleep and when. Include naps and note any waking periods during your sleep.

Day	Sleep Schedule
1	
2	
3	
4	
5	
6	
7	

Highlight the days when you felt well rested and energized. How was your sleeping pattern a factor?

_____
_____
_____
_____

Indicate the days you felt run-down. How did your sleep pattern affect how you felt? What can you do to make a positive change?

_____
_____
_____
_____

Judging from the information in the table, what seems to be the ideal sleep schedule for you? Describe it here, including number of hours, where you sleep, and when you sleep.

_____
_____
_____
_____

Exercise 4 Good and Bad Stress

In one column, list the positive changes that have occurred in your life over the past year. In the other, list the negative changes. Rate the stress level of each on a scale of 1 (not very stressful) to 10 (extremely stressful).

POSITIVE CHANGES	RATING	NEGATIVE CHANGES	RATING

Discuss what you consider to be the most stressful positive change and the most stressful negative change. What made each so stressful? How did you manage the situation? Do you feel you were successful in alleviating stress and dealing with the change?

Positive Change

_____
_____
_____
_____

MAINTAINING THE ESSENTIALS: TAKING CARE OF YOURSELF

Negative Change

_____
_____
_____
_____

Key to Cooperative Learning: Building Teamwork Skills

Solve the Problem of Stress

By yourself, make a list of anything that causes you stress. Then, in groups of two to four, see what causes are the most common among you. Assign one common cause of stress to each person. As a group, brainstorm ways to deal with each stress. Each person should note all of the coping strategies that correspond to the assigned cause of stress. Copy down the top strategies for the other causes as well. On your lists, circle the solutions you think would work for you. Keep your lists for reference.

Key to Self-Expression: Discovery through Journal Writing

You and Alcohol

Alcohol affects more lives than any of the other substances discussed in this chapter. Describe the role it plays in your life. How much do you drink, if at all? If you don't, why? If you do, are you comfortable with your drinking level? Do you want to change it? If so, how do you want to do it? What aspects of your life have been affected by alcohol—either your drinking or someone else's? How does alcohol make you feel?

_____
_____
_____
_____
_____
_____
_____
_____

KEY TO YOUR PERSONAL PORTFOLIO: YOUR PAPER TRAIL TO SUCCESS

Your Health Record

On a separate sheet of paper, draw up a "medical record" for yourself. Include the following:

- ❏ Health insurance plan and policy numbers
- ❏ Phone numbers of physicians and clinics; phone numbers of other important people to call in a medical emergency
- ❏ Immunizations: ones you have completed, and any you have yet to receive
- ❏ Surgery
- ❏ Hospital stays
- ❏ Illnesses and/or diseases
- ❏ Family history (parents, grandparents, siblings)
- ❏ Chronic health problems (arthritis, tendonitis, ulcer, etc.)
- ❏ Vision and/or hearing statistics if applicable
- ❏ Prescriptions used regularly and why

Highlight any conditions you feel you could improve with work or treatment. Choose one and draw up a problem-solving plan for making that improvement a reality.

Look again at the self-test in the chapter. Copy the questions and answer them on a separate sheet. If you feel that your score indicates a problem, write on the sheet what steps you intend to take to get help.

Make a list of the areas in which you enjoy exceptional health. For each, describe briefly how you maintain it.

Keep these lists up to date so you can monitor your health. If you change health plans or apply for a new job, you may need to furnish information about your health record. You'll have many opportunities to refer to this information.

B A L A N

Balance

8

Personal Power: Assuring Progress

Making progress along the road towards your goals takes more than just deciding what you want. You need to balance your drive with reasons why any given road you have chosen is the right one for you. You need to balance your desires with strategies that jump-start your engine and help to keep you going when you get tired or the process becomes more difficult or complicated than you had imagined. Plus, in order to maintain a balanced self-image, you need to know how to cope with success and failure along the way.

Because your personal qualities make up the content of your character, they have a great deal of impact on the success of your journey. In this chapter you will explore what *integrity* means, taking a close look at your values and ethics. You will examine *four power boosters: motivation, commitment, responsibility,* and *initiative.* Finally, you will discover coping mechanisms for *handling success and failure* as you strive to make the most of your opportunities and resources.

INTEGRITY

Integrity,
noun. The quality or state of having sound moral principles and ethics; honesty, uprightness, and sincerity

This important quality is one that will bring you great personal and professional rewards.

The concepts in the definition—*morals, principles, ethics, honesty, sincerity*—are familiar to you. Many of the decisions you make and act upon in your life are based on your underlying sense of what is "the right thing to do." Living with integrity puts that sense into day-to-day action.

A person of integrity

1. **Makes ethical family and work decisions based on moral principles.**

2. **Is honest.**

3. **Speaks and acts sincerely.**

4. **Considers the needs of others as well as his or her own needs.**

Following are some examples of how these principles might be applied to situations in daily life.

1. *Moral principles*: In order to share child care responsibilities with your spouse, you take advantage of your employers' flex-time policy.

2. *Honesty*: You tell your supervisor when you have made a mistake that cost the company some time.

3. *Sincerity*: You tell a fellow student that you will finish a project when she has to leave a study session early, and you follow through by completing the work.

4. *Consideration*: Your sister cares for your elderly father in her home where he lives with her; you spend a few nights a week with him so that she can take a course toward her degree.

How does living a life of integrity help you reach your goals? When you act with integrity, you become more trustworthy. In any work or personal relationship, trust brings freedom. If people can trust you to be honest, to be thoughtful of others, to do what is asked of you, and to make principled decisions, they will be more likely to encourage you to choose your own paths and to support you as you follow them. When you have increased freedom to make important decisions and pursue personal goals, you will experience greater progress.

Think of situations where a decision made with integrity has had a positive effect. Have you ever confessed to an instructor that your paper is late without a good excuse, only to find that despite your mistake you have earned the instructor's respect? Have extra efforts in the workplace ever helped you gain a promotion or a raise? Have your kindnesses toward a friend or spouse moved the relationship to a deeper level? Everyone wins when you decide to act with integrity.

Children are usually taught right from wrong by parents, instructors, and other authority figures; also, they gradually add to what they know through their life experiences. As they mature, they are faced with having to decide if and how they will follow what they have been taught. Acting with integrity goes beyond *knowing* how to live; it involves making an independent *decision* to live that way. A person of integrity isn't a perfect person, but one who makes the effort to live according to ethical principles, continually striving to learn from mistakes and to improve.

You're on your own in the real world; you establish your own integrity and make your own decisions. Here's a useful gauge: Judge what you do by how willing you would be to talk about it with someone you respect. If revealing a choice that you have made would make you feel deeply uncomfortable or ashamed—if you wouldn't be proud to defend your choice—chances are you haven't honored your sense of integrity. Take responsibility for making the right moves.

Values

Before you can begin to live according to a system of ethics, you need to examine the values that form the base of that system.

Your personal values are the goals and standards that are important to you. The sum total of all your values is called your *value system*. Your particular value system guides you in such areas as

❏ Getting along with others.

❏ Setting priorities.

❏ Raising children and living as a family.

❏ Accepting diversity.

People construct their value systems over time, using information from many different sources. Although you make the final decision about what means the most to you, your decision-making material comes from a number of sources: parents or guardians; relatives; friends; religious belief and study; instructors; mentors; and books, magazines, television, or other media.

Your job is to take in all of these ideas and opinions about what is important, moral, and necessary, and see what makes sense to you. Do you value family togetherness? Moving up the career track? Succeeding in class? Supporting your favorite football team? Volunteering? Maintaining physical fitness? Understanding what is most important to you will help you set your career and personal goals.

Values clarify, validate, and strengthen your goals; a wise goal-setter will base goals upon one or more personal values. If you value spending time with your family, your goals may include living near your parents, having dinner with your brother once a month, or writing your grandmother every week. If you value financial independence, goals such as working while going to school and keeping your credit card debt low reflect that value. You will experience a much stronger drive to achieve your goals if you build them around your values, because value-oriented goals involve what is most important to you.

Your value system is subject to change as you respond to the new perspectives that you encounter in your life. You will continually explore new perspectives as you take new jobs, study new subjects, meet new people, and become acquainted with new members (by birth, adoption, or marriage) of your extended family. If you allow yourself to consider different perspectives, you may find that new and different things will become important to you.

Additionally, new values come into the picture as life shifts bring new experiences. You may not have been too focused on family life until you marry and start to have children. You may not have thought much about being tolerant of other cultures until you move to a diverse urban area where your new job puts you in constant contact with people quite different from you. Allow your value system to change as you change.

Ethics

Once you know what's important to you, you can construct a code of ethics. Ethics are values and standards set in motion by the decisions you make. They are a "code," or system, that enables you to act and live according to your values and beliefs. Dr. Marvin T. Brown, an authority on ethics and the author of *The Ethical Process: A Strategy for Making Good Decisions*, describes ethics as an active process that allows

> **Values,** noun plural. The principles, goals, or standards held or accepted by an individual, class, group, or society

> **Ethics,** noun plural. The rules governing the conduct of a person or the members of a profession

a person to combine a variety of available ideas and resources in order to make the best possible decisions.

"The ethical process is a way of working together to make better decisions and fewer mistakes," says Dr. Brown. "Decisions are as good as the resources we use in making them. Many poor decisions occur not because decision makers wanted to make poor decisions, but because they lacked such resources as alternative points of view, relevant information, appropriate values, and other possible courses of action. As groups move through the ethical process, they will learn more than they knew before about each members' observations, values, and assumptions. This increase in knowledge, and in understanding, increases the likelihood that their decision will be the right one."

Dr. Brown suggests activating your ethical process by gathering and exploring the following resources when working through decisions:

1. **Proposals** Statements about what should be done.

2. **Observations** Descriptions of what is or is not possible.

3. **Value Judgments** Beliefs about what is important.

4. **Assumptions** Taken-for-granted notions of how things work.

5. **Alternative Views** Other observations, value judgments, and assumptions.

WORKING THROUGH THE ETHICAL PROCESS

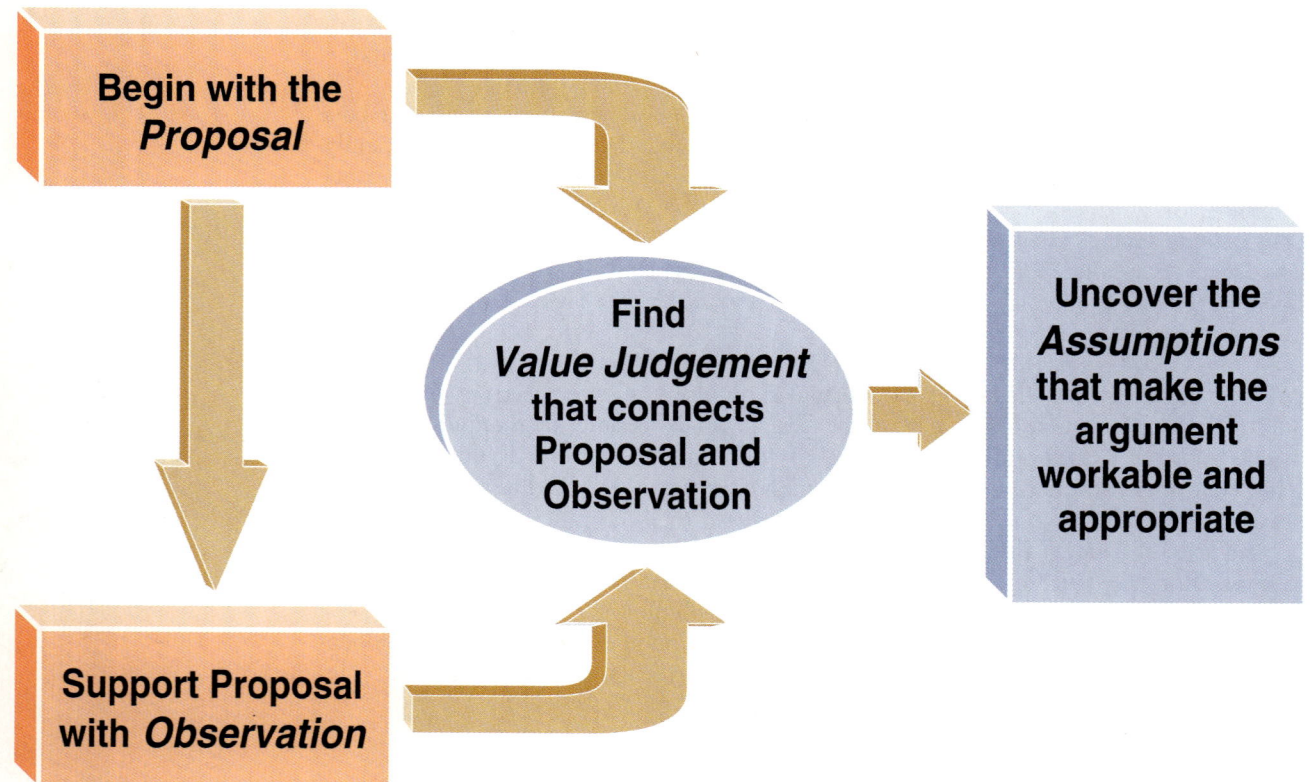

Source: Adapted from *The Ethical Process: A Strategy for Making Good Decisions*, by Marvin T. Brown, Ph.D., Prentice Hall, 1996.

FIGURE 8.1

Figure 8-1 illustrates how these components work together. You will obtain the greatest variety of these five resources when working with a group of people. The more different resources involved in the decision-making process, the greater the chance that an ethical decision will be made.

Suppose you work with a study group and feel that you do more than your share of the work. You attend class, take good notes, and give others the chance to benefit from your notes more than anyone else, in your perception. How can you make an ethical decision about how to change things?

At the next meeting of the study group you present the following:

- Your proposal: The group members should share the workload equally.

- Your observations: It is unfair for you to give so much and not to benefit from others' work and ideas. It is possible to even out the responsibility to some extent by asking that people attend class more often and share at group meetings.

- Your value judgment: It is important for everyone to contribute as equally as possible.

- Your assumption: Working in a study group is a necessary ingredient for success in school.

Alternative views emerge as you open the discussion to the group. One member observes that you, as a single person with no children, have fewer obligations than do some others who are spouses and parents. Another observes that if people have to miss class for any reason, they cannot possibly contribute to the discussion as substantially as someone who was there. Someone voices a value judgment that everyone needs to feel equally able to benefit from the group without feeling guilty when they cannot contribute as much.

After tossing around some other assumptions such as, "you take out what you put in," and, "we all depend on one another for information and help," your group arrives at a decision. Each week the group designates an individual member as "leader," a title that rotates to each member in turn. The leader is responsible for attending class and taking good notes so that the group is sure to have at least one reliable source of information, even if other group members miss class or don't have comprehensive notes. If a designated leader knows he or she cannot fulfill the obligation on an assigned week, he or she must switch weeks with another group member so that no week is skipped. Together, the group has arrived at an ethical decision that considers the needs of all concerned.

Your multifaceted integrity, involving the ethical process, discovery of values, and evaluation of professional and personal standards, shapes how you intend to live, both personally and professionally. Taking into account your needs and values as well as those of others, holding firm to your ethical process, and acting with truth, honesty, and sincerity will establish you as a person of integrity and move you ahead in pursuit of your goals.

> "Disagreement is not only a fact of everyday life, it is also the source for different observations, value judgments, and assumptions. Alternative views give voice to different aspirations. If groups agree to focus on reasons and not on the persons expressing them, they will increase the resources for making ethical decisions."
>
> Marvin T. Brown, Ph.D., Adjunct Instructor
> at The University of San Francisco

The Four Power Boosters

To really get moving on the road to success, you will need four power boosters: motivation, commitment, responsibility, and initiative. By promoting action in the face of change, this high-performance combination will move you ahead toward ever-increasing learning opportunities.

Motivation

When you are ready for the action to kick in, put your motivation to work. Motivation gives you energy that fuels your drive to achieve. There are many different things that motivate people. A few examples are:

- Self-improvement
- Learning a marketable skill
- Wanting to own your own business
- Making money
- Impressing friends or family members
- Supporting a family or moving to a better neighborhood
- Saving for the future

Everyone has energy highs and lows, and some days are better than others. How can you get motivated?

- *Decide what you want.* Focus your energy in a specific direction.

- *Establish a Reward.* Promise to do something nice for yourself when you succeed.

- *Remove obstacles.* An obstacle could be anything from a health problem to an overbearing authority figure to a persistently negative own self-image.

- *Take the first step.* It's usually the hardest part, often due to a fear of change and of the unknown. Imagine trying to exercise when you feel so sluggish that you can't imagine getting through the workout. After you give it a shot for five minutes, your energy may revive, enabling you to continue. A certain law of physics, Newton's first law of motion, says that things in motion tend to stay in motion. However, things at rest tend to stay at rest. Be a thing in motion.

For example, what if you were to decide you need to motivate yourself to keep your apartment neater? The clutter has gotten so bad that it interferes with your concentration. You decide to implement two strategies: one, you will set aside a two-hour period once a week to do a major spruce-up, and two, you will make a daily effort to pick items up and put them where they belong. You promise yourself that if you stick to it for at least a month, you will reward yourself with a purchase you've been wanting to make, maybe a cordless phone or a Walkman. You work on removing obstacles such as your habits of using TV as an avoidance technique and of throwing everything automatically to the floor. You take the first step; you schedule your first two-hour cleanup for tomorrow. If you keep it up, your motivation will pay off.

> **Motivation,**
> noun. That which impels, moves to action, provides incentive

Get motivated by removing obstacles on the road to success

Commitment

How do you focus your energy? Make a commitment.

Commitment means that you do what you say you will do. It requires honesty and trustworthiness. When you honor a commitment, you prove to others as well as to yourself that your words and intentions can be trusted. A committed person follows through on a promise.

Commitment often stretches over a period of time. You can commit to attending a meeting on a specific night next week, but more often you will commit to long-term endeavors, for example, "I'm committing to finishing school next year," or, "I've made a commitment to improving my marriage," or, "I'm committed to changing the way my company recycles." Not only have you made a promise, but you hold yourself to that promise for as long as the commitment demands.

Commitment requires you to focus your energy on something specific. In order to remain successfully committed, you must name your specific goal and the process you will use to achieve it.

Commitment,
noun. 1. A pledge or promise to do something
2. dedication to a long-term course of action

How do you go about making and keeping a commitment?

❑ *State your commitment concretely.* It's hard to commit to something like "I'm going to improve myself," because you haven't set yourself clear tasks. How are you going to improve? In body? Mind? Abilities? Commit to something specific such as, "I will walk two miles every day to work and back," and you will more likely see results.

❑ *Get started and note your progress.* The long road of a commitment can be daunting. Looking for improvements on the way, no matter how gradual or small, can help build momentum. For example, take that daily walk for a week and then evaluate what positive effects it has had.

❑ *Renew your commitment regularly.* How many times have you committed to waking up earlier, studying more, quitting smoking, reading the paper every day, trying not to yell—only to find your resolve has disappeared not long after? People have bursts of inspiration when they feel like they could commit to something forever, until the normal everyday fatigue sets in and clouds all of those good intentions. Don't feel like a failure if you lose steam—it's normal. Recharge yourself by reflecting on how your commitment benefits you and others around you. If you were to get busy with exams and skip your daily walk for a week, you could take a moment to remind yourself of how walking gave you more energy, boosted your metabolism, and reduced stress by giving your brain a rest.

❑ *Remind yourself of your commitment.* Find ways to make sure you don't forget the commitments you have made. Make a list of commitments to keep in your date book. If commitments involve events or projects that take place on specific dates, be sure to note them on the calendar. Post notes to yourself on your refrigerator, your wall, or your mirror. Tell people to remind you of what you have committed to should they notice you straying from your commitment. You may be more likely to walk if you tell your neighbors to call you when they don't see you out at your regular time each day.

Making and keeping your commitments benefits you in many ways. It helps you keep as steady a focus as possible on your most important goals. It gives you a sense of accomplishment as you experience gradual growth and progress. In addition, it earns you trust and respect from those to whom you have committed, which often results in people making valuable commitments to you in return.

Responsibility

When you are responsible, you respond to tasks or events with an appropriate course of action; through that kind of response, you become reliable and trustworthy.

A responsible person

❑ Does what needs to be done.

❑ Follows the most appropriate course of action.

❑ Does what needs to be done to the best of his or her ability.

❑ Does what needs to be done on time.

> **Responsible,**
> *adjective.* 1. Able to make moral or rational decisions on one's own and therefore answerable for one's behavior.
> 2. Able to be trusted or depended upon; reliable.

These guidelines may be simple to understand but they take effort to follow. Through them you can create an atmosphere in which instructors, supervisors, relatives and friends feel confident in your abilities. Trust gives you opportunities for growth; when others trust you, they tend to gradually give you chances to develop your skills through new tasks, since you have already shown what you can handle on your own. Trust, freedom, and success build upon each other.

Along with trust comes respect. When people trust how you take responsibility for yourself and your tasks, they will respect you as well. Respect, like trust, also leads to greater freedom and opportunities. Supervisors promote employees they respect; instructors give respected students special duties or assignments; respect deepens and strengthens a friendship. Even more important is the self-respect you develop when you prove to yourself that you follow through on your promises.

One example you have probably encountered involves your credit record. Through your mortgage payments, loan payments, and/or use of credit cards, you establish a record that indicates how responsibly you have repaid your debts. If you exhibit responsibility by making payments consistently on time and in the correct amounts, you earn the trust and respect of your creditors. In return, they reward your responsible actions with increased freedom to make use of credit and take out loans.

Responsible people earn power and opportunity by proving that they are capable of making the best of both. When you are given the opportunity to control a large number or a high level of tasks, you have the power to decide how to complete them and how well they turn out. That brings you full circle back to responsibility; with power comes the responsibility to use that power wisely. Keep the cycle going.

Initiative

You can't be responsible without initiative.

Initiative gets you off the ground. It spurs you to begin your task. It gets you over that difficult first hurdle of beginning your journey and keeps you moving as you follow through. It enables you to continually respond to whatever tasks roll your way.

When you use your initiative, you take the first step on your own instead of having to be dragged into something by people, rules, or requirements. You are taking initiative when you go to a counselor for help with a personal problem. You are taking initiative when you talk to a friend about something he or she said that upset you. You are taking initiative when you raise your hand to speak in a classroom, come up with a better way to do a job at work, or start doing fifty stomach crunches every morning.

Initiative also enables you to do more than is expected of you, which will often draw positive attention both at school and in the workplace. You are taking initiative when you complete an assignment a week early and ask your instructor about starting another ahead of time. You are taking initiative when you help a co-worker with a project after you have finished your own task. You are taking initiative when you offer a big thanks for a small favor, do someone an unexpected kindness, or volunteer your services to help people in need. Initiative is your spark plug. Even if you have all the other equipment, without initiative, you'll have trouble getting out of the parking lot.

> **Initiative,** noun. The power to begin or to follow through energetically with a plan or task; determination

Handling Success and Failure

In education, the workplace, and life in general, there are no guarantees. Someone started a rumor a long time ago that the perfect, trouble-free, ideal life is a possibility. Stop the rumor mill—it isn't true. This doesn't mean that a wonderful, engaging, challenging, fulfilling life isn't within reach. You can enjoy your life, but if you want to hang onto your sense of self-esteem, you should prepare to encounter stumbles along with your successes.

Dealing with Failure

Most people measure failure by comparing where they are to where they believe they should be. Since individual circumstances vary widely, so do definitions of failure. What you consider a failure may seem like a positive step for someone else. Imagine that your native language is Spanish. You have learned to speak English well, but you still have trouble writing it. Making writing mistakes may seem like failure to you, but to a recent immigrant from the Dominican Republic who knows limited English, your command of the language will seem advanced. If two people apply for work-study programs, one may see failure as receiving some offers but not the favorite one, while another may perceive failure as being wait-listed.

When you judge yourself as having failed, how can you deal with it?

- *Stay aware of the fact that you are a capable, valuable person.* Put your positive self-image in high gear—you'll need it. Remind yourself of your successes. Focus your energy on your best abilities. Know that you have the strength to try again.

- *Share your thoughts and disappointment with others.* Trading stories will help you realize you're not alone. You will find out that everybody fails. People refrain from talking about failures out of embarrassment, often feeling like no one else could have made as big a mess as they did. When you open up, though, you may be surprised to hear others exchange stories that rival your own.

- *Look on the bright side.* It may sound kind of worn-out, but you can gain from any failure. At worst, you at least have learned a lesson that will help you avoid similar situations in the future. Some people believe that everything happens for a reason. Try that approach and look for the positive results of what happened. If your romance flounders, the extra study time you suddenly have may help you boost your grades; if you fail a class, you may discover that you need to focus on a different subject that suits you better. What you learn from a failure may, in an unexpected way, bring you around to where you want to be.

- *Explore why you failed.* On one hand, it could have had nothing to do with you at all. You could have failed to win a job because someone else with equal qualifications was in line for it ahead of you. A family crisis that disrupted your sleep could have affected your studying, resulting in a failing grade on a test. In cases like those, the most you can do is learn a lesson from the experience and try to make adjustments in your approach to similar situations in the future. On the other hand, a limitation of yours may have directly or indirectly caused the failure. If so, identify that shortcoming and plan to make a change. Your efforts will give you the best possible chance next time, a chance that will enable you to say, "If I fail, it isn't because I was any less prepared or capable than I should have been."

Real World Perspective

Q Christine Grabovich, student at Trenton State College, Maple Shade, New Jersey

For many of my general education classes, adjunct instructors are used. Most of them seem to have no idea what they are teaching, and they don't seem to have investigated what we in the class had learned before. They don't have that much of an idea about how to teach at a college level. When I am in class listening to them and following the assignments they give, I feel like I'm still in high school. It is very frustrating.

I have approached some of these instructors to challenge their teaching style and to tell them what I thought about how we could learn best, but they thought they were doing what they were supposed to, and they haven't made any changes as far as I can tell. I don't think they have even sought out the advice of other teachers who probably could really help them. Since these are general education classes, they are required for graduation, and I can't just change to another class. I'm not willing to repeat a general education class either. I feel like I don't have a choice except to put up with these instructors. What can I do to improve my situation and feel like I am getting some benefit out of the time and effort I am investing in these classes?

A Patricia M. Lampkin, Associate Vice President for Student Affairs at the University of Virginia in Charlottesville, Virginia

I am pleased to see that you approached the professor to indicate your dissatisfaction with the course. The only way you can ever be assured of having input in your education is to take the opportunity to state your case. Unfortunately, what you can't control is whether change will occur once you take this step. If you do not notice changes and you are already into the semester of the course, you are always free to discuss your concerns with the Dean or Director of the department and at the very least take full advantage of an end-of-the-semester evaluation by providing honest, direct feedback.

Some other approaches center on the basic premise that you should strive to create the maximum number of options for yourself throughout your curriculum planning. Some ways to do this that relate to general education requirements might be to test out of some of these requirements. Many institutions accept AP credit for many of the general education requirements. It is a good way to receive the credit without having to take the time to complete the course. Your high school or college counselor can give you the procedures and registration information on this option.

You might also want to plan to take the general education requirements early in your college career so that if you want to switch sections or take a class during another semester you will not be locked into an undesirable class section on the last semester that you need to graduate. Finally, do your research before you register for the class. Talk to other students and talk to the professor before you register. Sections of the same class can vary tremendously according to who is teaching the course. Feel free to ask them what they plan to teach and what they expect of the students. If you take the initiative to investigate before you choose the class you will be able to make a better choice.

Dealing with Success

Success doesn't seem to need any specific coping techniques, but it can go to your head if you aren't careful. Be as cautious with it as you are with your failures.

❏ *First, celebrate!* You deserve it. Take time to congratulate yourself for a job well done—whether it be a good grade, an important step in learning a new language, a job offer, a promotion or graduation, or a personal victory over substance abuse. Bask in the glow a bit. Everybody hears about their mistakes, but people don't praise each other (or themselves) enough when success happens. Praise can give you a terrific vote of confidence. It's an assertion that you are of value.

❏ *Take that confidence on the road.* This victory is just the beginning of a long journey. Based on this success, you will be expected to prove to yourself and others that you are capable of growth, of continuing your successes and building upon them. Show yourself and others that the confidence is well founded.

❏ *Stay sensitive to others around you who may not have been so successful.* Remember that you have been in their place, and they in yours, and the positions may change many more times over in the future. Enjoy what you have, work to build on it and not to take it for granted, and support others as they need it.

Summing Up

When you live and work with integrity, using your value system and your ethics to guide your actions and decisions, you establish your trustworthiness and reliability to all with whom you work and live. Getting motivated, staying committed, taking initiative, and taking responsibility will keep you on the road toward your goals. Plus, as you encounter failures and successes on the way, you will be able to handle them with grace while continuing to learn and progress.

These personal qualities together make up the content of your character, something that carries more weight than any body of knowledge or specific skills. When you eventually pursue your chosen career, you will find that many companies search for good citizens first, valuing character above all else. A smart employer knows that while skills and rules can be taught, qualities like integrity, initiative, and motivation cannot. Build your future by building your character.

CHAPTER 8: APPLICATIONS

Keys for your Key Chain Skills Worth Keeping

List here what to you are the five most important keys, or skills, you have learned from reading this chapter.

1. _____
2. _____
3. _____
4. _____
5. _____

Key Into Your Life: Exercises to Apply What You Learn

Exercise 1 Your Progress

What would you like to be doing in two years? This exercise will help you determine a viable route to that goal. Start your map by determining point A—where you are—and *one* of what might be many points B—where you want to be. Describe your point B goal specifically. Pull it from any one of your five areas of interest: personal, family, career, financial, or lifestyle. Write here, as specifically as you can, what you want to happen.

_____
_____
_____

Now take a moment to think about where you are. What knowledge, resources, or experience do you have that puts you on the right road toward your goal?

_____
_____
_____

What do you lack at this point?

_____
_____
_____

Exercise 2 Get Motivated

What motivates you is unique to who you are. List seven motivators that get you moving.

PERSONAL POWER:
ASSURING PROGRESS

1. _____
2. _____
3. _____
4. _____
5. _____
6. _____
7. _____

Which three of these are the most important for helping you reach Point B in two years? Write each and indicate why it is so crucial.

1. _____
   _____
   _____
   _____

2. _____
   _____
   _____

3. _____
   _____
   _____

Exercise 3 Taking Initiative and Staying Responsible

How can you use your initiative to reach Point B?

_____
_____
_____

When you think of where you want to be in two years, what specific responsibilities do you have to take on in order to reach that place? What parts of the task are yours and yours alone? Name three responsibilities.

1. _____
   _____
   _____

2. _____
   _____
   _____

3. _____
   _____
   _____

Which of these is the hardest for you to keep up? Why? Talk about how can you take initiative to maintain it.

_____
_____
_____

Exercise 4 Overcoming Obstacles

Think through your plan to reach Point B. What obstacles could you encounter? Think of two, whether they are small stumbling blocks or larger problems, and discuss the best strategies to handle the failures they may cause.

1. _____

2. _____

Exercise 5 The Ethical Process

As you work toward your goal, you will be required to make ethical decisions. In this exercise, based on Dr. Marvin Brown's ethical decision model, you will work through the ethics involved in reaching your Point B. Using the sample in the chapter as a model, apply the ethical process. To help illustrate the exercise, examples are shown that work toward a goal to reduce student loan debt.

1. Offer your proposal. *Answer the question, "What?"* State a specific action you want to take toward your goal. Example: I want to pay my loan using my savings.

   _____
   _____

2. Make observations. *Answer the question, "Why?"* Look at what is true or possible about the situation as it stands. Examples: My savings is just enough to cover the loan. If I don't pay the loan now, I will owe interest for years to come. I don't have any other outstanding debts.

   _____
   _____

3. **Make a value judgment.** *Answer the question, "So What?"* Establish what you believe is important. Examples: It's more honest to live as debt-free as possible. It's better to be strapped now than pay interest later.

_____
_____
_____

4. **List assumptions.** *Answer the question, "What's the usual?"* State what you take for granted. Examples: Americans are naturally debtors throughout their lives. People go into debt to have the things they want. People who have no debt have less stress.

_____
_____
_____

5. **Find alternative views.** *Ask questions of others.* Talk to at least two other people. Ask for their observations, value judgments, and assumptions about your situation.

Person 1: _____(name and relationship to you)

_____
_____
_____

Person 2: _____(name and relationship to you)

_____
_____
_____

Considering the information you've gathered, reevaluate your proposal and make what you consider to be an ethical decision. Write your decision here.

_____
_____
_____

Has your opinion changed through the process? If so, indicate what thoughts and/or views affected it and how.

_____
_____
_____

Key to Cooperative Learning: Building Teamwork Skills

Overcoming Failure

Divide into groups of two to four. Each person should write on a sheet of paper one sentence that describes a kind of failure with which he or she is familiar (don't include your names). When you have finished writing, put the paper into a pile from which each person takes one; if you get your own, trade it back in for another. Take five minutes to list your own strategies for coping with the failure written on the paper you chose.

If you are in a group of four, divide into pairs. Share your ideas with your partner. If one person has thoughts about the other's strategies, add to the lists. After five or ten minutes, if you have separated, reconvene as a group. Each person should name the failure he or she worked on and share coping strategies with the group. Invite discussion: What do you all like about the strategies? Dislike? Which one would you use? Think of specific instances where each strategy would work well. When you have addressed all failures and revised the strategy lists according to the discussion, you will have a strategy packet that you can refer to for ideas.

Key to Self-Expression: Discovery through Journal Writing

Integrity

Describe a situation in which you compromised your integrity—where you did or said something that went against your values or ethical code. It doesn't have to be earth shattering. It can be something as simple as a "white lie" that seemed to cause no harm, but it should be something that made you feel uncomfortable. What happened? In arriving at a decision that you consider unethical, what was your process? What, if any, were the results? Did you expect them or not? What thoughts did your decision inspire in you? As a result, did you resolve to change anything about yourself or your behavior? Did you change? If so, how? If you did not make a change and would like to now, discuss how you would like to change.

_____
_____
_____
_____
_____
_____
_____
_____
_____
_____
_____

KEY TO YOUR PERSONAL PORTFOLIO: YOUR PAPER TRAIL TO SUCCESS

Put Yourself On Record

Making and keeping the following lists will help you develop self-knowledge and clarify your goals. First, draw up a list of your most important values. Don't restrict yourself; brainstorm and note everything that is important to you on any level. You can use the following categories as a guide:

- ❏ Career
- ❏ Family
- ❏ Personal qualities
- ❏ Academics
- ❏ Intellectual development
- ❏ Finances
- ❏ Appearance
- ❏ Physical fitness
- ❏ Ethics
- ❏ Lifestyle
- ❏ Skills
- ❏ Friends and social life
- ❏ Community
- ❏ Citizenship

You may want to list your values at random and then regroup them by category, or you can brainstorm them one category at time. Either way, you should end up with a categorically-organized list of values. You can draw on them whenever you need guidance in setting your goals.

Next, take a long sheet of lined paper and draw a line down the center. If you are working on a computer, turn your page into a table with two wide columns and lots of rows. Above the left column, write *Strengths*; above the right column, write *Stumbling Blocks* (although they cause trouble, you have the power to move them out of your way). Start with your strengths. List everything you perceive as being good, strong, or positive about yourself. These can be abilities, qualities, personality features, attitudes, ideas, ethical standards, values, or anything else. Be specific: "I am a nice person," isn't as revealing as, "I do yard work for my older relatives," or, "I take the time to thank people for their services when I am out doing errands." Then turn to the stumbling blocks, your problem areas, and list those as well. Go into the same kind of detail as you did with the strengths.

When you have finished, look over your lists. What jumps out to you? Highlight the five strengths that you feel you couldn't live without. Then highlight the five stumbling blocks that hinder you most—the ones that would make the most difference in your life if they were removed. Keep this list in your portfolio and refer to it as you work to improve yourself throughout the course. If you find that you have moved a stumbling block away or added a strength, make changes. Let the list reflect your changes and growth as you go along so it can be a reminder of where you are at any given time.

C O N N E C

Connect

9

The People Connection: Relating to Others

Nearly every moment of your life involves interaction with other people—family members, friends, peers, fellow students, co-workers, authority figures, strangers, clients, customers, and instructors. You focus a great deal of energy on your relationships. In return, when you keep the lines of communication open, you learn from them. As you see what others are all about, you discover yourself bit by bit, deciding what about you is similar and what is different. You become more aware of how the network of relationships in your life allows you to grow and progress toward your goals.

This chapter starts close to home with *human resources*, people both in and out of school who can help you. You will learn what *mentors* are and who yours might be. The section on *communication* describes the methods in which people communicate to one another and how you can use and improve them. You will examine ways to build successful *personal relationships* and *group relationships* through effective communication. Finally, you will explore how you relate to people different from yourself in *your diverse world*.

HUMAN RESOURCES

Just as the resources you examined in Chapter 1 offer services and materials that can help you cope, human resources are people who can provide assistance to you. It is worth your while to tap into the diverse knowledge that others possess. People in many different roles can give you useful information, provide you with coping strategies, help you learn, and offer support. It makes sense to pool resources and help each other out; as you know from your cooperative learning experiences, two or three heads are often better than one.

A great deal of what you learn comes from shared knowledge. Since you were born, you have learned by taking in information from verbal and nonverbal language. Even information that you read was written by someone who wanted to inform you, the reader; in that way the author shares information learned in turn from someone else. The chain of learning stretches back through time, each link formed by an exchange of information between people. As people pass knowledge along to one another, it develops and spawns new ideas, creating more than there was to start with.

You can find helpful, well-informed people both within your school population and administration as well as in your community outside of school.

In-School Resources

You have paid money in exchange for the service of an education. Get your money's worth by tapping into the human resources that come along with the package. *Instructors* are more than just lecturers during scheduled class time. They have spent years building up the knowledge that they pass on. Instructors usually make themselves available for consultation during posted office hours, and many instructors wish their students took more time to get to know them. Take them up on the offer; it is up to you to seek out your instructor. You generally have only one instructor per class, whereas your instructor has too many students to reach out to each one individually outside of class time. Use your study skills to make the most of class; then, take the initiative to develop an independent relationship with your instructor.

Instructors can help you in many different ways. Services will vary from instructor to instructor, since each individual has a unique base of knowledge and teaching style.

Help with classwork. Instructors know a lot about what they teach; you can ask them to clarify course material or lecture notes, discuss class topics, or go into further detail on specifics that interest you. Talking with an experienced, knowledgeable instructor will further strengthen and build your own knowledge. Instructors may also tutor privately or help you find someone who does, if you feel you need extra help.

Advice on course selection. Many schools assign an academic advisor to help each student with course selection. Sometimes you won't have an assigned advisor unless you have already declared a major. If your school does not offer this service, you may want to seek advice anyway. Ask a favorite instructor if you can schedule a meeting to talk about your academic goals. Instructors usually know a lot about what the school offers and requires. With your insight into your own needs, together you might come up with a terrific schedule. For example, if you had a required class to take but didn't know which of two sections to choose, an advisor might be able to help you decide by telling you more about the styles of the two different instructors.

Career advice. Instructors often have worked, or still do work, in the fields that they teach. They have a wide range of experience from which they have learned valuable lessons that they can pass on to you.

Personal advice. Instructors can be friends. If you want to talk about personal issues and an instructor offers a sympathetic ear, you might receive valuable advice.

Networking and contacts. Tapping into other peoples' networks can help you build your own list of contacts. From experience in the work force and in education, instructors have developed a wide range of contacts from which they might give you a few useful names. If you cultivate relationships with your instructors, they may feel they know you well enough to refer you to contacts who they believe can help you.

Administrators are charged with the task of delivering to you—the student consumer—a first-rate product. That product is the sum total of your education, comprising facilities, instructors, materials, and curricula. They are also responsible for ensuring that each student has the opportunity to benefit from this product. Schedule a meeting with your dean or other school administrator if you have an issue or problem to discuss, such as a clash of wills with an instructor, an inability to get into a required class, a desire to change your major or design your own, or a school rule or regulation with which you differ. If you take a problem to the top, you may have a better chance of seeing a change. Although administrators often do not routinely interact on a personal level with students, it is their business to know how efficiently their schools bring education to students. By getting to know an administrator, you can provide that person with a student perspective as well as tap into a new circle of contacts.

Counselors, depending on their specialty, can help with both the educational and personal sides of being a student. While an instructor is hired to teach and may choose to offer other services to you above and beyond teaching, a counselor's job is to provide information, advice, a listening ear, referrals, and any other aid that can help you maximize your educational benefits. You may want to seek out a counselor at least once a semester to talk over what's on your mind. You don't have to stick to school-related subjects; your personal life is just as relevant, especially since its ups and downs influence the stability of your academic life. You may be able to contact counselors through either the academic advising office or the student health center.

Out-of-School Resources

Family members, beyond being people you live with and see on holidays, have often had important experiences from which you can learn. If a parent, cousin, sibling, or other relative works in a field that interests you, set up an "appointment" to talk to him or her about their perspective on the workplace. Bring a notebook to write down what you learn. Even relatives who don't work in your chosen field may have contacts that you can add to your network.

Likewise, your *friends* have their own networks as well. Many people find jobs through casual conversations with friends. It can't hurt to "talk shop" with your friends. Someone who knows and likes you will be more likely to want to help you, just as you would want to help someone you care about. If you let friends know what your needs are, they will be more aware if they hear of a suitable opportunity for you.

Professional counselors provide services similar to what school-supported counseling does for you. If the counseling at school is nonexistent or unsatisfactory, you might want to seek help on the outside. Professional services often require payment, whereas school services usually are included in the cost of your tuition. However, some government-sponsored services may be free. Check your yellow pages under Counseling to discover what is available in your area, and call around to find out fees, schedules, and locations. Some counselors may charge fees on a sliding scale, meaning that the fee varies based on what you and the counselor together determine is comfortable for you to pay.

Real World Perspective

Q Dana Summoner, student at St. Mary's University in Oklahoma City, Oklahoma

Before I attended school, I was fairly creative. My siblings and I would always create plays and dramas. But when I got to kindergarten I had a really hard time. Because I couldn't read I was put into a "slow" class. My sister tried to teach me to read with Dr. Seuss books, but I was still in the lowest reading group. Through the next couple of years, as my reading slowly improved, I began writing. Just over ten years ago I wrote a little science fiction story. This was the last story I wrote for a long time.

When I was eleven my mom died of a terminal illness; the following year, my father died too. That was when I stopped writing for pleasure. It was really tough on me and my family, and throughout high school I still felt like I was "slow." I've always been an introverted person, and I still feel like I'm trying to come out. Writing was kind of a release and expression for me. I've been to see a counselor but she wasn't very encouraging. She didn't seem to pay attention to the quiet people, those who were on middle ground. A lot of people, including myself, feel neglected. I feel maybe she too has personal issues that result in miscommunication when she tries to help students. I would like to get involved with other people who can help me. How can I find a counselor, or a professor, who will understand me?

A Daphne Benyard, Counselor at the Center for Academic Skills for Essex County College, Newark, New Jersey

Counselors are people too, and although they are trained professionals, certain counselors may not suit you and your personality. As both a counselor and a graduate student, I know the importance of having a counselor or professor who can sense my feelings and communicate with me. If you are uncomfortable with any counselor, ask someone whose opinion you can trust to recommend someone to you. Also, if your school has student activity associations, you might benefit from attending a few meetings to get comfortable with the group and then asking students which counselors and professors they feel are sensitive to the needs of students.

People who work with counselors can help. Once my counselor was out ill. I felt lost. I consulted the secretary, assuming that since she worked with all of them she could direct me to someone helpful. She gave me two names; I was satisfied with both. Later, when my counselor took medical leave, I had two other individuals with whom I was comfortable. Look for a counselor who speaks honestly and personally instead of one who assumes the role of the all-knowing. Seek out a nonjudgmental person so that you can feel free to express and explore feelings and past experiences, not always easy things to do. As a counselor, I feel that the more we get in touch with ourselves and act what we feel instead of how others think we should, the more we open the lines of communication.

Mentors

You may go to many different people for help and advice throughout your life, and if you are lucky, you may find among them a true mentor.

A true mentoring relationship is rare; you cannot deliberately create it or force it to grow. It demands time and energy on both sides. Many people will offer you advice, but a mentor knows you well enough, continually keeping up with the changes in you, to be able to tailor advice and information to your specific needs. More than that, a mentor cares about you deeply enough to be devoted to your success and growth for your own sake, taking pleasure in your achievements and development.

Because it requires such depth and devotion, a mentoring relationship often evolves from a special personal relationship. Think about whom you go to when you are confused, troubled, need guidance, or seek support. A relative, instructor, friend, supervisor, or anyone else whom you admire and respect may become your mentor. A mentor can give you an understanding ear, a private audience for secrets and problems, advice tailored to your needs, a wealth of experience, support for your endeavors, guidance as you learn, and trust.

Like any exchange, mentoring is a two-way street. When a mentor makes the effort to help, you are responsible for respectfully taking the advice into consideration. It takes courage to be open to new ideas and to admit that you could benefit from some help. Friendship is also an important part of the exchange. You and your mentor can learn from each other and receive positive energy from the evolution of your relationship. You have the potential to grow and develop together.

> **Mentor,** noun. A wise and trusted counselor or instructor

Communication

No matter how hard you try, you can never really know what someone else is thinking. Your best bet is to listen well and to communicate as clearly as possible. As carefully as you attempt to craft your own messages, you still do not control the way those messages will be interpreted.

Communication is an exchange between two people; the "sender" speaks, and the "receiver" listens. The goal of the sender is to have the receiver receive the message exactly as intended.

If you say, "A," you want your receiver to both hear, "A," and to understand, "A," as you understand it. Two problems can interfere with the success of this endeavor. One, sometimes the information itself may not be clearly presented. Two, as people receive information, they often filter it through their own perspectives and interpret it in different ways. Therefore, the receiver's job is to send the message back to the sender to see whether it came through accurately. If not, the sender tries to find a way to clarify the message.

Andrew J. DuBrin, a professor and communications expert, says in his book *Human Relations for Career and Personal Success* that "to be successful in work or personal life, you usually have to be an effective communicator. You can't make friends or stand up against your enemies unless you can communicate with them. And you can't accomplish work through others unless you can send and receive messages effectively."

The Cycle of Communication

The exchanges that make up communication, along with the thought processes that occur for both sender and receiver, form a cycle. In Fig. 9-1 is a basic communication model, adapted from Mr. DuBrin's, which illustrates the cyclical path a message travels in the course of communication. If a student and an instructor were to play the roles of sender and receiver, this is how one course of action might proceed.

- **This is what I want to say (conceptualizing).** *The sender has an idea about what he or she wants to express.* The student, having gotten a C on a paper, wants to know where he fell short of the task, and develops the idea to ask the instructor about it.

- **This is how I want to put it (encoding).** *The sender makes a decision about how to transmit the message—what words to use, what tone to use, and what means of transmission to use.* The student decides how to express the disappointment to the instructor, in this case, by making an appointment to speak to her in her office that afternoon.

- **"I have something to talk to you about..." (transmission).** *The message is sent.* At the scheduled meeting, the student transmits the message orally; "I don't know why you gave me a C on this paper."

- **This is what I hear (receiving).** *The message is received by the receiver.* The instructor receives the message from the student. Not only does she *hear* the spoken words, she also *sees* the body language of the student, who sits still and maintains eye contact with her.

THE COMMUNICATION LOOP

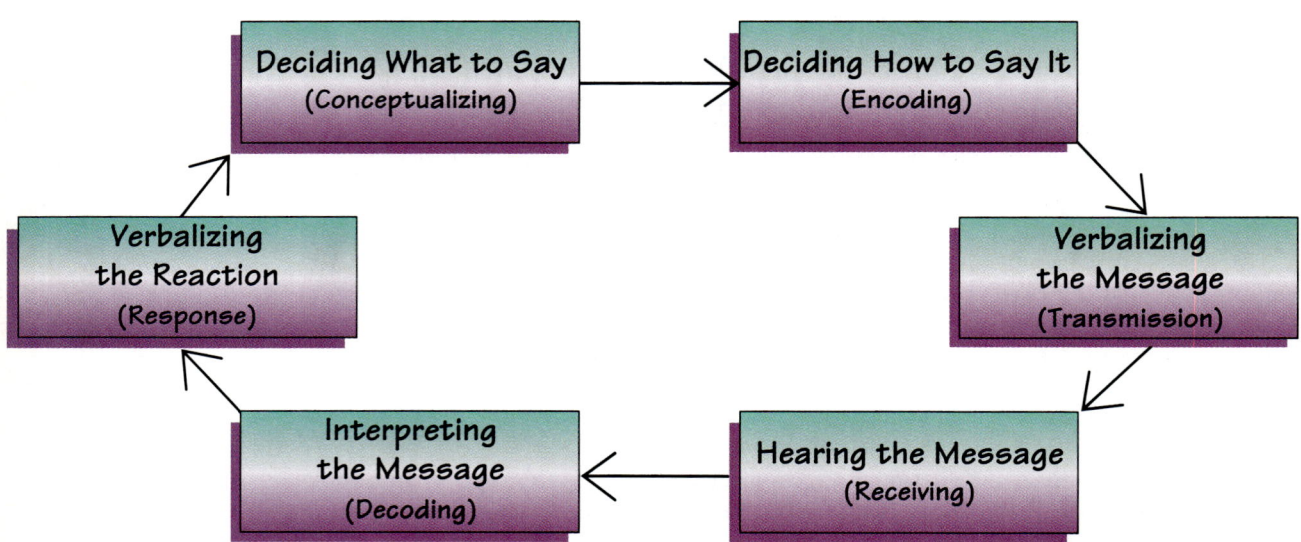

Source: Adapted from *Human Relations for Career and Personal Success*, by Andrew J. DuBrin, Fourth Edition. Prentice Hall, 1996.

FIGURE 9-1

❏ **This is how I think I should understand what I hear (decoding).** *The receiver interprets the message by examining tone, word choice, and any body language the sender may use.* The instructor decides that the student genuinely doesn't know why the paper didn't receive a higher grade and has done the best he could do at the time.

❏ **"I hear you and I feel…" (response).** *The receiver gives the sender a response to the message.* The instructor says, "I felt that your ideas were terrific but you made a lot of mechanical errors in punctuation, spelling, and sentence construction. I couldn't give you a higher grade just on content. If you would like, we can go over the errors together and then I will give you a chance to resubmit your paper for another grade."

Ways You Communicate

You communicate both *verbally*, expressing yourself by speaking words that others can hear, and *nonverbally*, expressing thoughts physically through the way you walk, sit, gesture, shift your eyes, or move facial features. People usually communicate both verbally and nonverbally at the same time, sometimes sending conflicting messages.

Verbal communication

Messages are communicated verbally through the spoken or the written word. The following strategies can help you communicate successfully:

Speak your piece. Say it or write it. No one can act on what you need until you communicate that need. You have the right to express your opinions, suggestions, and concerns.

Think before you communicate. Spoken too soon, ideas can come out sounding nothing like you intended them to. A little extra thought (and even some private rehearsal if you like) can help you choose the perfect combination of words. You have probably had to admit, at some time or another, "I didn't mean it that way!" Save the apologies—think it through and get it right the first time.

Communicate as soon as you are ready. One danger of holding back is that a problem or concern may only increase in severity if you wait to discuss it. Another is that when you don't express yourself, anger that may build up can emerge when you least expect it. You may have had the experience of becoming unexpectedly angry at someone over a minor issue, only to realize that most of your anger was caused by something different that you have kept bottled up. Wait until you have gathered and organized your thoughts, then take the first opportunity to communicate. Being prompt has two major benefits: (1) you solve the problem sooner, and (2) you are more likely to focus on the problem at hand than to let your anger spill over into other issues.

Be clear, precise, and brief. Unless you send a precisely worded message, you risk being misunderstood. Say exactly what you need to say. Link your ideas to clear examples, avoiding any extra information that can distract from the heart of the message. Get to the point and your efficiency will achieve the goal of your communication a lot sooner.

Be honest. Honesty creates brevity and clarity; it takes a lot more time to run verbal circles around the truth than it does to speak directly. Plus, no one to whom you speak can truly address your situation until you present it honestly. Even when honesty requires that you communicate something negative, it will help you earn respect in the long run. When others know they receive honesty from you, they will sense your integrity and feel safe sending you honest messages in return. Think about the people with whom you communicate best; you feel safe speaking honestly to them because they have proven that they will respond likewise.

Listen. Whether you are playing the role of sender or receiver, put your listening skills to work when you communicate. If you don't listen well, you will have trouble hearing messages accurately and may misunderstand their meaning.

Nonverbal communication

The way you send unspoken messages is the most basic form of communication. Even people who haven't any idea how to speak each other's language can communicate ideas through gestures and facial expressions. Your hand gestures, eye movement, facial expression, positioning of hands and arms, stance and posture, tone of voice, touching behavior, and use of personal space are all types of nonverbal communication.

What function does nonverbal communication have? Courtland L. Bovée and John V. Thill, in *Business Communication Today*, say that it works in tandem with verbal communication. "Our words carry part of the message, and nonverbal signals carry the rest. Together, the two modes of expression make a powerful team, augmenting, reinforcing, and clarifying each other." If you speak the same sentence three different times—once in a loud voice while standing up, once quietly while sitting with arms and legs crossed, and once while maintaining eye contact and taking the receiver's hand—you may send three entirely different messages.

Nonverbal communication strongly influences a first impression. First impressions emerge from a combination of nonverbal signals, tone of voice, and words spoken; the nonverbal elements usually come across first. Think about it; when you meet someone, you tend to judge the person upon sight, before either of you speaks a word. You make assumptions based on posture, eye contact, and speed and style of movement.

How can you use nonverbal communication to your advantage?

Become aware. Pay attention to what other people communicate nonverbally. If a friend compliments you with strong eye contact and a natural smile, you might feel genuinely flattered. If the same friend speaking the same words doesn't look you in the eye and is turned away or sitting with both arms and legs crossed, physically closed off from you, there might be something left unsaid. Also, start to examine what you convey with your own posture and gestures. Note when someone misinterprets what you have said; look for ways in which your nonverbal communication might have affected your message.

Don't contradict your words with your body language. Watch out for saying things with your body that go against what you speak; it confuses the receiver, who doesn't know what to believe. That confusion can result in your appearing dishonest. If you say to your advisor, "I don't care if I don't get into that class," with a tense tone of voice and aggressive posture, the advisor may misinterpret what you really feel.

Note cultural differences. In some cultures, casual acquaintances stand very close to one another when speaking; in others, the same distance may be used only in very intimate, personal conversations. General American culture encourages eye contact, interpreting it as honesty and openness; other cultures frown on it, interpreting it as a sign of disrespect. Some people shake hands readily and touch others aggressively when speaking; others refrain from touching, feeling that it is invasive and should only be used with intimate acquaintances. Within each conversation you have, you can discover what seems permissible by paying attention to what the other person does.

Strategies for Better Communication

It's all too easy to miscommunicate. You can convey unintentional meanings by not being specific enough, use words or tones that don't fit what you mean to say, or leave out important words or thoughts. Some of the most common communication problems follow along with strategies to help you combat them.

Problem: Poor or incomplete explanation
Solution: Support ideas with examples

As you learned in studying critical thinking, examples anchor ideas to reality. When you clarify a general idea by giving examples that illustrate how it works and what effects it causes, you will help your receiver understand what you mean and therefore have a better chance at holding his or her attention.

For example, think about the section you read in Chapter 7 about maintaining a healthy body. That section supports the idea that physical health is desirable by giving examples of the positive effects of eating properly, sleeping well, and exercising, as well as the negative effects of eating and sleeping poorly and being sedentary. If you were trying to convince a friend to take a certain class with you, you would communicate all of the positive effects that taking that class might have (progress towards a major, an excellent instructor, friendly study sessions). With examples and effects to back up an idea, you have a much greater chance of being able to apply the idea to your own life.

Problem: Attacking and accusing the receiver
Solution: "I" messages

Communicate your own needs rather than focusing on what you think someone else did wrong or should do differently. When a conflict arises, it is easy to blame someone else for the trouble. "You didn't lock the door!" "You never called last night!" "You left me out!" Attacking and accusing someone of wrongdoing (often without proof) immediately puts the other person on the defensive and effectively shuts down the lines of communication.

To generate a useful exchange, avoid blame by using *I* messages instead of *you* messages. "I felt uneasy when I came to work and the door was unlocked." "I became worried about you when I didn't hear from you last night." "I felt disappointed when I realized that I hadn't had a chance to go to the party." *I* statements soften the conflict and invite conversation by highlighting the effects of the other person's actions rather than the actions themselves. When you focus on your own response and needs, your receiver may feel more welcome in the conversation, perhaps offering help and even acknowledging mistakes. *I* statements leave room for the other person to offer an explanation that could help you better understand why the situation happened.

Think about how you communicate now. Do you often feel unresolved and tense after an exchange? If so, you probably need to work on conveying your own needs instead of blaming. As with any change, planning and effort are necessary. Think before you speak. Translate your anger into an *I* statement before speaking. Ask the other person, "Can we decide together how to improve this situation? How do you feel about what happened?" Using *I* statements will bring results.

Problem: Improper timing
Solution: Choose optimum listening conditions

A perfectly worded message won't get through to a receiver if the receiver isn't ready to receive. If you try to talk about a problem with your instructor when she is rushing out the door, coat half on and briefcase in hand, your message probably won't come across too well. If you drop a note on a paper-cluttered desk when no one is looking, it may very well get lost in the shuffle. Also, pay attention to the attitude of your receiver. If a friend has had an exhausting and traumatic week, you might not want to choose that time to ask a favor.

Time your messages according to when you feel you can create an open line of communication. Schedule an appointment during your instructor's normal office hours. Leave a message in a mailbox or with a reliable assistant. Ask a favor when a friend is in a good mood or when you have recently done that friend a good turn. When you need to talk to someone in person, choose a time and place convenient for both of you. Turn off the TV, leave the crowded room, schedule a chat ahead of time, and ask someone else to take your phone calls. Give the communication the best chance you can.

Problem: Passive or aggressive communication styles
Solution: Be assertive

Among the three major communication styles—aggressive, passive, assertive—the most efficient is the assertive style. The other two, while commonly used, favor either the receiver or the sender and throw the communication out of balance.

Aggressive communicators focus only on their own needs; they can become angry and impatient when those needs are not immediately satisfied. Examples of aggressive behavior are

> **Assertive,**
> *adjective. Able to insist on rights and express thoughts in a positive, confident, and persistent way*

Passive communicators doubt their right to be angry

- ❏ Loud, heated fighting
- ❏ Blaming, name-calling, and verbal insults
- ❏ Walking out of arguments before they are resolved
- ❏ Physically violent encounters

Passive communicators deny themselves the power that aggressive people hoard. They focus almost exclusively on the needs of others instead of their own. They experience frustration and tension that remains unexpressed. Passive behavior includes:

- ❏ Concealing feelings
- ❏ Denying anger
- ❏ Doubting the right to be angry

Assertive behavior strikes a balance between aggression and passivity. Assertive communicators express themselves without being nasty or overbearing. They involve others by making sure everyone has a chance to express his or her needs or opinions. People who are assertive listen carefully, but take an opportunity to speak as well. They use *I* statements to defuse arguments. Assertive communicators get the most mileage out of their style.

Personal Relationships

The relationships you have with friends, family members, and significant others often take center stage. Jobs and schools can come and go, but you rely on the people with whom you share your life. They are worth all of the energy and value you invest in them.

These influential relationships can affect other areas of your life. You have probably experienced conflict with a boyfriend or girlfriend that disturbed your ability to sleep, eat, or work. On the flip side, you probably also understand how the high of a successful relationship can have positive effects on other aspects of your life, increasing your success at work or at school. If you can manage your personal relationships, you will have a better chance at keeping the other areas of your life operational. Here are some suggestions.

Make personal relationships a high priority. Nurture the ones that you have, and develop new ones as they come along. Life is meant to be shared. In some marriage ceremonies, the bride and groom share a cup of wine that symbolizes life. One of the reasons given for this is that the sweetness of life is doubled by tasting it together, and the bitterness is cut in half because it is shared by two.

Keep personal problems in their place. Solve personal problems with the people directly involved and no one else. Bringing your emotions into class or work will disturb your concentration, hurting your performance while doing nothing to help your problem. If you are overwhelmed by a personal problem on a given day, consider taking the afternoon off so you can have some private time; it will save everyone some aggravation.

Invest time in your relationships. You devote time to education, work, and the other priorities in your life. Relationships need the same investment in order to thrive. You need it too—the time you spend with friends and family can relieve everyday stress and strain. When you make time for your friends, everyone benefits.

Work out tensions right away. Negative feelings often multiply when left unspoken. When you become angry with someone close to you over something small, you may often find that other unexpressed feelings have caused your anger over this one minor issue to grow out of proportion. A small annoyance over dishes in the sink can turn into a gigantic fight about everything under the sun if you let it ferment for too long.

Show appreciation. In this fast-moving, self-absorbed world, people don't thank each other often enough. If you think of something positive, say it. Thank someone for a service, express your affection, write a thank-you note. A little positive reinforcement goes a long way toward nurturing a relationship.

If you want a friend, be a friend. The Golden Rule, "Do unto others as you would have done unto you," never goes out of style. If you treat a friend how you would like a friend to treat you, by being loyal, available, positive, and supportive, you are likely to receive the same in return.

Risk. It can be frightening to reveal your deepest dreams and frustrations, to devote yourself to a friend, or to fall in love. Another option is not to reveal yourself or give yourself to a friendship at all, but when you don't give, you won't have much opportunity to receive. Take the plunge. Sure, you risk disappointment and heartbreak, but you stand to gain the incredible benefits of companionship, which for most people seem to far outweigh the risk.

Group Relationships

Groups have their own special chemistry and structure. Beyond who you are as an individual, you take on a certain role when part of a group. Since group interaction is an important part of your educational, personal, and working life, you should be aware of the role you will play when relating to others. Having a positive group dynamic is especially important when you work as a group to accomplish a goal, such as in a team project situation at work or a cooperative learning exercise in school. If you are comfortable in your role, you will help the group function more effectively because you will be more effective yourself.

There are three major roles to be played in the group experience: participating, leading, and negotiating. None is superior; a group needs all three to function successfully. Explore each one before you decide which is best for you.

Participating. Some people are happiest when participating in group activities that someone else leads and designs. They don't feel comfortable in a position of control or having the power to set the tone for the group as a whole. They trust others to make those decisions, preferring to help things run smoothly by taking on an assigned task and seeing it through. Participators don't mind not having the spotlight.

Leading. Some people like to initiate the action, make decisions, and control how things proceed. They have ideas they want to put into practice and enjoy explaining them to others. They are comfortable giving orders to people and directing group operations. Leaders often have a big picture perspective; it allows them to see how all of the different aspects of a group project can come together.

Negotiating. Negotiators are often also participators, since having less power can help a negotiator stake out a neutral ground. Negotiators help moderate group decisions and defuse conflicts. They don't want to be top dog, but they like a moderate level of influence. They are often calm, understanding, intuitive, and level-headed.

Look at a group project at work as an example. Say that four employees—call them *A*, *B*, *C*, and *D*—in the academic office of a school department need to figure out a way to transfer all of the student data, currently written on index cards, to a database in the computer. There is only one computer, so only one person can enter data at a time. *A* takes the reins, deciding that they should divide up the work by having one person put the cards in order, another read the information on each card aloud, a third enter the data that is read aloud, and a fourth proofread the entries afterwards. *A* thinks that *B* and *C* should be the pair at the computer, but *C* objects because he also has to answer the phones. *D* solves the conflict by volunteering to answer the phones while putting cards in order for *B* and *C*. *D* also offers the idea that *A* should proofread the entries, which will keep him free to supervise the operation as it progresses. Where would you fit in?

Whatever you decide works best for you, stay aware of group dynamics; they can shift quickly and move you into a new position you may or may not appreciate. If you don't feel comfortable, speak up. Reposition yourself where you will be more useful and happy. Also, realize that you may play different roles with different groups. You might be a participator at school and a leader in a self-help group. You could enjoy leading a religious group but prefer to take a back seat at work. You may only like to negotiate in small group situations. Find what suits you in each situation. The happier each group member is, the more effectively the group will function as a whole.

YOUR DIVERSE WORLD

Diversity is a fact of life, especially in a country like the United States that has made a longtime commitment to providing a free society for all different kinds of people. Although some refer to it as a "melting pot," the different peoples don't always "melt" together; some stick together in groups, making the multiculturalism of American society seem more like a tossed salad instead. The groups often interact; however, people gravitate toward those who share their experience.

It's natural to want to belong somewhere and to feel accepted as part of a group. Members of various groups share one or more common traits, whether they are skin color, a physical feature or disability, values, cultural background, beliefs, nationality, age, or gender. What you have in common is special and worth celebrating. It's important to feel positive about who you are, where you come from, what you believe, and how you practice your traditions.

Multiculturalism indicates a mix of many kinds of different cultures; the word *culture* refers to a system of behavior patterns, beliefs, and institutions belonging to a particular class, community, or group of people. People can be different in all kinds of ways. They can have different ethnic backgrounds (*ethnic* refers to a distinctive racial, national, or cultural heritage). They may be of different races (*race* indicates a population possessing genetically transmitted physical characteristics that distinguish them as a group). They may come from different nations or practice different religions. They may be male or female. They might be of difference sizes, of different age groups, or in different stages of life. They could have a physical disability or different value systems that define how they prefer to live.

Modern multiculturalism can affect your life in the following ways:

- ❏ You live, work, and study with people who are different from you.
- ❏ You become aware of different perspectives and different ways of doing things.
- ❏ You may socialize with and perhaps even marry a person from another culture.
- ❏ You patronize a diverse group of restaurants, services, and businesses in your community.
- ❏ You are exposed to different ways of life through television, movies, music, and other forms of popular culture.

Your role in this environment is to respect others. Finding what you have in common with other people will help you develop an appreciation for each other. Joining a club is one effective way for people to discover a common ground—an interest in computers, a love of music, or a desire to overcome an addiction. When you see how you are similar to people that at first seemed so unfamiliar, your shared thoughts, ideas, desires and emotions take the focus away from your differences.

Manage the diversity of your world by celebrating the differences you encounter in other people as you celebrate your own uniqueness.

This approach will enable you to relate to all kinds of people and will therefore increase your potential for success.

Racism and Discrimination

In the not-so-perfect world, individuals don't always receive the respect and treatment they deserve. When people choose not to accept the differences in each other, problems arise. Despite considerable progress in the last few decades, racism and discrimination are still a part of life in this country.

People often lash out when their needs are not fulfilled, and because they often feel that racism or discrimination has motivated someone to deny them their needs, they may direct their anger against a particular group. An African-American may clash with a Korean; someone in their twenties may not get along with someone in their sixties; a single person might not understand the circumstances of a parent of two children; a homosexual and a heterosexual may offend each other with their respective opinions. Your assumptions based on the appearances of others, along with peer pressure, may close your mind to the value of others and encourage you to see them as the enemy.

Racism and discrimination have many faces. Sheryl McCarthy, an African-American woman who writes a column in New York Newsday, speaks of being ignored by taxicab drivers. "Nothing is quite so basic and clear as having a cab go right past your furiously waving body and pick up the white person next to you," she says in her book, *Why Are The Heroes Always White?* "Sometimes you can debate whether racism was the motivating factor in an act; here there is no doubt whatsoever." A Hispanic person may be denied a chance to move up from a position in a restaurant kitchen because his English is heavily accented. A woman may lose out on a job because the fact that she is married and 30 years old leads the interviewer to assume that she will soon become pregnant and leave the company. So-called "majority" populations can experience discrimination as well; a qualified white man may be passed up for a promotion in favor of an equally-qualified female or minority employee in the attempt to diversify a quota.

Racism,
noun. The belief that race accounts for differences in human character or ability and that a particular race is superior to others

Discrimination,
noun. A showing of partiality or prejudice in treatment, specifically, action or policies directed against the welfare of a person or persons based on class or category rather than individual merit

The disabled and the obese are often targets of discrimination as well. Individuals with physical, mental, or emotional differences have just as much to contribute to society as anyone else; to think of them otherwise is to limit your view of human potential. John Hockenberry, a wheelchair-using journalist who lost the use of the lower half of his body in a car accident, challenges the idea that disabled people live lives of misery. "To rediscover my changed body was to explore the idea of the body and its relationship to the mind in a way no night class, self-help book, or therapist could. My body may have been capable of less, but virtually all of what it could do was suddenly charged with meaning. This feeling was the hardest to translate to the outside, where people wanted to believe that I must have to paint things in this way to keep from killing myself," he says in his memoir *Moving Violations*. "There was nothing odd about what I was doing…I was just reacting to each physical, human problem and solving it with the materials at hand."

The federal law states that it is unlawful for you to be denied work, the chance to apply for work, housing, or basic constitutional rights based on your race, creed, color, age, gender, national or ethnic origin, religion, marital status, arrest records, sexual preference, potential or actual pregnancy, or potential or actual illness or disability (unless the illness or disability prevents you from performing required tasks). Unfortunately, the law doesn't always catch everything. Some incidents go unreported or unnoticed; people are at times unwilling to make waves by standing up for themselves. People still have some evolving to do when it comes to treating each other equally.

What can you do? First and foremost, you are responsible for your own behavior. Make sure you never participate in or encourage discrimination. Second, if you are witness to a discriminatory act, decide if you can safely approach an authority about it. Third, if you feel you have been discriminated against, talk to the person who can most directly affect the situation—an instructor, your supervisor, a housing authority. Don't assume that people know something is wrong. It's unrealistic to expect that anyone will know your particular needs unless you communicate them clearly. For example, if you are disabled and you find that certain allowances haven't been made for you at work or school, speak up. Set up a time to meet and discuss your needs for transport, equipment, facilities, or a particular schedule.

> "The fear of cultures that are unknown is probably the most accurate explanation as to why racism exists. We are afraid of what we are unsure of because it is a part of our human nature. However, open and honest dialogue about racial issues increases understanding. Let your encounters with other races be free of assumptions and do not draw conclusions based on preconceived notions."
>
> Tamera Trotter and Joycelyn Allen, authors of *Talking Justice: 602 Ways to Build and Promote Racial Harmony*

If you don't find satisfaction and change at that level, try the next level of authority (an administrator, your supervisor's boss, a government official). If that doesn't produce results, you can opt to take legal action. Weigh all of the pros and cons carefully before making a decision; legal struggles can take a lot of time and drain a great deal of money out of your pocket. Evaluate whether the potential payoff and/or the principle are worth the fight.

You won't always get along with others or share opinions with people different than you. However, you owe them acceptance no matter what. Every human being on this earth has as much right to freely think and live as anyone else. Acceptance means you willingly and positively accept people's existence. You don't have to agree with people in order to accept them. When people feel accepted, they are happier, more friendly, more productive, and more forthcoming. You may discover more in common with them as they reveal themselves to you, and you may find that you learn from their perspectives. Even if you don't find much to agree with, you still have fostered a positive environment.

Be Part of the Solution

What can you do to promote the acceptance of diversity?

- Be aware of judgments based on externals such as skin color, body type, or gender.

- Cultivate relationships with people of different cultures, races, perspectives, and ages.

- Promote education. "We can empower ourselves to end racism through massive education," say Tamara Trotter and Joycelyn Allen in *Talking Justice: 602 Ways to Build and Promote Racial Harmony*. "The media has defined images for you which only serve to exacerbate the problem of racism. We encourage you to take advantage of books and people to teach you about other cultures. Empowerment comes through education. If you remain ignorant and blind to the critical issues of race and humanity, you will have no power to influence positive change."

- Be sensitive to the particular needs of others at school and on the job. Accept different styles, as long as they don't break rules.

- Be tolerant of views and perspectives that clash with or challenge your own.

- Help other people, no matter how different from you they may be. Sheryl McCarthy writes about an African-American man who, in the midst of the 1992 Los Angeles riots, saw a man being beaten and helped him to safety. "When asked why he risked grievous harm to save an Asian man he didn't even know, Williams said, 'Because if I'm not there to help someone else, when the mob comes for me, will there be someone there to save me?'" Fuel the cycle of kindness.

- Explore your own heritage and share it with others.

- Avoid blaming problems in your life on certain groups of people. Take responsibility for making changes instead of pointing the finger at someone else.

- Look for what you have in common—parenting, classes, career interests, sports, etc.

- Teach your children about other cultures and impress upon them the importance of appreciating differences while accepting all people as equal.

- Recognize that people everywhere have the same basic needs. Everyone loves, thinks, hurts, hopes, fears, and plans. Although people express themselves differently, their humanity unites them. There is only one race—the human race.

Summing Up

Unless you know of a well-stocked desert island to which you can escape and live comfortably, you will deal with other people every day for the rest of your life. Make the most of it by maintaining your connections, communicating with people efficiently, and accepting the diverse population of the world. Adaptable people who understand how to get along with others and can work well in groups will find both professional and personal success.

CHAPTER 9: APPLICATIONS

Keys for your Key Chain Skills Worth Keeping

List here what to you are the five most important keys, or skills, you have learned from reading this chapter.

1. _____
2. _____
3. _____
4. _____
5. _____

Key Into Your Life: Opportunities to Apply What You Learn

Exercise 1 Explore Human Resources at School

Make a point to interact with people at school who can enrich your experience. Schedule two meetings, one with an instructor and the other with a counselor, administrator, or job placement advisor. Report here on what happened.

Meeting 1

Name of the person you met:

_____

Position at your school:

_____

Something you learned about this person from your meeting:

_____
_____

Something new you found out that can help you with your studies or your working life:

_____
_____

The name of one new contact person you heard about in the meeting, and how he or she might be able to help you:

_____
_____

R

THE PEOPLE CONNECTION: RELATING TO OTHERS

Meeting 2

Name of the person you met:
_____

Position at your school:
_____

Something you learned about this person from your meeting:
_____
_____

Something new you found out that can help you with your studies or your working life:
_____
_____

The name of one new contact person you heard about in the meeting, and how he or she might be able to help you:
_____
_____

Exercise 2 Mentors

First, consider the people you go to with problems and questions, people that you trust and with whom you share a lot of yourself. Name up to five—don't fill the list unless you can really think of five people you trust.

1. _____
2. _____
3. _____
4. _____
5. _____

Examine your list. With which of those people do you feel you have a mentoring relationship? Discuss up to two; describe why you consider each to be a mentor of yours.

1. _____
_____
_____

2. _____

_____

_____

What, in your opinion, are the most important ways to respond to what a mentor gives to you?

_____

_____

If you are a mentor to anyone, describe your relationship; what do you learn from the person whom you mentor?

_____

_____

_____

Exercise 3 Say It With An "I"

In your quest to become a more successful communicator, rewrite the following sentences so that they are in the less accusatory *I* message style. Check your answers with other students and/or with your instructor.

1. You blew it completely.

_____

_____

2. Why didn't you tell me the meeting time changed?

_____

_____

3. You always forget to pick me up.

_____

_____

4. What does it take for you to understand how this machine works?

_____

_____

5. Where did you put the stapler? Did you lose it?

_____

_____

6. You never get that format right.

_____

_____

7. You are impossible to understand when you talk like that.

_____

_____

Exercise 4 Your Communication Style

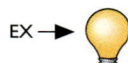

Read the following sentences. Circle the ones that sound like something you would say.

1. Get me the keys.
2. Would you mind if I stepped out just for a second?
3. Don't slam the door.
4. I'd appreciate it if you would have this done by two o'clock.
5. I think maybe it needs a little work just at the end, but I'm not sure.
6. Please take this back to the library.
7. You will have a good time if you join us.
8. Your loss.
9. I don't know, if you think so. I'll try it.
10. Let me know what you want me to do.
11. Turn it this way and see what happens.
12. We'll try both our ideas and see what works best.
13. I want it on my desk by the end of the day.
14. Just do what I told you.
15. If this isn't how you wanted it to look, I can change it. Just tell me and I'll do it.

Aggressive communicators would be likely to use sentences 1, 3, 8, 13, and 14.

Passive communicators would probably opt for sentences 2, 5, 9, 10, and 15.

Assertive communicators would probably choose sentences 4, 6, 7, 11, and 12.

In which category did you choose the most sentences?

What is your Communication Style? _____

If you scored as an assertive communicator, you are on the right track. If you scored in the aggressive or passive categories, what can you do to improve your skills?

_____
_____
_____
_____
_____
_____

Key to Cooperative Learning: Building Teamwork Skills

Discrimination and Sexual Harassment: How Far Will You Go?

In groups of three or four, divide a piece of paper into two columns, one headed Discrimination, the other headed Sexual Harassment. Together, brainstorm examples of either one that you have either seen, experienced, or heard about. Then rate the seriousness of each; talk over how you feel about each one and in what cases you would pursue justice. As a result of your discussion, divide the incidents into three groups—those for which you would go as far as legal routes to find justice; those for which you would go through more direct channels (administrators or supervisors) to try and change the situation, and those that you would ignore or put up with because the fight against them would be too difficult or too threatening to other needs of yours.

Key to Self-Expression: Discovery through Journal Writing

Your Diverse World

Do you interact with anyone you consider "different" from you? How are they different? How do you react to their differences? Has your approach to diversity changed from, say, five years ago? If so, why? Do you want to change further? Have you experienced prejudice or discrimination? Describe what happened. Were you the victim or one of the people who created the situation? How do you feel about what happened? Would you or should you have done anything differently? How did it change you?

_____
_____
_____
_____
_____
_____

THE PEOPLE CONNECTION: RELATING TO OTHERS

KEY TO YOUR PERSONAL PORTFOLIO: YOUR PAPER TRAIL TO SUCCESS

Your VIRs—Very Important References

For your portfolio, create a list of people who have served or could serve as references for you as you build your career. Brainstorm names from all areas of your human resources:

- ❏ Instructors
- ❏ Administrators
- ❏ Counselors
- ❏ Students
- ❏ Friends
- ❏ Family members
- ❏ Present/former co-workers
- ❏ Present/former employers
- ❏ Mentors

CHAPTER 9:
APPLICATIONS

In this chart, fill in the information for each reference. Reproduce the chart on a separate page if you have additional references.

Name	Address	Phone Number	How Associated
Jo Trenholm	727 Mercury Way Boston, MA	617/224-2808	Current supervisor

Update the information on this chart as you meet potential references or lose touch with old ones.

M A N A

Manage

10

Reality Resources: Managing Finances and Work

Money may not be the most important part of life, but it pays for a lot of what makes it livable. So much of what you do involves money—earning it, paying it out, studying so you can make more of it, borrowing it, worrying about it—that it's virtually impossible to function in society without money management skills. Although you may be in school primarily to improve your mind and build your knowledge, one of your goals is to eventually translate that knowledge into dollars. Whatever the current condition of your finances, you can benefit from efficient money management.

You will explore the management of your cash flow in the *budgeting* section. *Working now* will help you look into job opportunities while in school, touching on job choice, job-hunting, and tips for on-the-job success. *Loans and financial aid* will explain some of the grants, scholarships, and loans that can help fund your education. As you read about *banking services*, you will sort through what banks offer and how to tailor services to your particular needs. Finally, *smart spending and saving* offers reality-based savings strategies and tips for avoiding the pitfalls of credit.

Budgeting

Budget

verb. To plan activities and expenditures according to the amount of income available

You already budget your money. You do it every time you have some money in your pocket and have to figure out whether it will pay for what you want at that moment. It takes some thought and energy, though, to budget efficiently. The more money you can save each month, the more you will thank yourself later when you need it. Smart budgeting is a worthwhile investment in your future.

Budgeting is the process of setting goals with your money. As with your other goals, you have to consider resources and needs. **Resources** bring money in; **needs** cause money to flow out. A smart budget adjusts the money flow for the best possible chance that what comes in will be more than what goes out.

What steps can you take to budget?

1. Determine approximately how much money you will make (a month is a common time frame).

2. Determine your basic spending by estimating expenditures and examining amounts from previous months.

3. Subtract expenditures from income, and note what's left over.

4. Make decisions as needed about how to allocate your money for next month.
    a. Shift more money to areas that need it.
    b. Decide how much you can reduce spending on not-so-necessary items.
    c. Plan to reduce or cut spending in areas that may be unaffordable right now.

Determine how much you will make Do this by adding up your pay stubs from last month, if you currently have a regular full-time or part-time job. If you have received any financial aid, loan funding, or scholarship money, determine how much of that you can allow for each month's income and add it to your total.

Figure out how much you spend You may or may not have a handle on your spending; many people don't take the time to keep track. If you have never before paid much attention to how you spend money, take two weeks or even a month to examine your spending patterns. Record expenditures in a small notebook or on a piece of paper on a home bulletin board. You don't have to list everything down to the penny. Just indicate expenditures over $5, making sure to count smaller expenditures if they are frequent (a bus pass for a month, soda or newspaper purchases per week). In your list, include an estimate of the following:

- ❏ Rent/mortgage
- ❏ Tuition or educational loan payments (divide your annual total by 12 to arrive at a monthly figure)
- ❏ Books, lab fees, and other educational expenses
- ❏ Regular bills (heat, gas, electric, phone, car payment, water)
- ❏ Credit card or other payments on credit
- ❏ Food, toiletries, other household supplies

❏ Child care

❏ Entertainment and related items (eating out, books and publications, movies)

❏ Insurance

❏ Transportation

Look at how much money remains If there is any, decide how to save it if you can. Some months, you may not have any left over. If you end up with a negative number, indicating that you have spent more than you take in, make changes in your budget accordingly. When a negative number comes up for what seems to be a typical month, you may need to adjust your budget over the long term.

Adjust your spending according to your needs Some categories will have heavier spending in certain months, such as when you visit a dentist or put a deposit on a living space. Prioritize your expenditures and trim the ones you really don't need to make. Do you eat out too much? Can you live without cable? Be smart. Cut out unaffordable extras. You can also look at ways to take in more money to help support yourself. Taking a part-time job to help pay essentials may make sense. However, if the increased income would just pay for luxuries, it may not be worth the time it would take out of you schedule.

"Can You Live Without Cable"?

Figure 10-1 shows a sample budget of an unmarried student living with his parents. It will give you an idea of how to budget (all expenditures are general estimates, based on averages).

SAMPLE BUDGET

Part-time salary: $10 an hour, 20 hours a week. 10 x 20 = $200 a week x 4 weeks = $800
Student loan from school's financial aid office: $2000 divided by 12 months = $166
Total income per month: $966

Expenditures	Amount
Tuition ($6500 per year)	$ 542
Public transportation	$ 90
Phone	$ 40
Food	$ 130
Medical insurance	$ 100
Rent paid	$ 100
Entertainment	$ 100
Total spending	**$1102**

$966 (income) - $1102 (spending) = $-136 ($136 over budget)

FIGURE 10-1

This student already made some tough choices. In order to save money, he had asked his parents if he could move back home. They agreed as long as he paid them a small monthly fee—a stipend—similar to a low rent. That helped him put most of his money toward his tuition, which he wanted to cover himself, and saved him from having to pay heat and electric bills. He paid for his share of the phone bill and provided a lot of his own food. Sharing some family meals with his parents helped ease the money crunch too.

In spite of his planning, the student still went over budget. To make up the $136 shortfall, he must adjust his spending. He could rent movies or check them out of the library instead of going to the theater. He could socialize with friends at someone's apartment instead of paying high prices and tips at a bar or restaurant. Instead of buying CDs and tapes, he could borrow them. He could also shop for specials and bargains in the grocery store or go to a warehouse supermarket to stock up on staples at discount prices. He could make his lunch instead of buying it and walk instead of taking public transportation.

Not everyone likes the work involved in keeping a budget. While sequential, sensing, reflective, and verbal learners may more easily take to it, active, global, intuitive, and visual learners may resist the structure and detail. Visual learners might benefit from putting the budget on a chart like the one shown in the example or by constructing a Think Link that shows the connections between all the month's expenditures. Use images; picture a bathtub you are filling that is also draining at the same time. Dump all of your receipts into a big jar and tally them up at the end of the month. Even if you have to force yourself to do it, you will discover that budgeting is a very effective way of reducing stress and taking control of your finances and your life.

WORKING NOW

Eventual workplace success is probably at or near the top of the list of reasons you became a student. Unless you are lucky enough to have received an inheritance from a wealthy great aunt (odds are if you are reading this book you have had no such luck), you have to work in order to survive in society. What you are studying today will prepare you to find a job when you graduate that suits your abilities and brings in enough money to support your needs and lifestyle choices. In the meantime, though, you can make work a part of your student life for purposes of financial gain, career exploration, or both.

As the cost of education continues to rise, more and more students are working and taking classes at the same time. The 1989-90 National Postsecondary Student Aid Study says that approximately three-fourths of undergraduates reported working at some time during their enrollment in the academic year 1989-90, while about 40 percent reported working full-time. Students with part-time jobs were most likely to work throughout the academic year, while full-time workers combined work and classes during approximately 75 percent of their time in school. The most popular kinds of jobs were administrative support and service occupations. Figure 10-2 shows the rise of the adult student population, many of whom work, as well as the population of students working part time while in school.

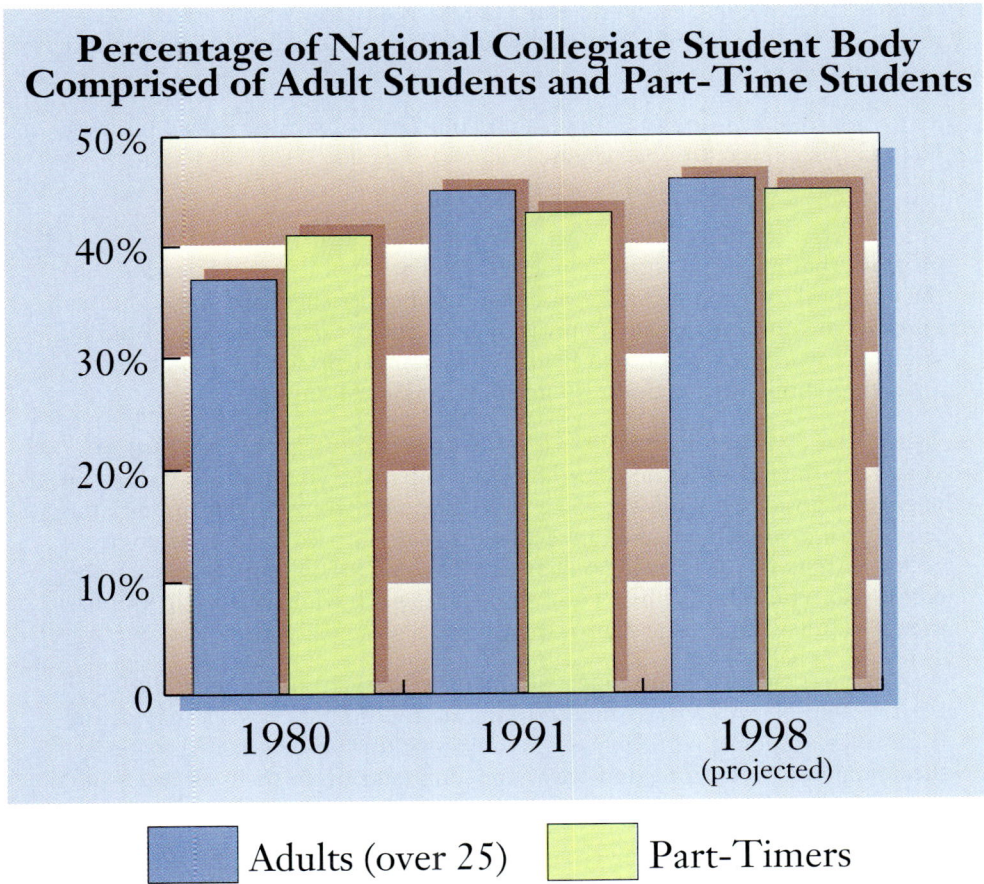

Source: Adapted from the U.S. Department of Education, National Center for Education Statistics, "Fall Enrollment in Institutions of Higher Education" surveys; Integrated Postsecondary Education Data System (IPEDS), "Fall Enrollment" surveys; *Projections of Education Statistics to 2004*; and U.S. Department of Commerce, Bureau of the Census, Current Population Reports, *Social and Economic Characteristics of Students*, various years, as reported in the *Digest of Educational Statistics*, 1994.

FIGURE 10-2

Working and taking classes at the same time isn't for everyone. Adding a job to the list of demands on your time and energy may create problems if it sharply reduces the time available for studying or being with your family. However, many people want to work and many need to work in order to pay for school. You are responsible for evaluating the positive and negative effects of any possible job situation and making a choice that you feel benefits you most. With careful job-hunting techniques, you may discover a work situation that doesn't force you to compromise your other priorities.

Positive and Negative Effects

Why might someone want to work while studying for a degree or certificate?

To earn money for essentials like rent, transportation, and food. Many people can't make it solely on the money from savings, loans or grants, and/or family members. A job can provide some crucial income to cover bills and keep from going under.

To earn spending money. Even if you have enough to live on and pay for school, it's nice to have something extra for an occasional luxury or an unexpected expense. You might want to take a day trip with friends; you might lose a contact lens when you least expect it. A small financial cushion can help you be prepared.

To help out with a family enterprise. If your family owns or runs a business, you may be expected to participate.

To gain general and career-specific experience and explore possible career options. Everyone, even not-so-active learners, can learn lessons from hands-on work that might not "take" when learned at school. Your education "in the trenches" can complement your classroom experience, and the additional knowledge you develop may improve your academic performance. Even if you don't work in your chosen field, you can apply principles within the areas of communication and responsibility to almost any job.

To maintain a position at work held prior to beginning school. It's hard to keep a job these days if you come and go; companies cannot afford to hold an important post open until you come back. Pregnant women often run into this problem; if a woman wants to take a longer maternity leave than her company policy permits, she may have no guarantee that her job will be there when she is ready to return. It may be a good strategy to work while you are in school even if you have to change your responsibilities or adjust your hours.

To stay busy. Work can provide a stimulating break from studying. In fact, the 1989-90 NPSAS reports that working up to 20 hours a week may actually enhance academic performance, because working students often manage their time more efficiently and may gain confidence from their successes in the workplace. The money isn't a bad benefit either.

To fulfill requirements as part of a work-study program. Part of your financial aid package may be a work-study program, requiring you to work in order to receive the promised financial benefits.

To establish or maintain connections inside and outside of school. You may have formed important relationships at work. The working world moves fast, though; if you don't keep in touch with your connections, they may become less aware of you in time. Maintaining your network of contacts by continuing to work may help you avoid losing ground. In addition, if you work for your educational institution, you may be able to develop beneficial relationships with instructors and administrators.

What can be difficult about combining work and school?

Making the time commitment. Whereas a non-working student splits time between academic and personal life, a working student must add a third, time-consuming factor. Working usually means having to cut back on study and personal time. The change in how you spend your time demands more efficient time management, because you have more responsibilities and less time for each.

Adjusting priorities. Depending on how much you work per week and how dependent you are on the money you make, the priority level of your job may vary. For a student who depends heavily on the income, work may take top priority, relegating other priorities like family time and studying time to lower rungs on the ladder. Take time to think carefully through your priorities if you decide to work while in school. Realize that you may have to cut back on your lesser priorities; depending on what those are, that may mean turning down some social activities, shorter study breaks, finding a workout that you can do at home instead of taking the time to travel to a gym, or cutting back on extracurricular involvement. Reconstruct your priorities to fit your needs.

Shifting gears. Unless your job complements your classroom curriculum perfectly, you may find it takes some effort to shift gears mentally as you move back and forth between academia and the workplace. Each environment has its own set of people, responsibilities, joys, and problems. If you can't shake off academic stresses while at work, and vice versa, your performance may suffer. Establish mental boundaries for yourself so that at any given time you can focus on the environment at hand.

If you decide to work, what next? What might you want in a job? Any number of factors might come into play.

Establish your needs first.

Salary/wage level. How much money do you aim to make? Start by considering the minimum you need, that is, the amount that justifies taking the time to work. If $300 a week will keep you going, and you find a job that offers $350 and takes exactly as much time per week as you can spare, take it. However, if that extra $50 means extra hours of work that should go toward studying or taking care of business at home, it might not be worth it. Find work that won't sabotage the rest of your life; think through the effects it can have on you.

Time of day. This depends on your school schedule. For example, if you take classes Monday, Tuesday, and Thursday during the day, you could look for a job with weekend or evening hours. If you attend evening classes, a daytime job could work fine.

Hours per week (part time vs. full time). Again, consider your needs. It's tough for a student to work full time; however, some people have to in order to finance their education. Such students have made the decision that the education is worth the sacrifice. If you can make enough money working part time, though, you will have more time to devote to studying and other priorities.

Duties performed. If you want hands-on experience in your chosen field, narrow your search to jobs that can provide it for you. On the other hand, if you just want a regular paycheck and don't really care what kind of work you do, consider your other priorities when choosing a job. Is there anything you absolutely can't stand? Working somewhere and/or doing something that makes you miserable may not be worth any amount of money.

Location. Where you work can make or break your schedule. Weigh the effects of each of your options. If work is a long drive or a problematic public-transportation haul away, getting there and back may cut deeply into your day. If you can take a bus and study on the way, you may not lose as much time. On the other hand, if the job gives you important experience that outweighs the commute, give it a shot. A job at or near your school, though, may give unparalleled convenience. When you know you can get to work quickly, you can schedule your day more tightly and get more done.

Flexibility. Even if your classes are at regular times, you might have other projects and meetings that take place at random. Do you need a job that offers flexibility, allowing you to shift your working time when you have to attend to an academic responsibility that takes priority? While you may be able to switch shifts at a restaurant, you might have a hard time backing out on a scheduled child-care stint. Choose according to the flexibility you require.

Affiliation with school or financial aid program. Some financial aid packages, especially if they involve funds from your school, can require you to take work at the school or a federal organization. In that case you would have to choose among the opportunities offered.

Job Listings and Networking

All routes to jobs have their origins in one of two areas: job listings or networking. Often the road to a job zigzags through both. A little effort can help you find a wealth of information.

Some of the best **job listings** are daily or periodic *newspapers*. They print extensive help-wanted sections in most issues, organized according to career field categories. At the beginning of most help-wanted sections you will find an index that tells you the categories and on what pages they begin in the listings. Individual ads describe the kind of position available and will give a telephone number or post office box for you to contact. Some ads will include additional information such as job requirements, a contact person, and the salary or wages offered. *Magazines* likewise often have help-wanted sections; usually not as extensive, they focus on the career areas related to the subject matter covered by the publication. In addition, you can access job search databases such as the Career Placement Registry (through DIALOG or CompuServe) and U.S. Employment Opportunities (CompuServe) through the *Internet*. Individual associations and organizations may also post job listings on the 'net.

Your school's employment services may have other materials for you to read. Generally, the *career planning and placement office* deals with post-graduation job placements, while the *student employment office* in conjunction with the financial aid office has more information about working while in school. At either location you might find *listings of job opportunities* and *contact information* for companies that may interest you. *Bulletin boards* at school, in the community, in libraries or at employment agencies might have help-wanted bills or other information about potential employment. Your school may sponsor *Job Fairs* where you can explore all kinds of job opportunities. *Employment agencies*, both government and private, may have similar collections of job listings.

Opportunities for **networking** occur every day. Networking refers to the method by which you make and keep contacts with the people around you, and is one of the most

Network,
noun. A group or system of interconnected or cooperating individuals

verb. To develop contacts and exchange information with others, as to further a career

important parts of finding and keeping jobs. The network of people who know each other makes the business world go 'round. People help each other find jobs through contacts and providing references, teach each other on the job, and boost business by promoting each other's companies. The working world operates through human exchange.

When you network, you open and maintain lines of communication with people who have the potential to help you.

Not everyone with whom you network will come through for you. Keep in contact with as many people as possible in the hope that someone will; you never know who that person might be.

You already have many networking possibilities. With each contact you make and maintain, you do more than just build your own network. You also tap into the networks already built by each person. Imagine a giant Think Link with all of your connections spreading out into a web of people just a couple of phone calls away.

Remember that the contacts with whom you network aren't just sources of job opportunities. They are people with whom you can develop lasting, valuable relationships. From their experience, they have information about many other aspects of your chosen career field. They may be happy to talk to you about such subjects as

- Getting established
- Challenges on the job
- A description of a typical day
- Salary and benefits
- Requirements such as clothing, certificates, degrees, or equipment

Friends and family members may know of work opportunities or might introduce you to potential contacts. At your school, you might hear of jobs or receive contact information about potential employers from *instructors, administrators,* or *counselors. People at the student employment office* or *career planning office* should know how to help you locate suitable work. Also, if you participate in a school-related financial aid program such as work-study, a *work-study officer* may help you find a job within the system. Some schools even have opportunities for students to interact with *alumni*; whether that is true of your school, you may know some alumni personally whose advice may help you.

Look to your present and past work experience for more job leads. *Employers* or *co-workers* may know someone who needs new employees. A *former employer* might even hire you back with similar or adjusted hours, if you left on good terms. Thank your contacts for their help and don't forget them. You may be in a position soon to repay the favor.

When you have gathered the information on the jobs you want, formulate a plan for pursuing them. Organize your approach according to what you need to do and how much time you have to devote to your search on any given day. Do you plan to make three phone calls per day? Will you fill out three job applications a week for a month? Keep a record—on 3x5 cards, a computer file, or in a notebook—of the following:

- People you contact
- Companies to which you apply
- Jobs you rule out (for example, jobs that become unavailable or which you find out don't suit your needs)

❏ Any response from your communications (phone calls to you, interviews, written communications) and the information on whoever contacted you (names, titles, times and dates)

Keeping accurate records will enable you to both chart your progress and maintain a clear picture of the process. You never know when information might come in handy again. If you don't get a job now, another one could open up at the same company in a couple of months. In the event of that occurrence, well-kept records would enable you to contact key personnel quickly and efficiently.

Give yourself the best possible chance at the job by following basic job-hunting etiquette. Format your résumé neatly; proof it for errors; type or print it on a heavier bond paper than ordinary copy paper. If you are called in for an interview, wear appropriate clothing. Don't forget to choose a nice pair of shoes; people notice. Avoid chewing gum. Don't smoke. Offer a strong handshake. Make eye contact. Show your integrity by speaking honestly about yourself. After the interview is over, no matter what the outcome, send a pleasant thank-you note as a follow up. Good luck.

Career Investigation

College is an ideal time to investigate what career may be the one for you. Students are in all different stages of thought when it comes to future careers. You may have never thought too much about it; you may have already had a career for years and are looking for a change; you may have had your heart set on a career and are now having second thoughts. Although it doesn't matter how far along you are in knowing what you want to do, now is the time to make progress.

You can apply any of a number of strategies to your investigation. Brainstorm about career areas. Network; learn from what instructors and fellow students know about different careers and job opportunities. Outline your job possibilities by seeking out information at your career center, the library, or the office of the department in which you have decided to major. One of the most inspiring books to read is *What Color Is Your Parachute?*, by Richard Nelson Bolles. Based in exploring personal values and goal-setting, it walks you through self-exploration, job hunting, and interviews in a comprehensive, friendly format. Says Bolles of his treatment of the job-hunting process, "Our goal in this book is to empower you, during this one experience in your life, so that you will know hereafter how to do this on your own."

Any kind of job experience can clue you in to something you may want to turn into a career. Look for internships in areas that interest you; even if they don't pay much or at all, they can give you valuable experience and connections that may later lead to a permanent job. Volunteer. Most importantly, keep an open mind. You never know what you might be doing when a career will reach out and grab you by surprise.

FINANCIAL AID

Seeking help from various sources of financial aid has become a way of life for much of the student population. Education is an important but often pricey investment; the cost for a year of school in 1993-4 ranged from two to twenty-two thousand dollars, with the national average hovering around $6,000 for public institutions and over $15,000 for private ones (Digest of Education Statistics, 1994). Not many people can pull cash for tuition out of their pockets and pay in full without aid. In fact, according to data compiled in the academic year 1989-90, forty-four percent of students enrolled received some kind of aid, and that percentage will almost certainly continue to increase along with rising tuition costs.

You are responsible for figuring out how you can finance your education (or you and your parents, if they currently help to support you). In most cases, sources of financial aid won't seek you out and present you with a big check unannounced. You need to do some research to find out what's available, weigh the positive and negative effects of each option, decide what would work best for you, and apply.

Cynthia and Phillip McKee, in their book *Cash for College: The Ultimate Guide to College Scholarships*, estimate that around twenty-eight billion dollars is available annually in the form of grants, loans, and scholarships from colleges, states, private funds, and the federal government. "The reality of today's economy makes the cost of tuition a major factor in deciding which college to attend and even whether to attend college at all. We can't stress enough how important it is to start as early as possible to investigate scholarship opportunities." You may be able to take advantage of all kinds of different financial aid opportunities if you take the time to hunt them down.

Loans

A loan is a sum of money given to you by a person, bank, or other lending agency, usually to put toward a specific purchase. You, as the recipient of the loan, then must pay back the amount of the loan, plus interest, in regular payments that stretch over a predetermined period of time. Interest is the fee that you pay for the privilege of using money that belongs to someone else. The lender determines interest by taking a variable or fixed percentage of the loan; that percentage is dependent on the type of loan.

What happens when you apply for a loan?

❏ **The loaning agency must approve you.** You will meet with someone who will ask about what you and any other family members earn, how much savings you have, your credit history, anything you own that is of substantial value (a home/business), and your history of payment on any previous loans.

❏ **An interest charge will be set.** Interest can range from 5 percent to over 20 percent, depending on the loan and the economy. Variable-interest loans shift charges as the economy strengthens or weakens. Fixed rate loans have one interest rate that remains constant.

❏ **The loaning agency will establish a payment plan.** Most loan payments are made monthly, although some may be quarterly. The amount of the payment depends on the total amount of the loan, how much you can comfortably pay per month, and the length of the repayment period. Methods of payment include pay by phone, a convenient way to make a payment using touch-tone technology; coupon books that require you to mail a check with the corresponding coupon for each payment; and automatic disbursement, where the loan payment is automatically deducted from your savings account.

The federal government administers or oversees most student loans. Following are the main loan programs to which you can apply if you are eligible. Amounts vary according to individual circumstances; contact your school, bank, or federal student aid office for further information. In most cases, the amount is limited to the cost of your education minus any other financial aid you are receiving.

Perkins Loans. Carrying a low, fixed rate of interest, these loans are available to those with exceptional financial need (need is determined by a government-determined formula that indicates how large of a contribution toward your education your family should be able to make). Schools issue these loans from their own allotment of federal education funds and set their own application deadlines. After you graduate, you have a "grace period" before you have to begin repaying your loan in monthly installments. Your grace period is nine months if you were a student more than half-time; under half-time, the grace period decreases.

Stafford Loans. Students with exceptional need may qualify for a "subsidized" Stafford Loan, for which the government pays your interest. However, you don't need to demonstrate exceptional need to apply for a regular Stafford loan; you just have to be enrolled at least half-time. These loans have variable interest rates. Banks and credit unions are the lenders; there is no set deadline for application. Like Perkins loans, Stafford loans are repaid monthly, beginning six months after you finish your education.

Plus Loans. Your parents can apply for a Plus loan if they currently claim you as a dependent. They must also undergo a credit check in order to be eligible, although the loans are not based on income. Interest is variable; banks and credit unions are the lenders. Your parents will have to begin repayment sixty days after they receive the last loan payment; there is no grace period.

Federal Direct Student Loans. Beginning in academic year 1994-95, some schools will be participating in this new program, which issues Stafford Loans and Plus Loans that have the federal government as the lender instead of a bank or credit union. Other details remain the same as with the "regular" versions of both loans.

Don't overlook the possibility of taking out a loan from relatives. If you have a close relationship with a family member who has some money put away, you might be able to talk to that person about the possibility of helping you with your education. If the idea comes across well, discuss the terms of the loan as you would with any financial institution, detailing how and when you will receive loan disbursements as well as how and when you will repay the loan. You may want to show your gratitude by offering to pay a fixed rate of interest.

Grants and Scholarships

These sources of aid, although harder to come by and (in the case of scholarships) often based upon the exhibition of exceptional talents, give your finances a terrific boost because they require no repayment.

The following are federal grant programs.

Pell Grants. These grants are need-based; your expected family contribution must fall below a certain number in order for you to be eligible. You must apply to your school for a Pell Grant; the funds are provided by the government. The Pell Grant serves as a foundation of aid to which you may add other aid sources. Pell Grants require no repayment.

SEOG (Supplemental Educational Opportunity Grants). Administered by the financial aid administrator at participating schools, SEOG eligibility depends on need. Whereas the government guarantees that every student eligible for a Pell Grant will receive one, each school receives a limited amount of federal funds for SEOGs, and once it's gone, it's gone. Schools set their own application deadlines. Apply early. No repayment is required.

Work-Study. This program is need-based and encourages community service work. You will earn at least the federal minimum wage and will be paid hourly. Jobs can be on-campus (usually for your school) or off-campus (often with a non-profit organization or a local, state, or federal public agency). Jobs should be related in some way to your course of study. A financial aid administrator at your school will take your class schedule, academic progress, and any health restrictions into account when setting your work hours.

Remember that you must be a citizen or eligible noncitizen and be enrolled in a program that the government has determined is eligible in order to receive aid from any federal source. Other important details about federal grants and loans are available in *The Student Guide to Financial Aid*, published by the U.S. Department of Education. You might find one at your school's financial aid office, or request one at this address:

> **Federal Student Aid Programs**
> **U.S. Department of Education**
> **Washington, D.C. 20202**

Outside the federal government, you may receive grants or scholarships from individual departments at your school or your school's independent scholarship funds, local organizations such as the Rotary Club, or privately operated aid foundations. Unions and companies may offer scholarship opportunities for children of their employees. Memberships such as scouting organizations or the Y might offer scholarships as well. Religious organizations such as the Knights of Columbus or the Council of Jewish Federations might be another source. If you are disabled, female, of ethnic background, a strong athlete, or a child of someone who draws benefits from a state agency (such as a POW or MIA), you might find special scholarship opportunities for students with your special qualities.

It takes work to locate sources of financing, because many scholarships and work-study programs aren't widely advertised. Ask about opportunities at your school's financial aid office—a little investigation and legwork might help you stumble on some helpful financing. Visit your library or bookstore and look in the section on "college" or "financial aid;" books like *Cash for College* and other extensive guides to funding sources catalogue thousands of organizations for you and help you search through them to find what fits you. The McKees advise you to use common sense when applying for aid. "A missed deadline is money lost. Being neat, orderly, and prompt are traits not all students have mastered, yet they are essential in giving the best impression possible to a scholarship committee."

> *"It's helpful to spend some time becoming aware of your areas of achievement, your abilities, your interests, and your ambitions. Your initiative in developing these aspects of your personality will influence your success [in locating financial aid]."*
>
> Cynthia and Phillip McKee, experts on financing college and authors of *Cash for College: The Ultimate Guide to College Scholarships*

Banking Services

Your money can do more than just pay for your needs and wants; it can make more money for you, with the help of your bank. Choose a bank with locations convenient to your school, home, or workplace; hours that fit your schedule, account fees that aren't too high, and a convenient network of ATMs (automatic teller machines). The banks that you explore may have any combination of the following services. Decide which are important to you.

Checking accounts. Most banks offer more than one checking plan. Some accounts include *check-writing fees*, a charge (around 25 cents) that some banks put on every check you write or on any checks above a certain number per month. Some accounts are called *free checking*, meaning no fees per check and unlimited check writing—but be careful, you will often have to maintain a minimum balance in your account to qualify. Some accounts charge a *monthly fee* that is standard or varies according to your balance. *Interest checking* pays you a low rate of interest on your balance, although you may have to keep a certain balance or have a savings account at the same bank. If you open a *joint checking* account with another person, either of you can sign a check to make it valid.

Savings Accounts. The most basic, the *interest savings* account, pays a rate of interest to you determined by the bank and based on the economy. Many interest savings accounts do not have a required balance. However, a *high-yield savings* account usually does; this account may also have restrictions about how long you must leave the money in the bank untouched. In return, you receive a higher rate of interest. You may pay a penalty for taking money out early. A *certificate of deposit* (CD) or a *money market savings* account will also yield greater interest. CDs are purchased for a fixed amount of money to which you cannot add, and like a high-yield account, you may not take it out without penalty during a specified period of time. In contrast, money-market-account interest rates rise and fall as the economy changes, but you have unpenalized access to your money.

Smart Spending and Saving

You work hard to earn your wages and study hard to hold on to your grants and loans. Stay in control of where and how fast your money goes by following two important rules.

Live Beneath Your Means To live *beyond* your means is to spend more than you make, creating a debt; to live *beneath* your means is to spend less than you make, creating a savings. Even if you spend one dollar less than you make, you're moving in the right direction. Any amount of savings will give you a buffer zone that can help with emergencies or bigger expenditures. You won't always be able to live beneath your means; sometimes your most basic needs will create a deficit. If you find, however, that you're going into debt with extraneous purchases, adjust your spending. The pleasure that luxuries provide isn't worth the stress created by debt. A new CD player won't be much consolation in a financial crisis.

Pay Yourself First When you have that one dollar or more saved from your monthly expenses, put it in your savings account. Paying yourself helps you store money in your savings where it can grow until you need it. That savings could become security when you grow older, financing for your children's college education, help with a financial crisis, or a down payment on a large purchase. Don't think of the money left after paying bills as extra. If you include it in your budget as a payment to yourself that carries equal weight with your mortgage or rent payment, you will honor your commitment to yourself and to your success in life.

Savings Strategies

Here are some suggestions for saving a little bit of money here and there. You'd be amazed at how it adds up after a while.

❏ Reuse grocery bags for food storage and garbage.

❏ Hand-wash items you ordinarily dry-clean.

❏ Rent movies or attend bargain matinees.

- ❑ Check movies, CDs, tapes, and books on tape out of your library. Frequently there is no charge.

- ❑ Make popcorn instead of buying bags of chips.

- ❑ Walk instead of paying for public transportation.

- ❑ Buy detergent, paper products, toiletries, and other staples in bulk.

- ❑ Shop in secondhand stores or make your own clothing.

- ❑ Keep your possessions neat, clean, and properly maintained—they will last longer.

- ❑ Take advantage of weekly supermarket specials and bring coupons when you shop.

- ❑ Return bottles for deposits if you live in a state that accepts them.

- ❑ Trade clothing with friends and barter services (plumbing for baby-sitting, for example).

- ❑ Buy display models of appliances or electronics (stereo equipment, TVs, VCRs).

- ❑ Take your lunch instead of buying it.

- ❑ Make long-distance phone calls in the evening and on weekends, or write letters.

- ❑ Save on heat by dressing warmly and using lots of blankets; save on air conditioning by using fans.

- ❑ Have pot-luck parties; ask people to bring dinner foods or munchies.

Although budgeting is important, be careful not to sacrifice all of the little extras that make life enjoyable. Life is too short to restrict all of your fun activities for the sake of saving money. You may know people who have worked so hard throughout their lives that by the time they retire they have no energy to take advantage of the money they have saved—don't join that club. Make your fun less expensive fun—or save up for a while to splurge on a really special occasion.

Credit

Credit can be an incredible lifesaver or a black hole of debt. As Eric Clapton says in one of his well-known tunes, "it's in the way that you use it!"

Some businesses or stores offer credit in the form of accounts; your purchases go "on account" and you pay for them in installments (usually monthly). Most credit, though, comes in the form of a powerful little plastic card. You need to have a good credit history in order to be eligible for a credit card. When choosing a card, pay attention to the *annual fee* and *interest rates*, the two ways in which a credit card company makes money from you. Some cards have no annual fee; others may charge a flat rate of $10 to $50 per year. Interest rates can be fixed or variable. A variable rate of 12 percent may sound terrific until it shoots up to 18 percent in an economic downturn; you might be better off with a mid-range fixed rate that you can always count on.

Credit, noun. A sum of money made available by a bank or credit card company, on which a specified person or firm may draw

Real World Perspective

Q Aida Ramos, student at St. Mary's University in San Antonio, Texas

When I entered college I received a scholarship based on my performance in high school. Later I received another based on my academic success in college. One of the scholarships covers some of my funding throughout four years, but the other only applied to my first year of school. Both of them together still couldn't cover all my costs. Therefore, I have taken a job to supplement my income. I spend about 20 hours a week at a work-study job that I got through my school. I do secretarial work, and it keeps me very busy. Even that didn't do it all. I eventually also got a Stafford loan, which I found out about and applied for through my school's financial aid office.

I know that I haven't explored all of the solutions out there. It's hard to find time. Sometimes funding my education is overwhelming—I try to tell myself not to worry about it. I have also received a ton of credit card applications, and they are tempting. It seems that a lot of credit card companies target college students because they need money. I know that credit can be dangerous. How can I successfully take advantage of the funding opportunities out there in order to intelligently finance my education?

A Mr. William D. Leith, Director of Student Financial Aid, the University of Maryland at College Park, Maryland

You are on the right track. The three primary mechanisms for financing a higher education, all of which you are exploring, are grants, loans, and work. Of these, grants (or scholarships) are most advantageous because they do not need to be paid back. Eligibility for grant assistance is based on financial need as determined by a defined standard, merit, or both. Pursue available grant funds through the Financial Aid Office and academic departments at your institution as well as private outside sources (check your library for reference books). Perhaps the most important step is to apply early. Students that apply for grant funds early have a higher probability of receiving funds.

Once all sources of grant funds have been exhausted, many students (as you have found) need to work, borrow money, or both, to meet the financial obligation of higher education. Employment generally offers the student money, via a pay check, on a regular basis and may allow the student to gain valuable work experience. Work programs can, however, affect the amount of time and effort you can put into your educational pursuits. Weigh the pros and cons and decide on a schedule that you can handle.

Student loans are a common way of financing educational costs. Federal student loans allow students to borrow funds; students must generally begin repayment after graduation. In addition, federal loan programs will offer a cap on the interest rate over the life of the loan. There are also private loan programs available; however, their interest rates are usually tied to market conditions and will not offer interest rate caps.

Your intuition about the danger of credit cards is accurate. Their use to fund an education—whether through payment of tuition/room/board or through extensive use to cover other bills left unpaid because of educational costs—will be extremely expensive relative to using federal and private hours, and should only be used as a last resort.

What are the positive effects of using credit?

Establishing a good credit history. If you use your credit card moderately and pay your bills on time every month, you will make a positive impression on your **creditors** (the people to whom you owe money). Companies such as TRW track credit histories of everyone who has any sort of credit. If you are conscientious, you will establish a good **credit history** (the record of your credit use) and **credit rating** (the score a company like TRW will give you based on how good or bad your history is). How promptly you make loan payments and pay mortgage and utility bills affects your credit rating as well.

Emergencies. Few people carry enough cash to handle unexpected expenses. Your credit card can help you in emergency situations, for example, if you were stranded because of a car problem and needed lodging.

Record of purchases. Credit card statements give you a monthly record of purchases made, where they were made, and exactly how much was paid. Using your credit card for purchases that you want to remember, such as work expenses, can help you keep records for tax purposes.

Taking advantage of sales. Items that you need may go on sale when you don't have the cash to take advantage of the lower price. However, if you use your credit card, you can make the purchase at the sale price and pay it off gradually.

Bonuses offered by credit card issuers. In recent years, many companies have issued credit cards that offer bonuses based on a percentage of the money you spend using the card. For example, airlines offer free miles, oil companies offer free gasoline, and automobile dealers offer discounts on future car financing. If you know that you will use a card consistently and you have a real need for the bonus it offers, you may benefit from using this type of card.

What are credit's negative effects?

You are spending someone else's money. The money you spend belongs to the credit card company. The company then pays the retailer, counting on the fact that you will pay later. It can be tempting to overspend when the money isn't really yours and you don't have to face up to paying it right away. That can lead to trouble if you find you are unable to make your monthly payments.

You are taking out a high-interest loan. Buying on credit is similar to taking out a loan—you are using money with the promise to pay it back. However, loan rates, especially for fixed-interest loans, are often much lower than the 11 to 23 percent you will pay on credit card debt. Fifteen percent interest per year on a credit card debt that averages $2000 is approximately $300; five percent interest per year on a loan in the same amount is $100. Even if month by month it doesn't seem like much of a difference, you lose money if you pay more interest on your credit card debt than you earn on your savings. If you can't pay off your credit card every month, at least keep the debt lower than the amount of money you have saved.

Credit can be addictive. Using credit can be like a drug. It's fun because the pain of paying is put off until later. If you get hooked, though, you can wind up thousands of dollars in debt to creditors. The high interest will compound your debt, and if you fail to make payments, your credit rating will fall, potentially hurting your eligibility for loans and mortgages. You may lose your credit cards altogether.

Bad credit ratings can haunt you. Any time you are late with a payment, default on a payment, or in any way misuse your card, a derogatory statement will be entered on your credit history, lowering your credit rating. If a prospective employer or loan officer investigates and discovers that, you may seem less trustworthy and could lose the chance at the job or the loan.

Don't cause yourself credit trauma. Stay in control by having only one or two cards and paying bills regularly. Try to pay in full each month; if you can't, at least make as much of a dent in the bill as you can.

If you get into trouble, use this three-step Plan: Admit it, Fix it, Prevent it. *Admit* that you made a mistake, even though you may be embarrassed. Then you will be able to *fix* the problem by taking action to reduce your debt. Address the situation immediately and honestly in order to minimize the damages. Call the bank or credit card company to talk to them about the problem. Often they will help you draw up a payment plan that allows you to pay your debt gradually, in amounts that your particular budget can manage. Creditors would rather accept small payments than have no idea what the problem is.

Finally, *prevent* this problem from happening again. Figure out what got you into trouble and take steps to avoid it in the future if you can. Some financial disasters, such as medical emergencies, may be beyond your control. Overspending on luxuries, however, is something you have the power to avoid. Make a habit of balancing your checkbook. Cut up a credit card or two if you have too many. Don't let a high credit limit tempt you to spend. Pay every month, even if you pay only the minimum. If you work to clean up your act, your credit history will clean up as well.

Summing Up

Money isn't everything, but it certainly is a focus of modern life. If you control your money through detailed investigation of your finances and careful budgeting, you will have more resources with which to make intelligent financial decisions. When you want to increase your income, the opportunities are out there; exploring available loans, grants, and job opportunities will help you stay afloat as you complete your education. Controlling your spending and your use of credit will help you keep as much money in the bank as possible. If you can stay financially balanced while under the pressures of being a student, you will be that much more capable of managing your money when you have graduated and are working full time.

CHAPTER 10: APPLICATIONS

Keys for your Key Chain Skills Worth Keeping

List here what to you are the five most important keys, or skills, you have learned from reading this chapter.

1. _____
2. _____
3. _____
4. _____
5. _____

Key Into Your Life: Opportunities to Apply What You Learn
Exercise 1 Your Job Priorities

What kind of a job could you manage while you're in school? How would you want a job to benefit you? Discuss your requirements in each of the following areas.

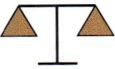

Salary/wage level
_____
_____

EX →

Time of day
_____
_____

Hours per week (part time vs. full time)
_____
_____

Duties
_____
_____

Location
_____
_____

Flexibility
_____
_____

Affiliation with school or financial aid program

_____

_____

What kind of job might fit all or most of your requirements? List three possibilities here.

1. _____

2. _____

3. _____

Exercise 2 Following your Job Leads

Choose one of the job possibilities you listed and follow up on it. What did you learn from your job leads about this type of work? Describe the results of your research in each of the following leads:

Help-Wanted listings in newspapers, magazines, or Internet databases

_____

_____

Listings of job opportunities/company contact information at your career center, student employment office, or independent employment agency

_____

_____

Bulletin boards at school or in the community

_____

_____

Contacts from friends or family members

_____

_____

Contacts from instructors, administrators, or counselors

_____

_____

Student employment office or career planning office personnel

_____

_____

School employees who administer work-study programs

_____
_____

Alumni

_____
_____

Current or former employers or co-workers

_____
_____

Exercise 3 Where Your Money Goes

Estimate your current expenses in dollars per month:

Expense	Amount
Rent/Mortgage payment	$
Utilities (electric, gas, heat, water)	$
Food	$
Telephone	$
Tuition	$
Books, lab fees, or other educational expenses	$
Loan payments (education or bank loans)	$
Car expenses (repairs, insurance, payments)	$
Gasoline/public transportation	$
Clothing/personal items	$
Entertainment	$
Child care (caregivers, clothing and supplies, other fees)	$
Medical care/insurance	$
Miscellaneous/unexpected	$
GRAND TOTAL:	$

The total is your total monthly expenses.

Exercise 4 Where Your Money Comes From

Calculate the money you take in each month. Divide any annual payments by twelve to derive the monthly figure.

INCOME SOURCE	AMOUNT
Regular work salary/wages (full time or part time)	$
Grants or work-study payments	$
Scholarships	$
Monthly assistance you may receive from family members	$
Any independent contracting work or private sale of items	$
Other	$
GRAND TOTAL:	$

Now, subtract the grand total of your monthly expenses (Exercise 3) from the grand total of your monthly income.

My income is $ _____ per month $ _____

My expenses are $ _____ per month   − $ _____

                                    CASH FLOW $ _____

Choose one: I have $ _____ positive cash flow.

                 I have $ _____ negative cash flow.

                 I pretty much break even.

Exercise 5 Adjusting Your Budget

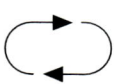

If you have a negative cash flow, you can either increase your income or decrease your spending. You may choose to do both. Start your adjustment by cutting spending. Increasing income often means taking on more work; you may or may not have the time for that now. Jot down here when and how you plan to cut your expenses.

EXPENSE	HOW YOU WILL CUT EXPENSES	AMOUNT SAVED
Rent/Mortgage		$
Utilities		$
Food		$
Telephone		$
Tuition		$
Educ. exp.		$
Loan payments		$
Car expenses		$
Gasoline/public trans.		$
Clothing/personal items		$
Entertainment		$
Child care		$
Medical care/insurance		$
Misc./unexpected		$
GRAND TOTAL:		$

Go back to your list of current expenses and subtract the amount you plan to save (the grand total from this exercise) from the total expenses per month. Recalculate your cash flow with that new number. If you had a negative cash flow before, have you moved into the positive? If you had a positive cash flow, how much more do you have the potential to save?

My current expenses: $ _____ per month $ _____

My planned savings: $ _____ per month   − $ _____

                      NEW EXPENSE AMOUNT $ _____

My income: $ _____ per month $ _____

New expense amount: $ _____ per month   − $ _____

                      NEW CASH FLOW $ _____

REALITY RESOURCES: MANAGING FINANCES AND WORK

Key to Cooperative Learning: Building Teamwork Skills

Savings Brainstorm

In groups of two to four, discuss the areas of your life where the lack of money causes problems and/or stress. Come up with five that you feel are the most important ones. Then, brainstorm strategies that can help; think of savings ideas, ways to control spending, and methods of alleviating the situations that cause financial trouble. Agree on a list of viable ideas for each area of financial trouble and share it with your class.

Key to Self-Expression: Discovery through Journal Writing

You and your Credit Cards

How do you use your credit cards? Are you conservative, overindulgent, or in-between? Do you pay on time or not? Do you pay off each card every month? How does using a credit card make you feel—powerful, excited, apprehensive, or nervous? For what sort of purchases do you use credit cards? What would you like to change about the way you use credit?

_____
_____
_____
_____
_____
_____
_____
_____
_____
_____

KEY TO YOUR PERSONAL PORTFOLIO: YOUR PAPER TRAIL TO SUCCESS

Financial History

Create for yourself a detailed financial picture. First, put your budget exercises, or copies of them, in your portfolio so that you have a record of your spending habits. Then answer on a separate sheet these questions and keep your work on file. Keeping accurate financial records is vital to being able to make intelligent financial decisions; your records are the facts and resources for decision making. Including your work record will help you maintain an accurate résumé and update it as needed.

In addition, you should always have a copy of important account and credit card numbers separate from your wallet or purse. That way, should you lose your cards, you have records of all of your credit card numbers and can cancel them immediately. Note: do NOT include any PINs (personal identification numbers) anywhere in your portfolio. Any record of PINs should be kept separately from credit cards or credit card numbers for your protection.

1. What sources make up your financial aid package? List school/federal/personal loans, scholarship funds, grants, and the amount that you pay out of pocket. Indicate all account numbers, payment plans, and records of payment, including dates and check numbers if applicable.

2. List bank accounts to which you have access, including all names on the accounts, bank names, type of accounts, and account numbers. Include any restrictions on the accounts such as minimum balances or time frames during which you will receive a penalty for removing funds.

3. List any non-academic loans you are currently repaying, noting the purpose of the loan, repayment schedule, loan payment amounts and dates of payments made, bank names and loan account numbers, and loan types.

4. List credit cards you use. Include major credit cards (American Express, Visa, MasterCard, Discover, etc.) as well as specific cards such as cards for gas stations or department stores. For each card, include:

❏ Name on the card

❏ Card number

❏ Expiration date

❏ Date you got the card

❏ Payment style (pay in full, pay minimum each month, etc.)

❏ Problems (late payments, lost cards, card fraud, etc.)

❏ Current balance and date

5. Detail your current job history. List the jobs you have had or currently have. Include the following information for each:

❏ Name of the company/business

❏ Job title

❏ Job descriptions (your duties and responsibilities)

❏ The dates of your employment there

❏ Personal contacts you made and have maintained (possible sources of references)

After you have completed this information, store it in your portfolio. Be sure to update it whenever there are changes.

G R O

Grou

11

Your Life:
Moving Ahead

Graduation is often referred to as *commencement*; the end of your student career is the beginning or continuation of your life as a full-time working citizen. When you end the single life by marrying, you start over as a spouse. Moving to a new state means ending your time in one place and beginning a new life in another. You can take any ending and find within it a new and different path to follow.

As you come to the end of your work in this course, you have built up a wealth of knowledge. Where will it take you? In what directions should you guide your studies, your career, and your personal growth? When you take responsibility for managing the constant change you will encounter, you will find that continuing to learn brings immense rewards.

The master key: lifelong learning will discuss ways in which you can making learning a habit for life. You will explore what can be positive about **when you fall short of your goals**, and **handling conflict and criticism** will help you turn problematic and tense situations into learning experiences. You will consider giving back to others and to the earth by investigating how you can **make a difference**. Finally, in *living your mission*, you will revisit your personal mission, molding it as you experience change and taking it with you into the future.

The Master Key: Lifelong Learning

As you change and the world changes, new knowledge and ideas continually emerge. Chances to learn something new filter through every moment of your time. Being a student is a gift and a golden opportunity; you are able to make learning your focus for a period of time, and your school focuses on you in return, adopting as its primary purpose your ease of access to all kinds of knowledge and experiences. Taking advantage of the academic atmosphere by developing a habit of seeking out new opportunities to learn will enable you to continue your learning long after you have graduated, even in the face of the pressures of everyday life. Visualize yourself as a lifelong student; make your vision a self-fulfilling prophecy.

Here are some ways you can continually explore new ideas.

Investigate new interests. All around you, information and events catch your attention. Take your interest one step further and find out more. If you are fascinated by a television show about animal rights, find out how you can get involved in your area. If a friend of yours starts to take yoga, try out a class with him. Turn the regretful, "I wish I had tried that," into the purposeful, "I'm going to do it."

Read books, newspapers, magazines, and other collections of words. Check out what's on the bestseller list at your bookstore. Ask your friends about books that have changed their lives. Stay on top of current change in your community, your state, your country, and the world by reading newspapers and magazines. Explore religious literature, old letters, and pages and newsgroups on the internet. Reading opens a world of new perspectives.

Spend time with interesting people. When you meet someone new who inspires you and makes you think, keep in touch. Have a dinner party and invite one person or couple from each corner of your life—your family, your work, your school, a club to which you belong, your neighborhood. Sometimes, meet for reasons beyond just being social. Start a book club, a play reading club, a hiking group, or an investing group. Learn something new from each other.

Pursue improvement in your studies and in your career. When at school, take classes outside of your major. After you have graduated, find time to continue your education both in your field and in the realm of general knowledge. Stay on top of ideas, developments, structural changes, and new technology in your field by seeking out continuing education courses. Sign up for career-related seminars. Take single courses at a local college or community learning center.

Talk to people of different generations than yours. Younger people can learn from the experienced, broad perspective of those belonging to older generations; older people can learn from the fresh and often radical perspective of those younger than themselves. Even beyond the benefits of new knowledge, there is much to be gained from developing mutual respect among the generations.

Delve into other cultures. Eat at a restaurant that serves food from a country you've never seen. Visit the home of a friend who has grown up in a culture entirely different from your own. Initiate conversations with people of different races, religions, and ethnic backgrounds, asking them about their experiences. Travel to different countries. Travel nearby to different neighborhoods or cities near you—they may be so different from what you are accustomed to that you may find them just as foreign.

Nurture a spiritual life. You can find spirituality in many places; it isn't just a benefit of regularly attending a house of worship. "A spiritual life of some kind is absolutely necessary for psychological 'health,'" says psychologist and author Thomas Moore in his book *The Care of the Soul.* "Fulfilling work, rewarding relationships, personal power, and relief from symptoms are all gifts of the soul. They are particularly elusive in our time because we don't believe in the soul and therefore give it no place in our hierarchy of values…we live in a time of deep division, in which mind is separated from body and spirituality is at odds with materialism." The words *soul* and *spirituality* hold different meaning for each individual. Decide what they mean to you. Whether you discover them in music, organized religion, friendship, nature, cooking, sports, or anything else, making them a priority in your life will help you find a greater sense of balance and meaning.

Experience what others create. Art is "an adventure of the mind" (Eugene Ionesco, playwright); "a means of knowing the world" (Angela Carter, author); something that "does not reproduce the visible; rather, it makes visible" (Paul Klee, painter); "a lie that makes us realize truth" (Pablo Picasso, painter); a revealer of "our most secret self" (Jean-luc Godard, filmmaker). Through art you can discover new ideas and shed new light on old ones. Explore all kinds of art and focus on any forms that hold your interest. Seek out whatever moves you—music, visual arts, theater, photography, dance, domestic arts, performance art, film and television, poetry, prose, and more.

Make your own creations. Bring out the artist in you. Take a class in drawing, in pottery, or in quilting. Learn to play an instrument that you have always wanted to master. Write poems for your favorite people or stories to read to your kids. Invent a recipe. Design and build a set of shelves for your home. Create a memoir of your life. You are a creative being. Express yourself, and learn more about yourself, through art.

Lifelong learning is the master key that unlocks every door you will encounter on your journey. If you keep it firmly in your hand, you will discover worlds of knowledge—and a place for yourself within them.

When You Fall Short of Your Goals

Things don't always go how you want them to go. Sometimes you will let yourself down or disappoint others. You may make mistakes or lose your motivation. Everyone does, no matter who they are or how smart or accomplished they may be. The distinction lies in how you choose to deal with what goes wrong. The best move is to accept falling short of your goals as part of being human. If you can forgive yourself, you will have the confidence to pick yourself up and keep going.

You have a choice when deciding how to handle a mistake, disappointment, or shortfall. You can blame the mistake on someone else or pretend it never happened, not taking responsibility for the consequences. You can heap blame on yourself, destroying your self-esteem with negative self-talk. On the other hand, you can analyze the causes and effects of what happened, make any amends that you can, and decide how to change your action or approach in the future. The latter choice is ideal. It allows you to take responsibility for what happened and learn from the experience without damaging your positive sense of self.

Sometimes it seems easier to blame others or to forget what happened because you can avoid the painful process of admitting personal flaws and trying to improve problem areas. However, taking the easy route denies you your opportunity to grow.

Real World Perspective

Q **Christine Carol Richardson, student at Southeastern Oklahoma State, in Durant, Oklahoma**

My first goal is to graduate with a bachelor's degree before I turn forty. I would eventually like my doctorate, but I have had to rethink my goals a few times. I'm an older, married woman with a home and a family, and I can't just move off to go to graduate school. When I decided to go back to college I found a small, local school with a good program; I picked the best school within driving distance. Sometimes I have to set my sights a little lower.

Being an older student, I've also encountered criticism for going back to school. People who have been in the work world for a while and return to school manage their time better than traditional students, and treat school more like a job, simply because they've had more experience. But many traditional students feel threatened by that. They feel that older students are robbing other students of a college experience. Others criticize me because I'm not at home with my family. Contrary to the "supermom" belief, I can't do everything. I've really had to rethink my values. My family supports me, and I couldn't do this without them. We know that we all have to sacrifice and do what we can to reach our goals. How can I keep a clear vision of my goals without being distracted from all of the expectations and criticism from those around me? What can I do to envision what I want from my future and take the steps I need to take to get there?

A **Barbara Crenshaw, executive coach, career consultant, and president of Crenshaw Associates, New York City**

Having a goal is the first step toward success. Believing it is attainable is the second step. The third step is staying focused on the ultimate result and taking one step at a time. First, focus on your undergraduate degree; then, the higher degree; and finally, as well as along the way in the jobs you take, your chosen profession. Your strength lies within. You can maintain your clear vision by writing down what you hope to achieve and setting a point in time when your goal will be reached.

Maintaining and expressing a positive self-image can improve reality. Explain your ambition to the people who try to diminish your efforts, showing them how your determination to succeed will bring you accomplishment and positive change in your life. Put the thought out to yourself, the universe, and your critics that everyone will gain from mutual support. Talk to others about how they can help you by offering encouragement, helping with babysitting during exams, etc. Cultivate new friendships with students old and young who share your goals and can work with you in projects and study sessions. Support each other as you share the road of learning, progress, and positive growth.

There will be sacrifices, of course; however, they won't seem that important when you look at the end result. Your accomplishment will set an example for your children and will instill in you the pride that you should rightfully take in your achievement.

Only the acceptance and investigation of the shortfall brings you new knowledge that will help you make better choices in the future.

For example, imagine that in the aftermath of a long night of studying you forgot to go to your part-time work-study commitment the next day. Because you weren't there, a crucial curriculum project that needed to be completed and sent was not touched. An entire class and instructor have been affected by your mistake. You could blame your supervisor who didn't post a new schedule, forget it ever happened, or make yourself miserable with guilt. However, the best response would be to realize that because you were overtired, you neglected to call and confirm your schedule. You could then apologize to the instructor and see if there were still a chance to finish up part of the work in the time remaining in the day. Finally, you could set a goal to try to remember to note your work schedule regularly in your date book and check it more often.

Think about the people you consider exceptionally smart and successful. They didn't rise to the top without taking risks and making their share of mistakes. They have built much of their success upon their willingness to recognize and learn from their shortfalls. If you keep up with national news, you'll notice that the President of the United States often has to publicly confess mistakes to the country's citizens, discussing what has been learned and what will happen differently in the future. You too can benefit from staying open to this kind of active, demanding, hard-won education.

Learning involves change and growth. Let what you learn from falling short of your goals inspire new and better ideas.

HANDLING CONFLICT AND CRITICISM

Conflict and criticism, as unpleasant as they can often be, are natural dynamics in the give and take of getting along with others. You can't avoid them, but you can control how you handle them. They too can be agents of change; if you stay open to the lessons they teach, you will be able to make positive changes based on what you have learned.

Conflict

Conflicts large and small arise when there is a clash of ideas or interests. You may have small conflicts with a housemate over food left out overnight, a door left unlocked, or a bill that needs paying. On the other end of the spectrum, you might encounter major conflicts with your significant other about finances, with an instructor about a failing grade, or with a friend about a secret that shouldn't have been revealed.

Conflict is one of the toughest hurdles you will encounter in your relationships. It can create anger and frustration, shutting down lines of communication and putting up hostile barriers that may stay in place for a long time. However, if calmly and intelligently handled, conflict can actually shed light on new ideas and help to strengthen bonds between those involved.

The primary key to conflict resolution is calm and open communication. Before you can apply the problem-solving process to the situation, you must be able to set aside your anger. Strong emotions can set up barriers to communication that foil even the best intentions. In order to steady yourself for conflict resolution, know your tendencies and work to counteract them. If you tend to be aggressive, give yourself time to cool down before you address a conflict. If you tend to be passive, make an effort to assert yourself by acknowledging and expressing your anger as soon as you can articulate it.

Once you are ready to calmly lay the issues on the table, apply your critical thinking skills.

> *Identify and analyze the problem.* This step can be difficult, as often the real problem hides behind other seemingly important issues. A student may approach an instructor regarding the problem of a failing grade in a course;

that problem is a mask for the real issue, which could involve the student's inability to work up to par or the instructor's inability to perceive the student's efforts. Dig deep and find the real cause of the problem; then, discuss the effects the problem has had on everyone involved.

Brainstorm possible solutions. What have you or other people done in a similar situation? What would take into account the needs of all concerned? What would cause the least stress? What would be the most honest?

Explore each solution. Evaluate the positive and negative effects of each solution. Why might each work, or not work, or work partially? Don't prejudge solutions until you have spent some time evaluating their possibilities. Make sure everyone has a chance to express an opinion.

Choose, execute, and evaluate the solution you decide is best. When you have implemented your choice, look at its effects. Did your solution turn out to have more negative effects or more positive ones? Was it a good choice?

One more hint: Use *I* statements throughout your exchange. Nothing shuts down communication during a resolution of conflict like a few well-aimed accusations. A friend with whom you are discussing a conflict will respond far more readily to "I was hurt when I wasn't included" than to the more accusatory "You didn't bother to call me. You left me out." If you keep the focus on the effects that the problem has had on you rather than on your interpretation of what happened, the other person will feel more willing to open up. The more you talk, the more you will both learn and change what you do in the future.

Criticism

Rarely do people get everything right all the time. Through criticism, people communicate what went wrong and discover how to improve. If you reject criticism without consideration, you reject an opportunity to learn something new and to improve yourself. Even if you eventually decide that you disagree with an item of criticism, you have still learned something about yourself from exploring the possibility. Be careful not to interpret criticism as a threat; you won't gain from being defensive and closing yourself off. Steel your self-esteem; know that you are strong enough to embrace criticism and become a better person because of it.

Different styles of criticism have different effects on the person on the receiving end. Criticism is considered constructive when it is offered supportively and contains useful suggestions for improvement. If it is delivered in a negative or harsh manner, criticism can create tension and bad feelings. If you can learn to give and accept criticism, making corresponding changes in your behavior, you will improve your relationships and your productivity. Well-handled criticism brings about substantial, lasting change.

When you offer criticism, use the following techniques to make it productive:

1. Make sure the behavior you intend to criticize is changeable. Chronic lateness can be changed; a physical inability to perform a task cannot.

2. Define specifically the behavior you want to criticize, refraining from dragging any side issues into the conversation.

3. Carefully choose a convenient time and a private place to talk.

4. Stay calm and be brief. Avoid threats, ultimatums, or accusations. Use *I* messages and choose positive, nonthreatening words.

5. Explain the effects caused by the behavior that warrants the criticism. Help the person understand why a change needs to happen, and talk about options in detail. Compare and contrast the effects of the current behavior with the effects of a potential change.

6. Offer help in changing the behavior.

Remember that repeated criticism is valid, even if you don't understand where it's coming from

When you find yourself on the receiving end of criticism, use these coping techniques:

1. Listen to the criticism and consider it carefully before you speak up. Resist the desire to defend yourself until you've heard all the details. Use your listening techniques.

2. If you accept the criticism as true, say so. If you are unsure, take time to think. Regularly repeated criticism is probably valid.

3. Ask for suggestions of how to change the criticized behavior. You could ask, "How would you handle this if you were in my place?"

4. Before the conversation ends, summarize the criticism and your response to it. Repeat it back to the person who offered it. Make sure both of you understand the situation in the same way.

5. If you feel that the criticism is valid, plan a specific strategy for correcting the behavior. Think over what you have learned from the change. If you don't agree with the criticism even after the whole conversation, explain your behavior from your point of view.

Accept and give criticism calmly, and you will learn from the experience. Even when you disagree, don't dismiss it right away. Did you ever reject criticism from a parent, only to realize months or even years later that he or she was right on target? Sometimes it will take you a while to face up to something you need to improve. Change takes time and courage.

Making a Difference

Everyday life is demanding; you have at any given moment a myriad of needs that require attention. It's easy to become so caught up in the issues of your own life that you neglect to look outside your immediate circle of need. However, you may have moments when you realize that your larger purpose may extend beyond your personal life. You have spent a great deal of time in this course working to improve yourself. Now that you've come so far, why not extend some of that energy and effort to the world outside? With all that you have to offer, you have the power to make all kinds of positive differences in the lives of others.

Your Imprint on the World

As difficult as your life can sometimes seem to be, looking outside yourself and into the lives of others can help put everything in perspective. Whereas you shouldn't negate your own hardships, you can see them more reasonably when you look at them in light of what is happening elsewhere in the world. Someone is always worse off than you; therefore, you always have something to give to others. Making a lasting difference in the lives of others is something to be proud of.

If you could eavesdrop on someone talking about you to another person, what would you want to hear? Would you want to be considered as a thoughtful, caring person? What you do for others makes an imprint that can have far more impact than you may imagine. Giving one person hope, comfort, or help can improve their perspective on life in a significant way. Then they in turn may be able to offer help to someone else. If each person contributes to this cycle of positive energy, many significant improvements can happen.

How can you make a difference? Many schools and companies are realizing the importance of community involvement and have appointed committees or established clearinghouses to find and organize volunteering opportunities. Make some kind of volunteering activity a priority on your schedule. Join a group from your company that tutors at a school. Organize a group of students to clean, repair, or entertain at a nursing home or halfway house. Look for what's available to you or create opportunities on your own. Here is a list of organizations that provide volunteer opportunities; you might also look into more local efforts or private clearinghouses that set up a number of different smaller projects.

- American Red Cross
- Amnesty International
- Audubon Society

- Big Brothers and Big Sisters
- Churches, synagogues, temples, and affiliated organizations such as the Ys
- Educational support organizations
- Greenpeace
- Hospitals
- Kiwanis/Knights of Columbus/Lions Club/Rotary
- Libraries
- Nursing homes
- Planned Parenthood
- School districts
- Scouting organizations
- Share Our Strength/other food donation organizations
- Shelters and organizations supporting the homeless
- Sierra Club/World Wildlife Fund

Sometimes it's hard to find time to volunteer when so many responsibilities compete for your attention. One solution is to combine other activities with volunteer work. Get exercise on a cleaning project or bring the whole family to help out at a nursing home on a weekend afternoon. Whatever you do, your actions will have a ripple effect, creating positive effects for those you help and those they encounter in turn.

Valuing Your Environment

Your environment is your home. When you value it, you help to maintain a clean, safe, and healthy place to live. What you do every day doesn't just affect you, it also has an impact on others around you and on the future. One famous slogan says that if you are not part of the solution, you are part of the problem. Every saved bottle, environmentally aware child, and reused bag is part of the solution. Take responsibility for what you can control—your own habits—and develop sound practices that contribute to the health of the environment.

Recycle anything that you can What can be recycled varies with the system set up in your area. When you notice products in the store that make use of recycled materials, patronize those companies—reward them for their dedication.

Trade and reuse items When children have grown too old for the crib, baby clothes, and toys, give away whatever is still usable. Trade clothes with your friends when you get tired of items and don't wear them anymore. Rinse out the clear produce bags you get at the supermarket and use them as sandwich baggies. Wrap presents in plain newspaper and decorate with markers. Use your imagination—there are many, many items that you can reuse, all around you.

Respect the outdoors You can find all different ways to participate in maintaining a healthy environment. Use products that reduce chemical waste. Pick up after yourself. Support the maintenance of parks and the preservation of natural, undeveloped land. Be creative; one young woman planned a cleanup of a local lakeside area as the main group activity for the guests at her birthday party (she joined them, of course). Everyone benefits when each takes part.

LIVING YOUR MISSION

As you learn and change, so may your idea of your life's mission. Whether you have changed your mission or solidified it, your progress has given you a greater sense of security in your choices. Think again about yourself. How has your idea of where you want to be changed since you first opened this book? How has your self-image changed? What have you learned about your values, your goals, your unique qualities, and your styles of communication and learning? Consider what has changed in your five goal areas: Personal, Family, Career, Financial, and Lifestyle. As you continue to grow and develop, keep your goals fluid, adjusting them to your changes and discoveries.

Stephen Covey says in *The Seven Habits of Highly Effective People*, "Change—real change—comes from the inside out. It doesn't come from hacking at the leaves of attitude and behavior with quick fix personality ethic techniques. It comes from striking at the root—the fabric of our thought, the fundamental essential paradigms which give definition to our character and create the lens through which we see the world."

It's a real risk to examine yourself deeply in that way. Most of all, it demands courage. People naturally resist change because it is much more difficult to question your established beliefs and face the unknown than it is to stay with a comfortable status quo. When you have the courage to risk the consequences of trying something unfamiliar, of admitting ignorance, or of challenging what you thought you knew, you give yourself unbounded opportunities to learn. You can see yourself safely through changes you never anticipated if you make the effort to be true to your mission each day, each week, each month, and for years to come.

> *"You would be wise not to try to approach this problem of 'your Mission in life' as primarily an intellectual puzzle... It is your will and your heart that must be involved in the search as well as your mind. To put it quite simply, it takes the total person to learn one's total Mission."*
>
> Richard Nelson Bolles, job-hunting expert and author of the 25th anniversary edition of *What Color Is Your Parachute? A Practical Manual for Job-Hunters and Career-Changers*

Bessie and Sadie Delany, sisters and accomplished African-American women both over one hundred years old, are two incredible examples of lives well led and choices well made. They took risks, becoming professionals in a time when women, especially minority women, were often denied both respect and opportunity. They learned from their hardships and were determined to teach to others what they learned, working hard to fight racial division and prejudice. They maintained their conviction that they are beautiful, intelligent, able people with an immense ability to give. As they look back on their lives, they can honestly say they have no regrets. Says Sadie in their *Book of Everyday Wisdom*, "If there's anything I've learned in all these years, it's that life is too good to waste a day. It's up to you to make it sweet."

Nothing significant is ever accomplished without sticking your neck out and taking risks. As a lifelong learner, you will always have a new direction in which to grow and a new challenge to face. Enjoy the richness of life by living each day to the fullest, developing your talents and potential into the achievement of your most valued goals.

CHAPTER 11: APPLICATIONS

Keys for your Key Chain: Skills Worth Keeping

List here what to you are the five most important keys, or skills, you have learned from reading this chapter.

1. _____
2. _____
3. _____
4. _____
5. _____

Key Into Your Life: Opportunities to Apply What You Learn
Exercise 1 Changes in Goals

Have you experienced any shifts in your goals? Think about what may have changed since you began this course about what you want out of life. List three major goals for each of the five goal areas. If any of these goals are significantly different from before, highlight the goal or goals and discuss why the change occurred.

 → EX

Personal

1. _____
   _____
2. _____
   _____
3. _____
   _____

Discuss changes:

_____
_____
_____

Family

1. _____
   _____
2. _____
   _____

3. _____
_____

Discuss changes:
_____
_____
_____

Lifestyle

1. _____
_____

2. _____
_____

3. _____
_____

Discuss changes:
_____
_____
_____

Career

1. _____
_____

2. _____
_____

3. _____
_____

Discuss changes:
_____
_____
_____

Financial

1. _____
   _____

2. _____
   _____

3. _____
   _____

Discuss changes:

_____
_____
_____

Exercise 2 Conflicts

Read the following scenario and analyze all of the different conflicts within. Offer suggestions for ways to solve each.

Andrea's husband Stuart, who works at night, reset the alarm clock improperly when he went to sleep at 6 A.M. and Andrea didn't wake up in time for work. She arrived late only to find that she had missed an important meeting with her supervisor about a project that had become top priority. Behind on her work and dealing with an angry supervisor, Andrea had to figure out a way to complete the work before she left at 1:00 P.M. She decided that she would have to stay late. Realizing that would make her late for her afternoon class, she called a classmate and asked her to let the instructor know the situation.

When she slipped into class later on, the instructor stopped the lecture to publicly acknowledge her lateness. Looking at her friend, Andrea realized that the friend had forgotten to give the instructor the message. The instructor gave Andrea a failing grade on that day's quiz since she had missed it at the start of class. Driving home, Andrea was so preoccupied about her day that she forgot to pick up a prescription that Stuart needed. He had to pick it up later himself and was in turn late to work. What a day.

Conflicts:

_____
_____
_____
_____
_____

Solutions:

___

Exercise 3 Criticism: Dishing It Out and Taking It

For each of the following problem situations, write two or three sentences of constructive criticism that can help to bring about a solution. Write in the first person (*I* messages).

1. Your sister borrows your sweater again without asking; this time, she makes a hole in it.

___

2. During a test, you spot a classmate reading information written on a crib sheet.

___

3. Your significant other arrives four hours after the expected time without having called you.

___

What is the most valid criticism anyone has given you in the last six months? How did you handle it when you were told? What have you done to address this criticism?

___

Exercise 4 Volunteering

Research volunteering opportunities in your community. What are the organizations? What are their needs? List five possibilities that would fit your schedule.

1. _____
2. _____
3. _____
4. _____
5. _____

Of these five, choose one that you know you will have time to try over the next two weeks. Schedule it and do it. Describe the experience. Would you do it again? If not, why not? What else would you consider?

_____
_____
_____
_____
_____
_____
_____
_____
_____
_____
_____

Key to Cooperative Learning: Building Teamwork Skills

Group Affirmation

Gather in groups of three to five. Each member of the group should independently write two goals on a piece of paper: one specific goal that he or she has attained, and one specific goal that he or she wants to work harder to achieve. When all are ready, sit in a circle. Each member should first take turns sharing details and thoughts about the successful goal. Show your support. Congratulate each other. If you know a group member well and have seen the difference hard work has made, say so. Then, go around the group again, giving each member a chance to bring up the goal that needs work. Offer suggestions and ideas. Boost each other's motivation by discussing the positive effects that can result from working on the goal.

Key to Self-Expression: Discovery through Journal Writing

Making Mistakes

Describe the biggest mistake you made in the last three months. What happened? How long did it take you to realize you had made a mistake? Were you able to remedy the situation? How? What did you learn from making this mistake? How has it changed you and your behavior?

Key to Your Personal Portfolio: Your Paper Trail to Success

Revised Mission Statement

Retrieve the mission statement you wrote at the end of Chapter 3. Give yourself a day or so to think it over; then, make any changes according to the changes that have occurred in you. Add new priorities and goals and delete those that are no longer valid. Continue to update your mission statement so that it reflects your growth and development, helping to guide you through the changes that await you in the future. Write your mew mission statement here.

REFERENCES

LEARNING AND THINKING

Lyman, Frank T., Jr. "Think-Pair-Share, Thinktrix, Thinklinks, and Weird Facts: An Interactive System for Cooperative Thinking." From *Enhancing Thinking Through Cooperative Learning*, edited by Neil Davidson and Toni Worsham. New York: Columbia University Teachers College Press, 1992. Pages 169-181.

Lyman, Frank T., Jr. "The Think Trix: A Classroom Tool for Thinking in Response to Reading," from *Reading: Issues and Practices*, edited by Joan Develin Coley. *Yearbook of the State of Maryland International Reading Association Council*, Vol. 4. Pages 15-18.

Toffler, Alvin and Heidi. *Creating a New Civilization: The Politics of the Third Wave*. Atlanta: Turner Publishing, Inc., 1995. Pages 19-40.

von Oech, Roger. *A Whack on the Side of the Head*. New York: Warner Books, 1990. Pages 11-168.

von Oech, Roger. *A Kick in the Seat of the Pants*. New York: Harper & Row Publishers, 1986. Pages 5-21.

STUDY SKILLS

Armstrong, William H. and M. Willard Lampe II. *Barron's Pocket Guide to Study Tips: How to Study Effectively and Get Better Grades*. New York: Barron's Educational Series, 1990. Pages 55-77, 229-245.

Lerner, Marcia. *Math Smart: Essential Math for these Numeric Times*. New York: Villard Books, 1995. Pages xi-59.

Lorayne, Harry. *Super Memory — Super Student: How to Raise Your Grades in 30 Days*. Boston: Little, Brown & Company, 1990. Pages 3-52.

WRITING

Friedman, Bonnie. *Writing Past Dark: Envy, Fear, Distractions, and Other Dilemmas in the Writer's Life*. New York: Harper Collins, 1993. Pages 1-8, 105-128.

Strunk, William Jr. and E.B. White. *The Elements of Style*. New York: Macmillan Publishing Co., Inc. 1979. Pages 15-33.

Troyka, Lynn Quitman. *Handbook for Writers*, Second Edition. Englewood Cliffs: Prentice Hall, 1990. Pages 2-159.

Troyka, Lynn Quitman. *Quick Access Reference For Writers*. Englewood Cliffs: Prentice Hall, 1995. Pages 1-27.

SELF-MANAGEMENT

Brown, Marvin T., Ph.D. *The Ethical Process: A Strategy for Making Good Decisions.* Upper Saddle River, New Jersey: Prentice Hall, 1995. Pages 1-32.

McKee, Cynthia Ruiz and McKee, Philip C. Jr. *Cash for College: The Ultimate Guide to College Scholarships.* New York: Hearst Books, 1994. Pages 3-13, 47-55.

Timm, Paul R., Ph.D. *Successful Self-Management: A Psychologically Sound Approach to Personal Effectiveness.* Los Altos, California: Crisp Publications, Inc., 1987. Pages 22-41.

PERSONAL DEVELOPMENT

Beattie, Melody. *Codependent No More: How To Stop Controlling Others and Start Caring for Yourself.* San Francisco: Harper San Francisco, 1992. Pages 27-95.

Bolles, Richard Nelson. *The 1995 What Color Is Your Parachute? A Practical Manual for Job-Hunters and Career Changers.* Berkeley: Ten Speed Press, 1995. Pages 11-23, 80-92, 446-450.

Chapman, Elwood N. *Your Attitude Is Showing: A Primer of Human Relations.* Chicago: Science Research Associates, Inc., 1987. Pages 16-20.

Covey, Stephen. *The Seven Habits of Highly Effective People.* New York: Simon & Schuster, 1989. Pages 70-144, 309-318.

Delany, Sarah and Elizabeth Delany with Amy Hill Hearth. Book of Everyday Wisdom. New York: Kodansha International, 1994. Page 123.

Moore, Thomas. *The Care of the Soul.* New York: Harper Perennial, 1992. Pages xi-xx.

HEALTH

Benson, Herbert, M.D. and Eileen M. Stuart, R.N., C.M.S. The Wellness Book. New York; Simon & Schuster, 1992. Pages 8-28, 103-123, 129-140, 154-165, 177-229.

Editors of the University of California at Berkeley Wellness Letter. *The New Wellness Encyclopedia.* New York: Houghton Mifflin, 1995. Pages 68-75, 77-85, 454.

Griest, John H., M.D. and James W. Jefferson, M.D. "*Dealing with depression: Taking Steps in the Right Direction.*" New York: Roerig, Pfizer, and Pratt pharmaceutical companies, 1992.

Louden, Jennifer. *The Woman's Comfort Book: A Self-Nurturing Guide for Restoring Balance in Your Life.* San Francisco: Harper San Francisco, 1992. Pages 33-37.

Schuckit, Marc Alan, M.D. *Educating Yourself about Alcohol and Drugs: A People's Primer.* New York: Plenum Press, 1995. Pages v-viii, 5-143, 368-370.

DIVERSITY

Hockenberry, John. *Moving Violations.* New York: Hyperion, 1995. Pages 15-86.

McCarthy, Sheryl. *Why Are the Heroes Always White?* Kansas City: Andrews and McMeel, 1995. Pages 135-137, 189-190.

Trotter, Tamera and Joycelyn Allen. *Talking Justice: 602 Ways to Build and Promote Racial Harmony*. Saratoga: R & E Publishers, 1993. Pages 3-81.

RELATIONSHIPS

Bovee, Courtland L. and John V. Thill. *Business Communication Today*, Third Edition. New York: McGraw Hill, Inc., 1992. Pages 28-48.

DuBrin, Andrew J. *Human Relations for Career and Personal Success*, Third Edition. Englewood Cliffs: Prentice Hall, 1992. Pages 120-134.

REFERENCE

The Columbia Dictionary of Quotations. New York: Columbia University Press, 1993. CD-ROM version on Microsoft Bookshelf 1994 version.

Harris, Sherwood. *The New York Public Library Book of How and Where to Look It Up*. New York: The Stonesong Press, 1991. Pages 9-78, 281-361.

Krol, Ed. *The Whole Internet User's Guide and Catalog*, O'Reilly & Associates, Inc., 1994. Pages xix-xxi, 1-11, 49-99, 101-110, 233-239, 287-294.

Lesko, Matthew. *Information U.S.A.* New York: Penguin Books, 1983. Pages 151-153, 512-514.

National Center for Education Statistics. *Digest of Education Statistics*, 1994. U.S. Department of Education Office of Educational Research and Improvement, 1994. Pages 167-323, 391-409.

The Student Guide 1994-95: *Financial Aid from the U.S. Department of Education.*

Index

Index

A

Abbreviations, 107
Abilities, 38-40
Acquired Immune Deficiency Disorder (AIDS), 168
Acronyms, 133
Active learners, 33
Active listening, 128
Active reading, 106
Addiction, 163-166
    self-test, 163-164
Administrators, 12
    as resource, 199
Adult Children of Alcoholics (ACOA), 166
Advisors, 12
African-Americans, 4, 210
Aggressive behavior, 206-207
Al-Anon, 166
Ala-Teen, 166
Alcohol, 159, 160
    abuse of, 164-166
Alcoholics Anonymous (AA), 165
Allen, Joycelyn, 210-212
Alumni, for networking, 229
American Red Cross, 254
Amnesty International, 234
Analogy, 83
Anderson, Cory, 114
Anorexia Nervosa, 163
Armstrong, William H., 107, 134
Asians, 4
Assertive behavior, 206-207
Attitude, 30-31
Audubon Society, 234

B

Bachelder, Adam, 130
Banking services, 233-234
Barron's Pocket Guide to Study Tips, 107, 134
Beattie, Melody, 165
Benchmarks, for steps toward a goal, 63
Benson, Herbert, MD, 159
Benyard, Daphne, 200
Big Brothers and Big Sisters, 254
Birth control, 166-167
Bolles, Richard Nelson, 230, 256
Bologna, Michelle Renee, 153
Bovée, Courtland, 250
Brainstorming, 86, 116
Brown, Marvin T., Ph.D., 180-181
Budgeting, 222-224
    sample budget, 224
    worksheets, 241-243
Bulimia, 163
Bulletin boards, 12, 228
Business Communication Today, 204
Business Periodicals Index, 14

C

C's, three, for writing, 112-113
Cardiovascular training, 155
The Care of the Soul, 249
Career investigation, 226, 230
Career planning/job placement office, 13, 228-229
Cash for College: The Ultimate Guide to College Scholarships, 231, 233
Categorization, 83
CD ROM, for library use, 14
Certificate of deposit (CD), 234
Change, handling, 67-70
Chapman, Elwood N., 30
Checking accounts, 233-234
Chin, Susan H., 68
Classification, 83
Clubs, 12
Code, for prioritizing scheduled tasks, 63
Codependency, 165-166
Codependent No More, 165
Codependents Anonymous, 166
Commitment, 183-184
Communication, 201-207
    cycle, 202-203
    nonverbal, 204-205
    strategies, 205-206
    styles, 206-207
    verbal, 203-204
Concentration, 129-131
Condition of Education Report, 5
Conflict, 251-252
    resolution through creative thinking, 85
Consequence, 83
Contacts, 228-230
Contrast, 83

Counselors, 12, 159, 165
    as resource, 199
Covey, Dr. Stephen, 56, 61, 256
Cox, Barbara, 114
Cramming, 135
Creating a New Civilization: The Politics of the Third Wave, 132
Creating/creative thinking, 84-87
    tips for, 86-87
Credit, 235-238
    history, 237
    positive and negative effects, 237
    rating, 237
    record, 185
Crenshaw, Barbara, 250
Critical thinking, 82-93
    mind actions, 83
    value of, 84
Criticism, 252-253

Daguillard, Nadja, 153
Date book/day planner, 62
Decision making, 88-91
Delany, Sadie and Bessie, 256
Delegating, 67
Depression, 158-159
Diagnostic and Statistical Manual of Mental Disorders, 4th Edition, 165
Dietary Guidelines (U.S. Depts of Agriculture and Health and Human Services), 152
Digest of Education Statistics, 4, 8, 225, 230
Discovery draft, for writing essays/papers, 117
Discrimination, 210-211
Dislikes, 36-38
Diversity, 209-212, 248
    promotion of, 212
Down time, 64
Drugs, 159-162
    abuse of, 164-166
    affects, 161
DuBrin, Andrew J., 202

Early, Jonathan, 68
Eating disorders, 162-163
Eating right, 152-154
Educating Yourself About Alcohol and Drugs: A People's Primer, 160-161
Education, reasons for, 5
    boosting income, 8
    definitions, 7-8
    and success, 8-10
Educational contract, 25
Electronic databases, for library use, 14
Electronic mail, 16, 131
Emerson, Ralph Waldo, 18
Enhancing Thinking Through Cooperative Learning, 82
Enrollment, growth and diversity of, 4
Environment, valuing, 255
Essay tests, 138-139
Essays, writing, 115-118
Essential tasks, 62-63
Ethical process, 180-181
The Ethical Process: A Strategy for Making Good Decisions, 179-180
Ethics, 178-181
Ethnicity, 209
Exercise, 154-155

Failure, 87
    dealing with, 186
Fear, 16-18
Federal Direct Student Loans, 232
Federal Student Aid Program, 233
Financial Aid Office, 14, 230-233
    grants and scholarships, 232-233
    loans, 231-232
Financial history, personal, 244-245
Flexibility training, 155
Focus, on goals, 57
    in commitment, 183
    when concentration, 131
    when listening, 129
Freewriting, 116

G

Generalization, 83
Ginsburg, Ruth Bader, 84
Global learners, 35-36, 61, 69, 105
Goal setting, daily and weekly, 61-62
    to avoid stress, 157
Goals, 56-60
    falling short of, 249-251
    lifelong objective, 57-58
    long-term, 58
    reevaluating and modifying, 67-69
    short-term, 58-59
    types, 59-60
Golden Rule, the, 208
Gopher, 16
Grabovich, Christine, 187
Grants, 232-233
Greenpeace, 254
Group relationships, 208-209

H

Habits, 31-32
    list, 99
Handbook for Writers, 111
Harris, Sherwood, 15
Have-to words, 29
Health services, school, 13
Health traps, 159-163
Highlighting, 105, 109
Hispanics, 4, 210
Hockenberry, John, 211
Hotlines, 13
Human Immunodeficiency Virus (HIV), 168
Human Relations for Career and Personal Success, 201-202

I

I messages, 205, 207, 252
If-there's-time tasks, 63, 65
Income, as affected by educational level, 8

Independence, 16
Information driven society, 102
Information USA, 14
Initiative, 185
Innovating, 86
Inquiring, 87-88
Instructors, 12
    as resource, 198-199
Integrated Postsecondary Educational Data System Fall Enrollment Survey (IPEDS), 4, 225
Integrity, 178-181
Interlibrary loan, 15
Internet, 15-16 for job search, 228
Intuition, 91
    mathematical, 140
Intuitors (learning style), 34, 61

J

Jacobs, Gregg D., Ph.D., 155
Jefferson, Thomas, 84
Job hunting, 228-230
Job listings, 228
Journaling, 113
Judgment, 83

K

Kelly, Nicole, 39
A Kick in the Seat of the Pants, 85
Kiwanis, 254
Knights of Columbus, 254
Krol, Ed, 15

L

Lampe, M. Willard II, 107, 134
Lampkin, Patricia M., 187
Leaders, in group communication, 208-209
Learner, Marcia, 139
Learning, basic rules of, 10
    lifelong, 248-249

Learning styles, 32-37
  inventory of, 42-45
Leith, William D., 236
Library, 11-15
Lifestyle, 7, 60
Likes, 36-38
Lions Club, 254
Listening, 128-29
  role in communication, 206
Loans, 231-232
Lopez, Charlene, 82
Lorayne, Harry, 132-133
Lyman, Frank Jr., Ph.D., 82, 84, 89, 109

Math, techniques for working with, 139-140
McCarthy, Sheryl, 210
McKee, Cynthia and Phillip, 231, 233
Medical record, personal, 175
Memory, 131-134
  association, 132
  mnemonic devices, 133-134
Mentors, 201
Mindus, Arlene
Minorities, 4, 210-211, 256
Mnemonic devices, 133-134
Money market account, 234
Mortazavi, Joubin, 92
Motivation, 66, 182
Moving Violations, 211
Multiculturalism, 209-210

N

Narcotics Anonymous, 165
National Association of Colleges and Employers, 68
National Center for Education, 4-5
  Profile of Older Undergraduates Contractor Report, 4
National Council on Alcohol and Drug Dependency, 160
National Institute on Alcohol Abuse and Alcoholism, 160
National Postsecondary Student Aid Study, 225

Native Americans, 4
Negative self-talk, 29
Negotiators, in group communication, 208-209
Networking, 228-230
New Wellness Encyclopedia, 152-154, 160
The New York Public Library Book of How and Where to Look It Up, 15
Nonverbal communication, 204-205
Northwest Airlines, mission statement, 56-57
Note-taking, 106-110
  habits, 106-107
  organizing, 107-110
  reviewing, 109-110
Numbers, techniques for working with, 139-140
Nursing homes, 254

Objective goals, 57-58
Objective tests, 137-138
Older/returning students, 4
On-line Computer Library Center (OCLC), 14
Outlining, 107-109, 116
Overeaters Anonymous, 165

P

Palken, Judith Lindsey, M.D., 162
Papers, writing, 115-118
Participators, in group communication, 208-209
Passive behavior, 206-207
Pell Grants, 232
Perkins loans, 231-232
Personal mission, 255-256
  statement, 56-57, 79, 263
Personal relationships, 207-208
Perspective, 91-93
Planned Parenthood, 167, 254
Planner, for daily schedule, 62
Plus loans, 232
Positive self-talk, 29-30, 40
Prediction, 83

Prentice Hall, mission statement, 57
Present, concentrating on the, 10-11
Preview, Read, Analyze, Review (reading technique), 104
Preview reading, 36, 104
The Princeton Review's Math Smart, 139
Priorities, 60-61
    shifting, 69-70
    with working while in school, 227
Prioritizing your schedule, 62-63
Problem solving, 88-89
Procrastination, 65-66, 157
Proofreading, 113-115, 118
Publications, school, 13
Purpose, 56-57
    for writing, 111

Q

Quality of life, 9
Quick Access Reference for Writers, 117

R

Racism, 210-211
Ramos, Aida, 236
Readers Guide to Periodical Literature, 14
Reading, 102-106
    for lifelong learning, 248
    textbook reading technique, 104-106
Real World Perspectives (student interviews), 6, 39, 68, 92, 114, 130, 153, 187, 200, 236, 250
Recycling, 255
Reference section of the library, 11, 14
Reflective learners, 33-34
Regular tasks, 63
Relationships, 207-209
    group, 208-209
    personal, 207-209
Repeating, when listening, 129
    for memory, 132
Resources, 11-16
    financial, 222
    in school, 198-199
    out of school, 199

Responsibility, 18, 61-62, 134, 152, 184-185, 212, 249
Reviewing notes, 109
Reviewing reading, 105-106
Rewards, for habits, 31
Richardson, Christine Carol, 250
Risk, 208, 256
Robbins, Jenny, 130
Rotary Club, 254
Rouse, James, 84

S

Savings accounts, 234
Savings strategies, 234-235
Schedule, 62-64
    adjusting, 70
Scholarships, 232-233
Schuckit, Marc Alan, M.D., 160
Schwartz, Bob, 162
Self-esteem, 28-29
Self-image, 28-29
Self-portrait, 52-53
Sensors (learning style), 34, 61
Sequential learners, 35, 61
The Seven Habits of Highly Effective People, 56, 256
Sexual harassment, 168-169
Sexual issues, 166-169
    birth control, 166-167
    sexual harassment, 168-169
    sexually transmitted diseases (STD's), 167-168
Sexually transmitted diseases (STD's), 167-168
Share Our Strength, 255
Short-term goals, 61
Sierra Club, 255
Single parents, 4
Sleep, 155-156
Soloman, Barbara, 33-34, 39
Spiritual life, 249
Stafford loans, 232
Strength training, 155
Stress, 156-158
Stuart, Eileen M., R.N., M.S., 159
Student body, characteristics of current, 4
Student employment office, 228-229
Subjective (essay) tests, 138-139
Substantiation, 83
Success, dealing with, 188

from knowing learning style, 37
noting, 29
Summoner, Dana, 200
Super Memory - Super Student, 132-133
Supplemental Educational Opportunity Grants (SEOG), 232
Support groups, 13, 165

T

Talking Justice: 602 Ways to Build and Promote Racial Harmony, 211-212
TELNET, 15
Tests, 134-139
    objective, 137-138
    preparing for, 134-136
    subjective, 138-139
    taking, 136-137
    types, 137-139
Thesis statement, 116
Thill, John V., 250
Think Links, 52-53, 105, 109-110, 116-117, 224
Thinktrix, 82-84
Time management, 61-67
    daily and weekly, 61-62
    procrastination, 65-66
    scheduling, 62-64
    to do lists, 64-65
Time traps, 66-67
Timm, Paul, 57, 59, 62-63
To do lists, 64-65
Tobacco, 159-160
Toffler, Alvin and Heidi, 132
Topic, choosing for paper, 116
Trends, educational, 5
Trotter, Tamera, 210-212
Troyka, Lynn Quitman, 111-112, 115, 117
Tutoring, 14

U

Usenet, 16

V

Values, 179, 194
van Oech, Roger, 85-86
Verbal communication, 203-204
Verbal learners, 35, 105
Visual learners, 34-35, 105
Volunteering, 254-255

W

Want-to words, 29
Weaknesses, 40
Weight control, 154, 162-163
Weight Watchers, 163
The Wellness Book, 155, 162
A Whack on the Side of the Head, 86-87
The Whole Internet User's Guide and Catalog, 15-16
Why Are The Heroes Always White?, 210
Why go to school, 5
Wilke, Earle, 6
Wilson, Jack, 92
The Woman's Comfort Book, 158
Wonder, Stevie, 84
Wood, Susan Elizabeth, 6
Work-study, 226, 229, 232-233
Working while in school, 225-230
    positive and negative effects of, 226-227
World Wide Web, 16
World Wildlife Fund, 255
Writing, 111-118
    audience, 111-112
    draft, 117
    essays and papers, 115-118
    establishing a subject, 116
    purposes, 111
    revising, 117-118
    specifying a topic, 116
Writing sample, 125

Yearlong goals, 58
Your Attitude is Showing: A Primer of Human Relations, 30

OTHER BOOKS BY CAROL CARTER